The Worship
of God

The Worship of God

Reformed Concepts of Biblical Worship

MENTOR

Copyright © Christian Focus Publications 2005

ISBN 1-84550-055-5

10 9 8 7 6 5 4 3 2 1

Published in 2005
in the
Mentor imprint
by
Christian Focus Publications,
Geanies House, Fearn, Tain,
Ross-shire, IV20 1TW, Scotland
and
Greenville Presbyterian Theological Seminary,
418 East Main St, Taylors, South Carolina, USA

www.christianfocus.com

Cover design by Alister MacInnes

Printed and bound in Scotland by
Bell & Bain, Glasgow

Contents

Acknowledgements

We would like to thank the contributors for their presentations at the conference and the work in preparing their messages for print. In addition to the papers delivered or preached during the conference, we have included an additional chapter written by Cliff Blair, who was a senior at Greenville Seminary at the time of the conference and is now pastor of Redeemer Orthodox Presbyterian Church in Charlotte, NC. To Mr. Blair we offer our thanks for his contribution. The editors are most thankful for several individuals who helped to see this project through to completion: Mrs. Paul Davies of New Zealand and Mrs. Caroline Brown, who spent many hours in giving editorial advice; Mrs. Sherri Crick, who transcribed some of the lectures; and Mr. Andy Wortman, librarian at Greenville Seminary, who coordinated between contributors, transcriber, and editors and did the initial layout. The editors also would like to thank the editorial staff at Christian Focus Publications for their willingness to publish this book and for their helpful advice in bringing it to publication.

It is our prayer that our Lord, who delights in receiving the worship of His people, will "bless the work of our hands" to the edification of many. Soli Deo Gloria!

The Editors.

Preface

Joseph A. Pipa Jr

Few issues have perplexed the modern church more than that of worship. The conflict over worship manifests itself in what have been called "the worship wars." While some grow impatient with the conflict, history teaches that we may not lightly dismiss this problem. Calvin taught that we may not overestimate the importance of worship:

I have also no difficulty in conceding to you that there is nothing more perilous to our salvation than a distorted and perverse worship of God. The primary rudiments by which we are wont to train those whom we wish to win as disciples to Christ, are these; viz., not to frame any new worship of God for themselves at random, and after their own pleasure, but to know that the only legitimate worship is that which He himself approved from the beginning. For we maintain what the sacred oracle declared, that obedience is more excellent than any sacrifice (1 Sam. xv. 22). In short, we train them by every means to be contented with the one rule of worship which they have received from His mouth, and bid adieu to all fictitious worship[1].

In another place the reformer wrote, "If it be inquired, then, by what things chiefly the Christian religion has a standing existence amongst us, and maintains its truth, it will be found that the following two not only occupy the principal place, but comprehend under them all the other parts, and consequently the whole substance of

---

1. John Calvin, A Reformation Debate, ed., John C. Olin (Grand Rapids: Baker Book House, 1976), 59.

Christianity, that is, a knowledge, first, of the mode in which God is duly worshipped; and, secondly, of the source from which salvation is to be obtained." [2]

Convinced of the importance of worship for the health of the Church, we offer this book to the public. The purpose of this book is to address a number of the major issues that create tensions in our practice of worship. Our intent, however, is not simply to critique those who differ from us, but also to offer a blueprint for a more biblical, God-honoring worship. Thus we deal with the purpose of worship, the rule for worship, and the practice of worship. We also seek to address some of the difficulties we have with contemporary worship models and contemporary Christian music. We address the arguments for exclusive Psalmody and those arguments for singing hymns as well as psalms.

Most of these chapters were originally delivered as lectures and sermons at Greenville Presbyterian Theological Seminary's 2003 Spring Theology Conference. Each year the seminary sponsors and hosts a theology conference designed to refresh and encourage church officers and members in the work of the Church.

---

2. John Calvin, The Necessity of Reforming the Church, trans. Henry Beveridge 1844 (Revised reprint Dallas: Protestant Heritage Press, 1995), 15.

Chapter 1

The Regulative Principle

Terry L. Johnson

There can be no more important issue than that of worship. There can be no more important question than that of how God is to be worshipped. Biblically this seems clear enough. There is a sense in which the entire Old Testament is about establishing and maintaining the true worship of the true God. In His exchange with the Samaritan woman Jesus says, "You worship that which you do not know; we worship that which we know, for salvation is from the Jews," (John 4:22). "Salvation" He says, "is of the Jews." Salvation? This was a debate about worship, not soteriology, was it not? Or are worship and salvation connected in some way about which we are unaccustomed to thinking? Indeed they are. To be "saved" is precisely to be rescued from idolatry, from false gods and false worship, for the true worship of the true God. The Samaritans were worshipping that which they "did not know" and so were lost. The Jews, however, had been rescued from Egypt ("let my people go that they may serve Me;" Exod. 7:16; 8:1,20, 27, 28; 9:1, 13 etc.; cf. 3:12, 10:25, 12:24), and then were led to Sinai, where they were given detailed instruction respecting worship. Subsequently they conquered and occupied the Promised Land precisely so that they might know, serve, and worship the true God truly.

The history of the Reformed churches also underscores the importance of worship. The Reformed wing of the Reformation conducted a *War Against the Idols*, as Carlos M. N. Eire entitled his superb study of the era. "The central focus of Reformed Protestantism was its interpretation of worship," he argues.[1] Not only on the continent, but in Great Britain as well, the pivotal issue was worship. The hundred-year war waged by the Puritans against the British monarchy was primarily over worship: would the worship of the English church be reformed along Genevan lines or retain the vestiges of Romanism found in the Prayer Book?

Current events also urge close consideration of the issue. "Worship Wars" rage across the land, dividing churches and denominations. Regrettably, worship is often treated atomistically, as though virtually any form of worship could be joined to any theological and ecclesiastical tradition, and that theological tradition be maintained. I am skeptical of this. More likely, the way we worship today will determine the shape and substance of our piety for generations to come. This is so because worship expresses our theology. Or, to put it another way, theology requires a worship service to express and sustain it. Indeed, worship services (e.g., the Roman Catholic mass, a Charismatic praise service, an Orthodox worship service) invariably are the expression of a theology that a given tradition currently holds, *or the one it soon will*. We need to be honest about this. We are either communicating our doctrine and convictions through the forms of our public worship, or we are not communicating them at all. Our public Sunday services are the only opportunities that we pastors have to reach a majority of our people, who attend then and at no other time. Either our forms are substantial enough to transmit the theology and piety of Reformed Protestantism (traditionally that has meant expository preaching, Psalm–singing, Scripture reading, and Scripture–based prayer) or we have, in fact if not intentionally, given up the project.

The "regulative principle" has historically been the principle through which the Reformed tradition has addressed the worship issue. I understand my assignment here not as considerations of two

---

1. Carlos M. N. Eire, *War Against the Idols: The Reformation of Worship from Erasmus to Calvin* (Cambridge: Cambridge University Press, 1986), 2.

different themes, one on the regulative principle and another on "heart worship."[2] Rather, I see this as two aspects of one theme, that of the regulative principle. This is because the regulative principle includes both "form" and "heart," both "truth" and "spirit." The regulative principle is concerned with: (1) Content and form, or truth; and, (2) Heart and motive, or spirit.

John 4 will serve as the primary text for our consideration of worship. In this setting, Jesus encounters the Samaritan woman at the well. He offers her living water, which she wants, but then introduces her current living arrangements: she has had five husbands and is now living with a man not her husband. Trapped, she diverts the direction of the conversation away from morality to religion, by asking whether the right place of worship is in Samaria or Jerusalem. She says, "Our fathers worshiped in this mountain, and you people say that in Jerusalem is the place where men ought to worship," (John 4:20). His startling answer is, "Woman, believe Me, an hour is coming when neither in this mountain, nor in Jerusalem, shall you worship the Father." Jesus partially sides with the Jews in that debate saying, "You worship that which you do not know; we worship that which we know, for salvation is from the Jews," (John 4:22).

Knowledge counts. Truth is essential. Samaritan worship was in error. Samaritans and, by implication, all people, must look to the Jews, and in particular the book of the Jews, the Bible, in order to learn how to worship God and thus possess salvation. Then Jesus repeats the substance of verse 21 by adding, "But an hour is coming, and now is, when the true worshipers shall worship the Father in spirit and truth; for such people the Father seeks to be His worshipers. God is spirit, and those who worship Him must worship in spirit and truth" (John 4:23, 24).

I believe that this is the single most revolutionary statement that Jesus ever made. Clearly He is saying that the place of worship no longer matters, rather the spirit. He is marginalizing the externals of worship while giving prominence to the internal. Jerusalem was important because the temple was there, and within the temple, the

2. See Chapter 7 for the author's address on "heart worship".

altars, the priests, and the sacrifices. If the place of worship is no longer significant, the whole Old Testament system is being swept away. Typological Old Testament worship, with its symbols of our Great High Priest and the Lamb of God who would take away the sin of the world, is abolished with a word and contrasted with that which shall stand in its place. Over against that which is temporary, typological, and external shall be new covenant worship offered in "spirit and truth." What does this mean? It means this: over against Samaritan errors, worship must be "in truth," that is, according to God's revelation of truth; over against concern for the externals of place and procedure, worship must be "in spirit," that is, in the right spirit, which is a matter of the heart, of the motive.

Note that there are two sides to worship, and we "must" deal correctly with both of them. There is the heart of worship (its spirit) and its content and form (its truth). Both are necessary. Both are commanded. Periodically the question is raised, "Are you saying that God is not pleased with the worship of such and such group of very earnest, sincere, devout Christians?" The answer we give is, form is not irrelevant. God cares about the form and content of worship as well as its spirit. One may be very sincere, and yet sincerely wrong, offering worship to God in a manner that He has not authorized. The extreme case of this is found in pagan worship, such as the worship of the prophets of Baal on Mt Carmel, who practiced self-mutilation amidst their ceremonial dance and frenzied cries (1 Kings 18:25-29). Were they earnest, sincere, devout? Absolutely. Likewise the ancient Canaanites offered their infants to Molech in human sacrifice. A more zealous expression of religious devotion can scarcely be imagined. But the manner was utterly unauthorized, without Divine command, and wrong.

Content matters. Jesus says worship must be conducted with both the right attitude and in the right manner, with both spirit and truth.

The Regulative Principle
Jesus says worship must be "in truth." This is at the center of what we mean by the regulative principle. We should understand "truth" in two senses. **First, worship that is "in truth" is according to**

Scripture. The Samaritans were not different from the rest of humanity. "You worship that which you do not know," Jesus told the Samaritan woman. There are almost limitless ways in which God might be worshiped. Jesus is insisting that we get it right. We must worship God according to His self revelation. If we are to worship in truth, we must submit to scriptural revelation.

Calvin argued that "lawful" worship is that which the Lord has established "by Himself."[3] He called for "the rejection of any mode of worship that is not sanctioned by the command of God."[4] This principle has become known as "the regulative principle."[5] The Catholic, Lutheran, and Anglican understanding may be called a "normative principle" – general norms for worship are given, but whatever is not expressly forbidden by Scripture is permitted. The Reformed practice was much more rigorous. It stated that whatever is not enjoined by Scripture (whether by command, example, or by deduction from broader principles) is forbidden. The Westminster Confession of Faith expresses it in this way: "But the acceptable way of worshiping the true God is instituted by himself, and so limited by his own revealed will, that he may not be worshiped according to the imaginations and devices of men, or the suggestions of Satan, under any visible representation, or any other way not prescribed in the holy Scripture," (Chapter XXI. 1).

Where does the Bible teach this? Certainly the point is made in the very detailed prescriptions for worship found in Exodus 25–40 and Leviticus, but also in the following:

---

3. John Calvin, *Institutes of the Christian Religion* (Philadelphia: The Westminster Press, 1960), II.8.17.

4. John Calvin, "On the Necessity of Reforming the Church" in *Selected Works* of John Calvin, (1844; reprint, Grand Rapids: Baker Book House, 1983), 133.

5. One approaches despair when John Frame, *Worship in Spirit and Truth* (Phillipsburg, NJ: P&R Publishing, 1996), ostensibly distinguishes his own methodology from the Puritans' as simply "obeying everything that God says in Scripture about worship," (54). And, "We must simply search the Scriptures to determine what is appropriate and inappropriate to do when the church meets to together as a body in the name of the Lord Jesus," (55). What, if not this, has Reformed Protestantism been aiming at for the past 480 years? 6. *Institutes*,

- *Cain and Abel* (Gen. 4:3-8). This was the first "worship war." Abel offered "the firstlings of his flock and their fat portions," but Cain offered "the fruit of the ground." The Lord "had regard for Abel and for his offering; but for Cain and for his offering He had no regard." Why? The Lord's rebuke, "If you do well, will not your countenance be lifted?" implies that either the spirit or truth of the offering was deficient. It was either an unauthorized offering or an authorized offering offered in the wrong way.

- *The Second Commandment* (Exod. 20:4). In prohibiting worship through images, God declares that He alone determines how He is to be worshiped. Though their use seem to be ever so sincere and sensible (as aids to worship), images are not pleasing to Him, and by implication, neither is anything else that He has not sanctioned.

- *The Golden Calf* (Exod. 32). The image was probably a representation of Jehovah (see vv. 4, 5, 8), but totally unacceptable for use in worship because unauthorized and forbidden.

- *Nadab and Abihu* (Lev. 10). They offered up "strange fire" to the Lord, that is, an offering presented in a manner "which He had not commanded them" (10:1), and God struck them dead. In so doing God made a statement to the ages – "By those who come near Me I will be treated as holy..." (10:2, 3), which could only mean that those who approach God must do so in a way consistent with what He has commanded.

- *Warnings* not to add to or take away from God's commandments (Deut. 4:2; 12:32).

- *The rejection of Saul's unwarranted worship*, and the principle "obedience is better than sacrifice" (1 Sam. 105:22). Obedience to what? Obedience to God's commands regarding worship.

- *The rejection of pagan rites* "which I never commanded or spoke of, nor did it ever enter My mind," (Jer. 19:6; 32:35). We may deduce that the rites performed in Israel were to be only those that God had spoken of or commanded.

- *Jesus' rejection of Pharisaic worship*, citing the words of Isaiah who said, "in vain do they worship Me, teaching as doctrines the precepts of men" (Mark 7:7, cf. Matt. 15:9; Isa. 29:13).

- *The rejection of Samaritan worship* by Jesus because they worship "what (they) do not know," (John 4:22). "True" worship is impossible for them as long as they devise their own worship. Worship that is in "truth" is based upon the knowledge of what God has commanded.

- *The rejection of what the old divines called "will worship"*, is translated in a modern version of Colossians as "the commandments and teachings of men ... self-made religion and self-abasement and severe treatment of the body," all no doubt sincere religious practices, but unacceptable because humanly devised, (Col. 2:22, 23 NASV).

This is just a sampling of the passages that could be cited. Clearly they teach that we are not free to improvise in our worship. Calvin warns of the "snares of novelty." Furthermore, the regulative principle is rooted not merely in the several above proof-texts, but is the necessary implication of the fundamental principles of Reformed theology. The rejection of the regulative principle necessarily would involve compromising the central tenets of the Reformed faith. Consider the following outline, first suggested in the writings of T. David Gordon:

- *The Doctrines of God and Man.* No system of theology has given as much emphasis to the creator/creature distinction as has Biblical Calvinism. No other has so emphasized and celebrated the great gulf between the infinite God of heaven and earth, and finite man. His thoughts are not our thoughts, and His ways are not our ways, (Isa. 55:8, 9). "Who has known the mind of the Lord?" the Apostle Paul asks (Rom. 11:34). The creature cannot know what worship will be pleasing to God apart from His self revelation. Is not this the obvious implication of a Reformed view of the natures of God and man?

The Doctrine of Sin. Again, no system of theology has emphasized the extent of the effects of the fall on human nature as has the Reformed faith. Total depravity has been the phrase that we have used to describe the corruption of all of man's faculties, mind, will, and affections. "The hearts of the sons of men are full of evil," says Ecclesiastes (9:3). "The heart is more deceitful than all else and is desperately sick," says Jeremiah (17:9). "There is none righteous ... there is none who does good ... there is none who seeks for God" (Rom. 3:10-12). The Westminster Confession of Faith says of the fall that Adam and Eve and their posterity were "wholly defiled in all the parts and faculties of soul and body" and "are utterly indisposed, disabled, and made opposite to all good, and wholly inclined to evil," (VI. 2, 4). It has never been stated more strongly than this, nor more accurately. The effect of this radical corruption of man is to take us beyond the finite's ignorance of the Infinite discussed above, to the positive principle of idolatry. Man is by nature an idolater (Rom. 1:18-32). He cannot and will not get it right. The human heart is "a perpetual factory of idols," said Calvin.[6] We are not competent to devise God honoring worship. If we follow our natural, even commonsense inclinations, we will get it exactly wrong. A humble acceptance of this requires that we look to God to tell us that which He desires from us.

- *The Doctrine of Scripture.* No other tradition has elevated the authority and sufficiency of Scripture to the heights that the Reformed tradition has. Sola Scriptura is a fundamental principle of the whole Protestant and Reformed heritage. Our final authority in all matters of faith and conduct is Scripture. "The supreme judge by which all controversies

---

I. XI. 8.

of religion are to be determined … can be no other but the Holy Spirit speaking in the Scripture," (WCF I. 10). For this task of ordering faith and life, the Scripture is sufficient. The Apostle Paul writes, "All Scripture is inspired by God and profitable for teaching, for reproof, for correction, for training in righteousness; that the man of God may be adequate, equipped for every good work," (2 Tim. 3:16,17). The saints are adequately equipped for "every good work" by Scripture. It teaches, reproves, corrects, and trains us for life's tasks and trials. Through Scripture alone we are "thoroughly equipped" (NIV) for "every," not some or most, but "every good work." The all important work of worship would not only be included, but would be at the top of any list of works for which Scripture is designed to equip us. Again, we cite the Confession: "The whole counsel of God, concerning all things necessary for His own glory, man's salvation, faith, and life, is either expressly set down in Scripture, or by good and necessary consequence may be deduced from Scripture: unto which nothing at any time is to be added (I.6).

- *The Doctrine of the Church*. The Reformed tradition has sharply limited the church's authority and power to those areas specifically delegated to it by Christ. Its authority is extensive (the "keys" of Matt. 16:18ff; 18:18ff), yet is "ministerial and declarative." It may administer what Christ calls it to administer, and it may declare what Christ calls it to declare, argues T. David Gordon, "but it does not have discretionary power to frame new ordinances or laws."[7] The church may not "bind the conscience" by creating rules not expressed or implied by Scripture. The regulative principle is the necessary application of this principle in the area of worship. The Church may require of its members only that which Christ requires, that and no more. Thus the people are free from the traditions and devices of mere men.

---

7. T. David Gordon, "Presbyterian Worship: Its Distinguishing Principle," (unpublished manuscript, n.d.)

Perhaps the *doctrine of God's sovereignty*, that doctrine which does so much to give substance and shape to Reformed thought, best summarizes our point. Because our God is a sovereign God, He is sovereign over His worship. He alone can rightly order His worship (because we are finite and fallen), and He alone does order His worship (through His word, to which His Church is subject). He is not obligated to accept whatever worship finite and fallen man might devise, or even what redeemed ecclesiastical officials might create. He is Lord. He is sovereign. He alone can and does authorize the worship that pleases Him.

Thus we do in worship that which is "according to Scripture." We limit ourselves to those things which God Himself has authorized and has promised to bless. This is not an odious or burdensome requirement. It is simply a matter of embracing those activities or elements in worship with which God is pleased and to which He has attached His promises. *The regulative principle flows necessarily from the whole system of Reformed theology.*

Elements, Forms, Circumstances
This then leads to the question, what specifically has He authorized? What are the elements which He has ordained for worship? The Confession provides specifics: "Prayer with thanksgiving ... the reading of the Scriptures with godly fear, the sound preaching and conscionable hearing of the Word ... singing of psalms with grace in the heart ... the due administration and worthy receiving of the sacraments instituted by Christ, are all parts of the ordinary religious worship of God," (XXI. 3, 5).

In addition, the Confession speaks of occasional elements such as "religious oaths" and "vows" (as in Creeds, membership covenants, and ordination vows) as legitimate parts of "religious worship" (XXI.5, XXII.1). Texts such as Acts 2:42 provide a glimpse of the early church in worship, in simple services of the word, sacraments, and prayer. We also see the Apostle Paul regulating prayer (1 Cor. 11:2-16; 14:14-17; 2 Tim. 2:13), the singing of praise (1 Cor. 14:26, 27; Col. 3:16; Eph. 5:19), the ministry of the word (1 Cor. 14:29-33; 1 Tim. 4:13; 2 Tim. 4:1, 2), the collection (1 Cor.

16:1,2), and the Lord's Supper (1 Cor. 11:17-34). These all appear to be regular elements of the worship of the apostolic church. *Prayer, the reading of Scripture, the preaching of Scripture, the singing of Psalms*, the administration of the sacraments, and religious oaths are all "according to Scripture," modeled by apostolic example, regulated by apostolic command, and accompanied by divine promises of blessing.

At this point, a detractor might ask about pulpits and hymnals and lights and microphones, and question the consistency with which the regulative principle is being applied. Where, he might ask, is the Scriptural warrant for these innovations? The Reformed tradition generally, and *The Westminster Standards* specifically, distinguish between elements (which are Scripturally determined and unchanging), forms (the contents of the elements, regarding which there is considerable freedom), and circumstances, which are governed by broader considerations. For example, the element of prayer may be expressed through a written or extemporaneous form. The element of preaching may be textual or topical in form. The element of Scripture reading may be expressed in various forms: a few verses or a chapter or more, from Genesis or Revelation, or from anywhere in between. In each case the form is the content and structure through which the element is expressed.

Are there any restrictions on forms? Indeed there are and must be, lest the integrity of the element be undermined. Forms are not limitless. The basic principle is this: A form must be consistent with the nature of the element. One may not "dance the sermon," primarily because a sermon by nature is spoken communication. Dance is not a form of preaching, but a new element, the arguments of its proponents notwithstanding.[8] Still, there is a range of choices. T. David Gordon acknowledges that this category "appears to be

---

8. Frame sees drama as "a form of preaching and teaching," pointing out that "biblical preaching and teaching contain many dramatic elements" (*Worship*, 93). This is a classic example of the argument of the beard. Preaching and drama do lie upon a spectrum as do clean shaves and beards. There are dramatic sermons and sermonic dramas even as there are six o'clock shadows and light beards. But a clean shave is not a beard and a sermon is not a skit. We can distinguish between these things and speak meaningfully of the difference.

less well-known than the categories "element" or "circumstance." Nevertheless, it has been an important part of the discussion of worship since the Reformation. For example, Calvin's Genevan worship was entitled a *Form of Church Prayers* (1542), the *Larger Catechism* and scores of Reformed authors have referred to the Lord's Prayer as a form of prayer, and various forms of family prayer and public prayer have been published over the years. Also, a debate over "free" *vs.* "fixed" forms of worship has been carried on by Presbyterians since the days of the Puritans. A cursory acquaintance with the literature of classical Protestantism will verify this assertion. "Form" is the word traditionally used to identify the content of an element and the way it is structured.[9]

Circumstances are addressed by the Confession in I.6: "there are some circumstances concerning the worship of God … common to human actions and societies, which are to be ordered by the light of nature and Christian prudence, according to the general rules of the Word, which are always to be observed." The "light

---

9. Gordon provides the following support: "Larger Catechism Question 186 says: 'The whole Word of God is of use to direct us in the duty of prayer; but the special rule of direction is that form of prayer which our Savior Christ taught His disciples, commonly called the Lord's Prayer.' Again, Shorter Catechism Question 99 says: 'The whole Word of God is of use to direct us in prayer; but the special rule of direction is that form of prayer which Christ taught His disciples, commonly called the Lord's Prayer.' Similarly, the following directions from the *Directory of Worship of the Presbyterian Church in America* would find parallel in the older, earlier forms of government from which these statements had been derived:

"47.6. The Lord Jesus Christ has prescribed no fixed forms for public worship but, in the interest of life and power in worship, has given His Church a large measure of liberty in this matter. It may not be forgotten, however, that there is true liberty only where the rules of God's Word are observed and the Spirit of the Lord is, that all things must be done decently and in order, and that God's people should serve Him with reverence and in the beauty of holiness.

"524. Ministers are not to be confined to fixed forms of prayer for public worship, yet it is the duty of the minister, previous to entering upon his office, to prepare and qualify himself for this part of his work, as well as for preaching.

"633. Family worship, which should be observed by every family, consists in prayer, reading the Scriptures, and singing praises; or in some briefer form of outspoken recognition of God."

T. David Gordon, "Some Answers About the Regulative Principle," *Westminster Theological Journal* 55 (Fall 1993): 326, n. 18.

of nature," "Christian prudence," and "general rules of the word" are to help us resolve circumstantial issues that are "common to human actions and societies," that is, common to public gatherings. For example, all public assemblies must resolve the questions of illumination, of sound projection or amplification, of meeting time and place, and, if group singing or reciting is to take place, of how to provide texts for the group. How are they to be resolved? By the "light of nature" and "Christian prudence" or what we might call sanctified common sense. We are not to expect Scripture texts for these questions. Returning to the example of prayer, I may pray in worship (it is an authorized element), a free or written prayer (matters of form), using an unaided voice or a microphone (matters of circumstance). I may preach (element) from Mark's gospel or Luke's (form) in an assembly hall illuminated by electric lights or oil lamps (circumstances).

Thus, there is a consistency in the application of the regulative principle, one which recognizes the important distinctions between elements, which require scriptural sanction (by command, example, or implication), freedom in forms limited only by the requirement that the form be consistent with the nature of the element, and common sense in circumstances. The regulative principle as outlined demonstrates what Reformed people have meant by worship that is "according to Scripture." It summarizes the Reformed view of worship. Indeed it is "Calvinism at worship," as T. David Gordon has said. It is the historic principle by which the Reformed church has articulated its understanding of the command of Jesus that we worship "in truth."

Filled with Scripture
Thus far we have shown that worship that is "in truth" is according to Scripture. Now, in the second place we shall prove that **worship "in truth" must be filled with Scripture.** Worship is not only governed by the Word, but is also saturated with the Word. The Samaritans do not "know" what they worship. Christians are to know. Old Testament worship expressed much of its truth in external, physical, typological form. The New Testament, with its

spiritual worship, will not. The truth expressed will have greater emphasis in the new era because the truth represented will be diminished. The Bible provides both the structure and the content of our worship. Much of pagan worship is noncognitive. Pagans pray with "meaningless repetition" and "many words" (Matt. 6:7). This is typical. Pagan worship functions on the level of feeling and experience rather than thought. Christian worship is thoughtful and filled with content. We are to love God with our minds (Matt. 22:37). Our "spiritual service of worship" is offered with renewed minds (Rom. 12:1, 2). As Calvin pointed out (and Augustine before him), herein lies "the difference between the singing of men and that of birds." The parrot may speak cleverly and the nightingale may sing beautifully, "but the unique gift of man is to sing knowing that which he sings."[10] Our "psalms, hymns, and spiritual songs" "teach and admonish," (Col. 3:16). Our worship is a two-sided conversation in which God speaks to us intelligibly in His word, and we speak back intelligibly in words that He has taught us. Our minds are never to be "unfruitful." Rather, we are to "pray with the spirit" and "with the mind also." We are to "sing with the spirit" and "with the mind also" (1 Cor. 14:14, 15). What God has joined together ought not ever to be broken asunder.

Thus, our praise is modeled on Biblical Psalms, our confession of sin on Biblical repentance, our confession of faith on Biblical doctrines, and our preaching on Biblical texts. We address God intelligently (in Biblical praise and confession) and He addresses our understanding (through His Word). To put it simply, in worship we pray the Word, sing the Word, read the Word, preach the Word, and see the Word (in the sacraments). The language of Christian worship is the language of Scripture. Why? Because this is what converts, sanctifies, and edifies God's people.

The Apostle Paul teaches that "faith comes from hearing the Word of God" (Rom. 10:17). How are we born again? By the Spirit and Word of God (1 Pet. 1:23-25). How do we grow in Christ? By the "pure milk of the word" (1 Pet. 2:2). How are we sanctified?

---

10. Preface to the Psalter, 1543.

"Sanctify them in the truth: Thy word is truth," Jesus said (John 17:17). Matured? Conformed to the image of God? By the Word of God performing its work in us (1 Thess. 2:13). The gospel (*euangelion*) is the power of God (Rom. 1:16; 1 Cor. 1:18, 24). The gospel message (*kerygma*) comes "in demonstration of the Spirit and power" (1 Cor. 2:4). It comes "in power and in the Holy Spirit with full conviction" (1 Thess. 1:5). Consequently, our worship is full of Biblical content.

One might have thought that this would be obvious to anyone who has a Protestant evangelical background. Regrettably, we can no longer count on this to be so. Biblical content is rapidly disappearing from evangelical worship. Some observers attempt to evaluate "our time" by looking only at particular songs or sermons and asking, "What's wrong with this?"[11] We think that one must step back and look not at isolated examples, but identify the trajectory of evangelical worship from a generation ago to today. A mere generation ago substantial portions of Scripture were read among Protestant evangelicals, sermons were expository, hymns were loaded with Biblical content, and prayers were full of Biblical content and allusions. Typically today little Scripture is read. Sermons are topical. Songs have comparatively little Biblical content, and what little there is of it is repeated with mantra-like frequency.[12] Prayers are short or nonexistent, and are expressed with language that is overly familiar, and only superficially Biblical. The sacraments, which

---

11. John Frame's books are particularly deficient at this point. He spends much of his effort defending this or that song or practice, but never surveys the big picture. He never considers the trajectory. Where have we come in the evangelical world? Where are we going? It is impossible to give an adequate evaluation of the parts without considering the whole.

12. David Wells has analyzed the theological content of the 406 songs of the two most popular contemporary songbooks, *Worship Songs of the Vineyard* and *Maranatha! Music Praise Chorus Book*. He compared them with the 662 hymns of *The Covenant Hymnal*. He summarized his findings saying, "the large majority of praise songs I analyzed, 58.9 percent, offer no doctrinal grounding or explanation for the praise; in the classical hymnody examined it was hard to find hymns that were *not* predicated upon and did not develop some aspect of doctrine" (emphasis mine). In addition, important Biblical themes are largely ignored. For example, the theme of the church is found in 1.2% of the songs; sin, penitence and longing for holiness in 3.6%; the holiness of God in 4.3%. *Losing OurVirtue* (Grand Rapids: William B. Eerdmans Publishing Co., 1998), 44.

require considerable Biblical reading and explanation in order to be properly administered, are infrequently observed or even moved to midweek. Evangelical and Reformed Protestants cannot be pleased about these developments. One need not be a prophet to sense trouble coming down the road. What shall we call "worship" when the Bible is not read, not preached, not sung, and not prayed except in token doses? Shall we call it a service? an event? a celebration? Since it is "sacred writings which are able to give (us) the wisdom that leads to salvation through faith which is in Christ Jesus," what kind of church will be left after a generation of "worship" in which these "sacred writings" are largely absent (2 Tim. 3:15)?

We may outline our principles as follows:

- Read the Bible. The Westminster Assembly's Directory for the Publick Worship of God commends the reading of whole chapters of Scripture. Paul told Timothy, "devote yourself to the public reading of Scripture, to preaching and to teaching" (1 Tim 4:13). In Reformed worship we read not just a verse or two here and there, but extended passages of Scripture.

- Preach the Bible. "From the very beginning the sermon was supposed to be an explanation of the Scripture reading," says Hughes Old, arguing from Nehemiah 8. It "is not just a lecture on some religious subject, it is rather an explanation of a passage of Scripture."[13] "Preach the word," Paul tells Timothy (2 Tim. 4:2). Expository, sequential, verse by verse, book by book, preaching through the whole Bible, the "whole counsel of God," (Acts 20:27), was the practice of many of the church fathers (e.g., Chrysostom, Augustine), all the Reformers, and the best of their heirs ever since. The preached word is the central feature of Reformed worship.[14]

---

13. Hughes Old, *Worship*, 59, 60.
14. Remarkably, Frame writes, "there is no specific Biblical command, so far as I can tell, to have sermons in worship" ("Some Questions," Westminster Theological Journal, 54 (1990), 366, n. 10). One wonders about a brand of "biblicism" that considers it necessary to make such a statement. Where in all of the Bible do the people of God assemble and not read and explain the Scripture? (e.g., Deut. 26:1ff; Exod. 24:1-11; Neh. 8:1-8; Luke 4:14-21; Acts 20:7ff; etc.) For an overwhelming case against Frame at this point, see Hughes O.

- Sing the Bible. Our songs should be rich with Biblical and theological content. The current divisions over music are at the heart of our worship wars. Yet some principles should be easy enough to identify. First, what does a Christian worship song look like? Answer, it looks like a Psalm. Reformed Protestants have at times exclusively sung Psalms. But even if that is not one's conviction, one should still acknowledge that the Psalms themselves should be sung and that the Psalms provide the model for Christian hymnody. If the songs we sing in worship look like Psalms, they will develop themes over many lines with minimal repetition. They will be rich in theological and experiential content. They will tell us much about God, man, sin, salvation, and the Christian life. They will express the whole range of human experience and emotion.

  Second, what does a Christian worship song sound like? Many are quick to point out that God has not given us a book of tunes. No, but He has given us a book of lyrics (the Psalms) and their form will do much to determine the kinds of melodies that will be used. Put simply, the tunes will be suited to the words. They will be sophisticated enough to carry substantial content over several lines and stanzas. They will use minimal repetition. They will be appropriate to the emotional mood of the Psalm or Biblebased Christian hymn. Sing the Bible.[15]

- Pray the Bible. The pulpit prayers of Reformed churches should be rich in Biblical and theological content. Do we not learn the language of Christian devotion from the Bible? Do we not learn the language of confession and penitence from the Bible? Do we not learn the promises of God that we are to believe and claim in prayer from the Bible? Do we not we learn the will of God, the commands of God, and the desires of God for His people, for which we are

---

Old, *The Reading and Preaching of the Scriptures in the Worship of the Christian Church*, Volumes 1 & 2 (Grand Rapids: William B. Eerdmans Publishing Co., 1998).
15. These ideas are worked out in more detail in Terry Johnson, *The Pastor's Public Ministry* (Greenville: Reformed Academic Press, 2001), 25-30.

to plead in prayer, from the Bible? Since these things are so, public prayers should repeat and echo the language of the Bible throughout. This was once widely understood. Matthew Henry[16] and Isaac Watts[17] produced prayer manuals that trained Protestant pastors for generations to pray in the language of Scripture, and are still used today. Hughes Old has produced a similar work in recent years.[18]

- *See the Bible*. Augustine first referred to the sacraments as the "visible word." The sacraments are accompanied by extensive Bible reading (e.g., the words of institution and warning) and theological explanation (e.g., the covenant and the nature of the sacraments). They are themselves visual symbols of gospel truths. In Reformed worship the word and sacrament are never separated. Why? Because faith comes by hearing the word of God (Rom. 10:17).

Thus the worship of Reformed Protestantism is simple. We merely read, preach, pray, and sing the Bible, but more about its simplicity later. Sometimes this emphasis on the Bible in Reformed worship has been criticized as being overly "cognitive" or "intellectual,"[19] as well as anti-emotional and against the arts. While this is not the place to take on all these issues (e.g., a theology of art, a theory of human

---

16. J. Matthew Henry, *A Method for Prayer*, ed. J. Ligon Duncan III (1710; reprint Greenville: Reformed Academic Press, 1994).

17. Isaac Watts, *A Guide to Prayer* (1715; reprint, Edinburgh: The Banner of Truth Trust, 2001).

18. Hughes Old, *Leading in Prayer* (Grand Rapids: William B. Eerdmans Publishing Co., 1995).

19. Robert Webber and John Frame both typically say things like this. "For centuries the focus of Protestant thought about worship has been on worship as a cerebral act," and "What made worship worship was the sermon," (Robert Webber, "Reaffirming the Arts," Worship Leader 8, no. 6, [November/December, 1999]:, 10). Also Frame, *Worship*, 7778. Frame is concerned that traditional hymns have too much Biblical/theological content. For example, "'Shine, Jesus Shine' stands up pretty well against 'Of the Father's Love Begotten'" says Frame, because the latter "states too many doctrines too fast to be truly edifying" (Contemporary, 116). By this standard one supposes that the Psalms could never be sung, or for that matter the book of Romans could never be read (too many doctrines flying by too fast). He regularly biases his argument by referring to the "intellectual content" of songs and sermons rather than the Biblical content, their real essence (Contemporary, 98ff).

psychology, a philosophy of learning and so on), we would simply answer: worship must be "according to Scripture." In addressing the understanding, Scripture addresses the whole man: mind, will, and emotions. Scripture filled sermons, songs, and prayers are not "cerebral" or "academic," any more than a human father's loving and firm communication to his beloved child can be so classified. It is singularly odd that they should have even come to be considered such.

Conclusion

The regulative principle is not difficult. It is not heavy or burdensome. It merely requires that we worship "according to Scripture." We are both to structure our worship with Biblical elements, and fill those elements with Biblical content.

Those who attend a Reformed worship service will hear a steady stream of sanctifying Biblical content. They will be called to worship with a Biblical call such as Psalm 95: *Come, let us worship and bow down; let us kneel before the Lord our Maker. For He is our God, and we are the people of His pasture, and the sheep of His hand* (vv. 6, 7)

Reformed worshippers will sing an opening hymn of praise that is rich with Biblical language and themes.

> *O worship the King all glorious above,*
> *O gratefully sing his pow'r and his love;*
> *Our Shield and Defender, the Ancient of Days,*
> *Pavilioned in splendor and girded with praise.*
> *(1st stanza, "O Worship the King")*

They will hear an invocation that echoes the language of Biblical praise such as that found in 1 Timothy 1:17 and 6:15-16: "Now to the King eternal, immortal, invisible, the only wise God, …the blessed and only Sovereign, the King of kings and Lord of lords; who alone possesses immortality and dwells in unapproachable light; whom no man has seen or can see. To Him be honor and eternal dominion!"

They will recite a summary of Biblical doctrine in the language in one of the historic creeds. They will hear the Biblical language of confessions, thanksgiving, and intercession in the "pastoral prayer." A significant portion of each testament will be read, and a complete Psalm (or large section of a longer Psalm) will be sung. The sermon will be an exposition of Scripture that explains, applies, and exhorts on the basis of a Biblical text. The closing hymn, like the opening, will be rich in Biblical language and allusion. Finally they will hear a Biblical benediction, such as the Aaronic:

> *The Lord bless you and keep you,*
> *The Lord make His face to shine upon you,*
> *and be gracious unto you.*
> *The Lord lift up His countenance upon you,*
> *and give you His peace.* (Numbers 6:24-26).

Do not underestimate the cumulative impact of this weight of Scripture week in and week out throughout the life of the members of Reformed churches. Does faith come by hearing the word of God (Rom. 10:17)? Are we sanctified by the truth (John 17:17)? If so, and we are, we will not want this content diminished.

It should be clear by this point that the real battleground today is not over elements but forms. Only a small minority of Reformed churches believe that dance and drama are legitimate elements of worship, and an even smaller minority will ever implement their use. Even the newest of New School theologians continue to affirm the regulative principle. The real debate is whether contemporary forms are adequate for the expression of the Reformed faith. Can contemporary buckets carry Calvinistic water? Can an informal, casual setting and tone, pop/rock music, minimal prayer and Bible reading, and needs based topical preaching produce a new generation of Puritans, Huguenots, and Covenanters – that is, brave, uncompromising souls who will shape civilizations? Those churches that abandon traditional forms for contemporary alternatives are unlikely to experience that depth of sanctifying grace, since it is in our Sunday public services that Reformed convictions receive their widest dissemination,. We will not see reproduced broadly in our generation the characteristics that were typical of Reformed people of previous generations; namely, warm piety (because they look gratefully to Christ alone), moral precision (because they hold to the third use of the law), steadfastness in hardship (because they believe in Romans 8:28 and the sovereignty of God), strong families (because they are aware of their covenantal responsibilities), and self-government (because Presbyterian government has taught them to regard highly the rights and responsibilities of the governed). We are convinced that it will not happen precisely because contemporary forms are not up to the task. Only the historically Reformed worship can do the job. Only Presbyterian buckets can carry Presbyterian water.

What ought we to do in worship? What has God promised to bless? The reading, preaching, singing and praying of the Scriptures, along the traditional lines outlined above, along with the sacraments Biblically explained and administered.

Chapter 2

Calvin and the Worship of God

W. Robert Godfrey

John Calvin is a hero for Reformed people. He is a hero because he was such a profound teacher of biblical Christianity. His systematic theology and his biblical commentaries remain models of brilliant scholarship and sensitive faith. While not necessarily agreeing with Calvin at every point and certainly not regarding him as an absolute authority, Reformed people continue to follow basically the theological map charted by Calvin.

Ironically, however, many Reformed people today do not follow Calvin's view of worship. Many are not even acquainted with his views. If Calvin is as biblical and as theologically profound as many Reformed people believe him to be, perhaps his approach to worship needs to be reconsidered.

Importance of Worship
The first surprise for students of Calvin is likely to be the great importance that he attached to worship. In 1543 he wrote a treatise entitled "On the Necessity of Reforming the Church." The work was written as an explanation and defense of the Reformation to be presented to Emperor Charles V. Near the beginning Calvin wrote:

> If it be inquired, then, by what things chiefly the Christian religion has a standing existence amongst us, and maintains its truth, it will be found that the following two not only occupy the principal place,

but comprehend under them all the other parts, and consequently the whole substance of Christianity, viz., a knowledge, first, of the mode in which God is duly worshipped; and, secondly, of the source from which salvation is to be obtained.[1]

Remarkably Calvin put worship ahead of salvation in his list of the two most important elements of biblical Christianity.

This prominence given to worship by Calvin is repeated often. In the *Institutes*, Calvin noted that the first four commandments of the Decalogue relate to worship. He concluded: "Surely the first foundation of righteousness is the worship of God."[2] In his celebrated defense of the Reformation, "Reply to Sadoleto," Calvin noted that "there is nothing more perilous to our salvation than a preposterous and perverse worship of God."[3]

Why is worship so important? For Calvin worship was the key meeting place of God and his people: "let us know and be fully persuaded, that wherever the faithful, who worship him purely and in due form, according to the appointment of his word, are assembled together to engage in the solemn acts of religious worship, he is graciously present, and presides in the midst of them."[4] The restoration of the fellowship between God and his people is expressed most fully in worship. As that fellowship was broken by sin and rebellion, so its restoration must be expressed in obedience to God. "Only when we follow what God has commanded us," wrote Calvin, "do we truly worship Him, and render obedience to His Word."[5]

Calvin's approach to worship later came to be called the regulative principle. This principle holds that the Scriptures must so regulate

1. John Calvin, "On the Necessity of Reforming the Church," in Selected Works of John Calvin, ed. Henry Beveridge (Grand Rapids: Baker Book House, 1983), 1:126.
2. John Calvin, *Institutes of the Christian Religion*, ed. J.T. McNeill (Philadelphia: Westminster Press, 1960), II.viii. 11.
3. John Calvin and Jacopo Sadoleto, *A Reformation Debate*, ed. by John C. Olin, (New York: Harper and Row, 1966), 59.
4. John Calvin, *Commentary on the Book of Psalms*, (Grand Rapids: Baker Book House, 1979), 1:122.
5. John Calvin, *Calvin's Commentaries: The Epistles of Paul The Apostle to the Romans and to the Thessalonians*, ed. D. W. Torrance et al (Grand Rapids: William B. Eerdmans Publishing Co. 1973), 118 (on Romans 5:19).

public worship that only what is explicitly commanded in the Bible may be an element of worship.[6] Calvin was eloquent on the theme:

> I know how difficult it is to persuade the world that God disapproves of all modes of worship not expressly sanctioned by His Word. The opposite persuasion which cleaves to them, being seated, as it were, in their very bones and marrow, is, that whatever they do has in itself a sufficient sanction, provided it exhibits some kind of zeal for the honour of God. But since God not only regards as fruitless, but also plainly abominates, whatever we undertake from zeal to His worship, if at variance with His command, what do we gain by a contrary course? The words of God are clear and distinct, 'Obedience is better than sacrifice.' 'In vain do they worship me, teaching for doctrines the commandments of men,' (1 Sam. xv. 22; Matt. xv. 9.) Every addition to His word, especially in this matter, is a lie. Mere 'will worship' [Col. ii. 23] … is vanity. This is the decision, and when once the judge has decided, it is no longer time to debate.[7]

Calvin knew the human tendency to think that sincerity and fervor can substitute for truth and faithfulness, but he rejected any such notion absolutely.

Calvin based his great caution about worship on the Fall. One of the most profound effects of the Fall for Calvin was that men have become idolaters.[8] The seed of religion left in them does not lead them to the true God, but leads them to fashion gods of their own design.[9] "Experience," suggested Calvin, "teaches us how fertile is

---

6. Attempts have been made at times to argue that the regulative principle is a Puritan invention foreign to the thought of Calvin. Such a division cannot be maintained. It is true that Calvin's application of the principle was not always in harmony with some Puritan applications, but Puritans differed among themselves on the application of the principle. This crucial distinction between principle and application is missed in Ralph J. Gore, Jr., "The Pursuit of Plainness: Rethinking the Puritan Regulative Principle of Worship," Ph.D. dissertation, Westminster Theological Seminary, 1988, and therefore the relationship between Calvin and the Puritans on this point is fundamentally misunderstood.

7. Calvin, "On the Necessity," Selected Works, 1:128ff.

8. See the excellent discussion of Carlos M. N. Eire, *War Against the Idols. The Reformation of Worship from Erasmus to Calvin* (Cambridge: Cambridge University Press, 1986), 195-233.

9. Ibid., 209.

the field of falsehood in the human mind, and that the smallest of grains, when sown there, will grow to yield an immense harvest."[10] Even among Christians the temptation to idolatry remains strong. Calvin states it poignantly when he says, "The mind of man, I say, is like a work place of idolatrie"[11] and "every one of us is, even from his mother's womb, a master craftsman of idols."[12]

The temptation to idolatry requires that Christians be very careful and vigilant in regulating their worship by the Scriptures. Calvin reminded Christians that "too much diligence and care cannot be taken to cleanse ourselves wholly from all sorts of pollutions; for as long as any relics of superstition continue among us, they will ever entangle us...."[13]

Calvin's great caution and concern on matters of worship reflected his belief that Christians too often want to please themselves in worship rather than please God. "Nor can it be doubted," he argued, "but that, under the pretense of holy zeal, superstitious men give way to the indulgences of the flesh; and Satan baits his fictitious modes of worship with such attractions, that they are willingly and eagerly caught hold of and obstinately retained."[14] Calvin sharply warned of the great difference between the attitudes of God and man toward worship: "This single consideration, when the inquiry relates to the worship of God, ought to be sufficient for restraining the insolence of our mind, that God is so far from being like us, that those things which please us most are for him loathsome and nauseating."[15] He related this warning particularly to the human tendency to want worship which is pleasing to the senses when

10. Ibid., 223 (citing Calvin, Corpus Reformatorum, 13.85.)
11. Cited by T. Brienen, De Lituraie bij Johannes Calviin, (Kampen: De Groot Goudriaan, 1987), 145 (from a sermon by Calvin on Deuteronomy 11.)
12. Eire, War Against the Idols, 208 (citing Calvin's Commentary on the Acts of the Apostles, CR, 48.562.)
13. John Calvin, Commentaries on the Twelve Minor Prophets, (Grand Rapids: Baker Book House, 1984), 1:108 (on Hosea 2:17).
14. John Calvin, Commentaries on the Four Last Books of Moses, (Grand Rapids: Baker Book House, 1984), 3:346.
15. Eire, War Against the Idols, 208 (citing Calvin's Commentary on the Gospel of John, CR 47.90.)

he wrote: "And undoubtedly this is the origin of all superstitions, that men are delighted with their own inventions, and choose to be wise in their own eyes rather than restrain their senses in obedience to God."[16] His conclusion on various activities and ceremonies in worship is striking: "the more it delights human nature, the more it is to be suspected by These matters are so serious for Calvin because "nothing is more abominable in the sight of God than pretended worship, which proceeds from human contrivance."[18]

For Calvin, worship was not a means to an end. Worship was not a means to evangelize or entertain. Worship was an end in itself. Worship was not to be arranged by pragmatic considerations, but was rather to be determined by theological principles derived from the Scriptures. The most basic realities of the Christian life were involved. In worship God meets with his people to bless them. What could be more important? What should require more care and faithfulness?

The Practice of Worship

The importance Calvin placed on worship is reflected in his active involvement in reforming worship. He not only had a theology of worship, but also a keen pastoral involvement in worship. He frequently led worship as pastor and preacher. He prepared service books or liturgies that his churches in Strasbourg and Geneva followed. He eagerly promoted the preparation of the Genevan Psalter that ultimately included all of the Psalms in metrical form to be sung by the congregation.

> Calvin was concerned about the environment of worship. He "purified" the cathedral church of Geneva, St. Pierre's, where he preached. All religious symbols including crosses were removed from the interior of the church. The exterior cross on the top of St Pierre's was not removed, but when it was destroyed by lightning, it was not replaced.

---

16. John Calvin, *Commentary on the Book of the Prophet Isaiah* (Grand Rapids, Michigan: Baker Book House, 1979), 4:381.

17. Calvin, *Institutes*, IV.x.11.

18. Calvin, *Commentary on Isaiah*, 4:385.

As he worked on the reform of worship, several important influences played a role in the formation of his thought. The Bible was of course the most important. Calvin always sought to test his ideas against the standard of the Bible. But Calvin was no rugged individualist. He also sought the wisdom and insight of other Christians into the Bible's teaching on worship. He carefully studied the ancient fathers of the church for their insights, as is clear in this statement to the Roman Catholic bishop Jacopo Sadoleto:

> I will not press you so closely as to call you back to that form which the Apostles instituted (though in it we have the only model of a true church, and whosoever deviates from it in the smallest degree is in error), but to indulge you so far, place, I pray, before your eyes, that ancient form of the Church, such as their writings prove it to have been in the age of Chrysostom and Basil, among the Greeks, and of Cyprian, Ambrose, and Augustine, among the Latins; after so doing, contemplate the ruins of that Church, as now surviving among yourselves.[19]

Calvin's genuine concern to follow the wisdom of the fathers can be further seen in his title for the Genevan service book, "The Form of Prayers and Manner of Ministering the Sacraments according to the Use of the Ancient Church." Also in his "Preface" to the Genevan Psalter (1545) Calvin acknowledged especially the influence of Augustine and Chrysostom.

Of Calvin's contemporaries clearly the most influential on worship was Martin Bucer of Strasbourg. Calvin spent his years of exile from Geneva (1538–1541) in Strasbourg, and Calvin closely followed Bucer's approach to the liturgy. Calvin's Sunday morning liturgy in Geneva was very similar to Bucer's. The basic order was as follows:

---

19. Calvin, *A Reformation Debate*, 62.

Liturgy of the Word	Liturgy of the Upper Room
Call to worship: Psalm 124:8	Collection of offerings
Confession of sins	Prayers of intercession and a long
Prayer for pardon	paraphrase of the Lord's Prayer
Singing of a Psalm	Singing of Apostles' Creed (while
Prayer for illumination	elements of the Lord's Supper are
Scripture reading	prepared)
Sermon	Words of Institution
	Instruction and Exhortation
	Communion (while a Psalm is sung
	or Scripture read)
	Prayer of thanksgiving
	Benediction (Num. 6:24 26)[20]

This pattern is the one regularly used by Calvin on Sunday mornings except that communion was not administered weekly. Calvin desired a weekly communion, but could never get permission from the city government to do so. On the matter of the frequency of communion Calvin wrote as late as 1561: "I have taken care to record publicly that our custom is defective? so that those who come after me may be able to correct it more freely and easily."[21]

While Calvin was quite content to use form prayers and liturgies in the Sunday morning service, he also recognized a legitimate role for freedom from specific forms in worship. Before presenting the ordinary Sunday service Calvin's "Form of Prayers" stated: "On ordinary Meetings the Minister leads the devotions of the people in whatever words seem to him suitable, adapting his address to the time and the subject of the Discourse which he is to deliver, but the following Form is generally used on the Morning of the Lord's Day."[22]

---

20. This listing basically follows William D. Maxwell, *An Outline of Christian Worship* (London: Oxford University Press, 1958), 114ff. For the similarities between Calvin and Bucer on the structure of the liturgy, see Maxwell, 87ff.

21. Cited in *The Liturgy of the Church of Scotland*, Part I. Calvin's Liturgy, ed. Stephen A. Hurlbut (Washington, D.C: The St. Albans Press, 1944), 6 (from Calvini Opera, x, i, 213).

22. Calvin, "Form of Prayers," Selected Works, 2:100.

Basic Principles of Worship

Calvin nowhere neatly listed his basic principles of worship. But a study of Calvin's writings and work points to several principles that flow from and reflect his theology. The first principle is, of course, the centrality of the Word of God. The Word not only directs worship, but is also very largely the content of worship. The Word is read and preached, and the Word is also sung and seen (in communion). The worshiper meets God through the Word.

Criticism of Calvin's approach to worship often focuses on his stress upon the Bible. One such criticism is that Calvin is a Biblicist in his approach to worship. Such a criticism declares that there is no Book of Leviticus in the New Testament and so the church has great freedom to worship as it sees best. Calvin's response would be that the absence of a Levitical book in the New Testament reflects more the simplicity of the church's worship in Christ than creative freedom. For Calvin the teaching of the New Testament is full and complete as a guide and warrant for the simple worship of the children of God in the Spirit. No more freedom is given in the New Testament to invent forms of worship than was given in the Old.

Calvin certainly recognized that incidental matters of worship are not specified in the Bible. In such areas the church has freedom under the general guidelines of the Word to reach specific decisions that will be edifying for the church.[23] For example the Bible does

---

23. Calvin makes this point clearly in *Institutes*, IV.x.30: "Let us take, for example, kneeling when solemn prayers are being said. The question is whether it is a human tradition, which any man may lawfully repudiate or neglect. I say that it is human, as it is also divine. It is of God in so far as it is a part of that decorum whose care and observance the apostle has commended to us? But it is of men in so far as it specifically designates what had in general been suggested rather than explicitly stated.... I mean that the Lord has in his sacred oracles faithfully embraced and clearly expressed both the whole sum of true righteousness, and all aspects of the worship of his majesty, and whatever was necessary to salvation; therefore, in these the Master alone is to be heard. But because he did not will in outward discipline and ceremonies to prescribe in detail what we ought to do (because he foresaw that this depended upon the state of the times, and he did not deem one form suitable for all ages), here we must take refuge in those general rules which he has given, that whatever the necessity of the church will require for order and decorum should be tested against these.... Indeed, I admit that we ought not to charge into innovation rashly, suddenly, for insufficient cause. But love will best judge what may hurt or edify; and if we

not specify when on Sunday the church should gather for worship. But some time must be chosen and that choice should be based on what will best facilitate gathering for worship. Such decisions can be changed when necessary and can never be viewed as binding the conscience as if they were necessary for salvation.[24]

Another criticism of Calvin's stress on the Word is that Calvin's worship becomes too intellectual or didactic because of an excessive concentration on the Bible. Calvin's defenders would respond that the Bible itself points to the importance of preaching and teaching, which is especially vital when knowledge of sound doctrine is at a low ebb. But defenders would also insist that his worship service is not solely or overwhelmingly intellectual. Congregational praise and prayer are key elements and in Calvin's ideal service communion weekly draws the worshiper back to the heart of the gospel. The Lord's Supper for Calvin was a rich experience. Calvin could write: "Now, if anyone should ask me how this [Christ lifting believers up in the Supper to heaven to commune with him] takes place, I shall not be ashamed to confess that it is a secret too lofty for either my mind to comprehend or my words to declare. And, to speak more plainly, I rather experience than understand it."[25]

A second basic principle for Calvin was simplicity. The maturity of the children of God in the new covenant meant that Christians were not dependent on the childish props of the old covenant. In Christ the Christian is already seated with Christ in the heavenlies and the need of visible supports for faith is greatly diminished:

---

let love be our guide, all will be safe." The Westminster Confession of Faith makes basically the same point in its distinction between elements of worship which must be warranted by Scripture, and the circumstances of worship, about which the church has a measure of freedom (see chapters I.6; XX.2; XXI.1).

24. Calvin, Institutes, IV.x.27: "We see that some form of organization is necessary in all human society to foster the common peace and maintain concord. We further see that in human transactions some procedure is always in effect, which is to be respected in the interest of public decency, and even of humanity itself.... But in these observances one thing must be guarded against. They are not to be considered necessary for salvation and thus bind consciences by scruples; nor are they to be associated with the worship of God, and piety thus be lodged in them."

25. Ibid., IV.xvii.32.

What shall I say of ceremonies which, with Christ half buried, cause us to return to Jewish symbols? 'Our Lord Christ,' says Augustine, 'has bound the fellowship of the new people together with sacraments, very few in number, very excellent in meaning, very easy to observe.' How far from this simplicity is the multitude and variety of rites, with which we see the church entangled today, cannot be fully told.[26]

Simplicity did not mean the absence of liturgical structure. Calvin's service with its movement from confession to praise to preaching to intercessions to communion reveals that. Simplicity meant the removal of physical symbolism and ceremonies that were not instituted in the Bible. Simplicity is closely linked to spirituality. In the simplicity of the Spirit's power, Christ is present among his people in the preaching and sacrament. Nothing may be added to that divine arrangement. Simplicity rather than "showiness" serves the pure worship of the church: "For Paul is urging the Corinthians to value or strive after, above all, those gifts which are the most effective for upbuilding. For the fault of caring more for ostentation rather than beneficial things was rife among them."[27] The eye of faith rather than the eye of the flesh is to be active in worship.

Closely related to simplicity is a third basic principle: worship is spiritual ascent. For Calvin, Christians ascend into heaven while worshipping. Worship draws the Christian into heaven in communion with the ascended Christ. This ascent in worship is mysterious – even for Calvin – but a foundational current in his thought.[28]

The idea of ascent is part of the pattern of Christian experience flowing from Christ's saving work. Christ descended in his incarnation to lift us to heaven.

---

26. Ibid., IV.x.14.

27. John Calvin, Calvin's Commentaries. *The First Epistle of Paul the Apostle to the Corinthians* (Grand Rapids: William B. Eerdmans Publishing Co., 1973), 272 (on 1 Cor. 12:31).

28. Calvin uses the idea of the believer's ascent into heaven in his theology of the Lord's Supper. He teaches that the believer communes with the body and blood of the ascended Lord in heaven and, as noted above (p. 12) acknowledges that this communion in heaven is a mystery.

Now that the Mosaic ceremonies are abolished we worship at the footstool of God, when we yield a reverential submission to his word, and rise from the sacraments to a true spiritual service of him. Knowing that God has not descended from heaven directly or in his absolute character, but that his feet are withdrawn from us, being placed on a footstool, we should be careful to rise to him by the intermediate steps. Christ is he not only on whom the feet of God rest, but in whom the whole fullness of God's essence and glory resides, and in him therefore, we should seek the Father. With this view he descended, that we might rise heavenward.[29]

Christ continues to help us heavenward as his Spirit descends to empower the Word and sacraments of the church. "It is thus that the Holy Spirit condescends for our profit, and in accommodation to our infirmity, raising our thought to heavenly and divine things by these worldly elements.[30] The worshipper needs these means – or "ladders" – that God provides to help with that ascent:

He does not enjoin us to ascend forthwith into heaven, but, consulting our weakness, he descends to us.... This ... may well suffice to put to shame the arrogance of those who without concern can bear to be deprived of those means, or rather, who proudly despise them, as if it were in their power to ascend to heaven in a moment's flight.... We must not, however, imagine that the prophet suffered himself to rest in earthly elements, but only that he made use of them as a ladder, by which he might ascend to God, finding that he had not wings with which to fly thither.[31]

A visually elaborate context would interfere with our spiritual ascent, binding our minds too much to earth. "Such is the weakness of our minds that we rise with difficulty to the contemplation of his glory in the heavens."[32] False worship – especially idolatrous worship – panders to human weakness and tries to force God to descend to earth when his will is for the Christian to ascend to heaven:

---

29. Calvin, *Commentary on Psalms*, 5:150.
30. Ibid.
31. Ibid., 2:129f.
32. Ibid., 4:52.

> The reason why God holds images so much in abhorrence appears very plainly from this, that he cannot endure that the worship due to himself should be taken from him and given to them ... when men attempt to attach God to their inventions, and to make him, as it were, descend from heaven, then a pure fiction is substituted in his place.... Averse to seek God in a spiritual manner, they therefore pull him down from his throne, and place him under inanimate things.[33]

Christians are called to worship the heavenly God in heaven, God's true temple.

A fourth basic principle for Calvin was reverence. Reverence is indeed a basic element of Christianity for him:

> Here indeed is pure and real religion: faith so joined with an earnest fear of God that this fear also embraces willing reverence, and carries with it such legitimate worship as is prescribed in the law. And we ought to note this fact even more diligently: all men have a vague general veneration of God, but very few really reverence him; and wherever there is great ostentation in ceremonies, sincerity of heart is rare indeed.[34]

The worship of God must express a decorum and dignity appropriate to the meeting of God with his children: "we have been adopted for this reason: to reverence him as our Father."[35]

In the contemporary church Calvin's concern for reverence has undergone sharp criticism. Critics insist that Calvin's worship had too little emotion and particularly too little joy. Calvin was not opposed to emotion and believed that a full range of emotion – not just joy! – should be expressed in Christian life and worship:

> For the principle which the Stoics assume, that all the passions are perturbations and like diseases, is false, and has its origin in ignorance; for either to grieve, or to fear, or to rejoice, or to hope, is by no means repugnant to reason, nor does it interfere

---

33. Ibid., 4:350f.
34. Calvin, *Institutes*, I.ii.2.
35. Ibid., III.xvii.6.

with tranquillity and moderation of mind; it is only excess or intemperance which corrupts what would else be pure. And surely grief, anger, desire, hope, fear, are affections of our unfallen (*intergrae*) nature, implanted in us by God, and such as we may not find fault with, without insulting God himself.[36]

But Calvin did insist that emotion must be moderate. Self-control is a key fruit of the Holy Spirit.

Moderation is proper even in expressing joy. The Psalmist declares, "Worship the Lord with reverence, and rejoice with trembling" (Ps. 2:11). Calvin wrote:

To prevent them from supposing that the service to which he calls them is grievous, he teaches them by the word rejoice how pleasant and desirable it is, since it furnishes matter of true gladness. But lest they should, according to their usual way, wax wanton, and, intoxicated with vain pleasures, imagine themselves happy while they are enemies to God, he exhorts them farther by the words with fear to an humble and dutiful submission. There is a great difference between the pleasant and cheerful state of a peaceful conscience, which the faithful enjoy in having the favour of God, whom they fear, and the unbridled insolence to which the wicked are carried, by contempt and forgetfulness of God. The language of the prophet, therefore, implies, that so long as the proud profligately rejoice in the gratification of the lusts of the flesh, they sport with their own destruction, while, on the contrary, the only true and salutary joy is that which arises from resting in the fear and reverence of God.[37]

He made a similar comment on the biblical text, "let us be thankful, and so worship God acceptably with reverence and awe" (Heb. 12:28): "although readiness and joy are demanded in our service, at the same time no worship is pleasing to Him that is not allied to humility and due reverence."[38]

---

36. John Calvin, *Commentaries on the Four Last Books of Moses* (Grand Rapids: Baker Book House, 1979), III: 346 (on Exodus 32:19).

37. Calvin, *Commentary on Psalms*, 1:23f

38. John Calvin, Calvin's Commentaries. *The Epistle of Paul the Apostle to the Hebrews* (Grand Rapids: William B. Eerdmans Publishing Co., 1963), 203.

Part of the reverence of Reformed worship is found in the role of the minister. He speaks for God to the people and for the people to God. Some criticize this practice as limiting the participation of the people in worship. Calvin's response would be twofold. First, such a criticism misses the importance of the ministry in Christ's church: "For neither the light and heat of the sun, nor food and drink, are so necessary to nourish and sustain the present life as the apostolic and pastoral office is necessary to preserve the church on earth."[39] The ministers as they preach faithfully speak for God: "he [God] proves our obedience by a very good test when we hear his ministers speaking just as if he himself spoke."[40] Second, Calvin would argue that the congregation does participate actively in worship. They must listen actively in faith to the preaching of the Word. They must join in the sung praise of God. They must pray with the minister lifting their hearts and minds to God. Such activities are the reverent participation to which God calls his people.

Music for Worship

Calvin's position on music is one application of his theology of worship. Calvin's view of music focuses most sharply the differences between Calvin and many contemporary evangelicals, even those who would call themselves Reformed. Music was important to Calvin. He wrote of music: "we find by experience that it has a sacred and almost incredible power to move hearts in one way or another. Therefore we ought to be even more diligent in regulating it in such a way that it shall be useful to us and in no way pernicious."[41]

Calvin greatly simplified the use of music in worship in comparison with the musical developments of the late medieval period. Calvin eliminated choirs and musical instruments from public worship. The only music in worship was congregational singing unaccompanied by musical instruments. The simplicity of singing and the unity of

---

39. Calvin, *Institutes*, IV.iii.2.
40. Ibid., IV.i.5
41. John Calvin, "Preface" to the *Genevan Psalter* (1545), 3. This and subsequent quotations are from an English translation (from the "Calvini Opera", 6:172ff) by Charles Garside, Jr. as part of an unpublished bachelor's thesis at Princeton University.

the congregation was best preserved, Calvin believed, by singing in unison.

Singing was a basic element of worship for Calvin because he saw singing as a particularly heartfelt way to pray: "As for public prayers, there are two kinds. The ones with the word alone: the others with singing."[42]

Calvin believed that the Psalms were the best songs for the Christian community to sing:

> Moreover, that which St Augustine has said is true, that no one is able to sing things worthy of God except that which he has received from him. Therefore, when we have looked thoroughly, and searched here and there, we shall not find better songs nor more fitting for the purpose, than the Psalms of David, which the Holy Spirit spoke and made through him. And moreover, when we sing them, we are certain that God puts in our mouths these, as if he himself were singing in us to exalt his glory.[43]

Calvin elaborated on his strong feelings about the value of the Psalms to the Christian community in the preface to his Psalms commentary:

> I have been accustomed to call this book, I think not inappropriately, 'An Anatomy of all the Parts of the Soul'; for there is not an emotion of which any one can be conscious that is not here represented as in a mirror ... in short, there is no other book in which we are more perfectly taught the right manner of praising God, or in which we are more powerfully stirred up to the performance of this religious exercise.[44]

Calvin's approach to music may well seem strange and idiosyncratic today. Calvin believed, however, that he was simply restoring the use of music sanctioned by the Bible and followed by the ancient church. From reading the fathers (especially Athanasius,

---

42. Ibid., 2.
43. Ibid., 4.
44. Calvin, *Commentary on Psalms*, 1:xxxvi xxxix.

Chrysostom and Augustine) Calvin learned that the ancient church
sang exclusively (or almost exclusively) Psalms in unison without
instrumental accompaniment.[45] He believed that he was purifying
the church from recent musical innovations in the western
church.

On the issue of musical instruments Calvin was convinced that
the fathers rightly saw that the new covenant required abandoning
instruments for public worship:

> To sing the praises of God upon the harp and psaltery unquestionably
> formed a part of the training of the law, and of the service of God
> under that dispensation of shadows and figures; but they are not now
> to be used in public thanksgiving. We are not, indeed, forbidden to
> use, in private, musical instruments, but they are banished out of
> the churches by the plain command of the Holy Spirit, when Paul,
> in 1 Cor. xiv. 13, lays it down as an invariable rule, that we must
> praise God, and pray to him only in a known tongue.[46]

Calvin linked the movement of New Testament worship away
from instruments to the greater simplicity of the new covenant:
"musical instruments were among the legal ceremonies which Christ
at His coming abolished; and therefore we, under the Gospel, must
maintain a greater simplicity."[47] Calvin's statements show that his
criticism of instruments was primarily directed against any role for
musical instruments independent of accompanying congregational
singing, but in practice he did eliminate instruments completely
from worship.

Calvin argued that the instruments were instituted for the Jews
to wean them gradually from the dissolute ways of the world: "that
he might lead men away from those vain and corrupt pleasures
to which they are excessively addicted, to a holy and profitable

45. For the accuracy of Calvin's understanding of the ancient church, see Johannes Quasten, *Music and Worship in Pagan and Christian Antiquity* (Washington, D.C: National Association of Pastoral Musicians, 1983). The Eastern Orthodox churches to this day do not use musical instruments in their churches.
46. Calvin, *Commentary on Psalms,* 3:98. See also, 1:539.
47. Calvin, *Commentary on the Four Last Books of Moses*, 1:263. See also *Commentary on Psalms,* 3:312.

joy."[48] But the maturity of the church after the appearance of Jesus made such "puerile instruction" unnecessary and detrimental to spirituality.

> But when they [believers] frequent their sacred assemblies, musical instruments in celebrating the praises of God would be no more suitable than the burning of incense, the lighting up of lamps, and the restoration of the other shadows of the law. The Papists, therefore, have foolishly borrowed this, as well as many other things, from the Jews ... but we should always take care that no corruption creep in which might both defile the pure worship of God and involve men in superstition.[49]

Calvin's concern for proper worship extended also to the tunes to be used for the Psalms. He carefully supervised the preparation of the Genevan Psalter over the years to insure the composition of appropriate music and in the providence of God was blessed with composers of extraordinary talent like Louis Bourgeois. Calvin expressed his basic position on tunes in these words: "Touching the melody, it has seemed best that it be moderated in the manner we have adopted to carry the weight and majesty appropriate to the subject, and even to be proper for singing in the Church...."[50] The music for the songs of the church must be reverent in relation to God and "singable" for the congregation.

Calvin's critics suggest that his approach to music is dominated by the very cautious attitudes of Plato toward music. Certainly Plato, both directly and mediated through the fathers, was a great influence on Calvin. Calvin did refer to Plato's attitude toward music quite favorably both in the "Preface" to the Genevan Psalter and elsewhere: "we all know from experience how great a power music has for moving men's feelings, so that Plato teaches, quite rightly, that in one way or another music is of the greatest value

---

48. Calvin, *Commentary on Psalms*, 5: 320.
49. Ibid., 1:539.
50. Calvin, "Preface" to Genevan Psalter, 4. See a detailed look at this and related matters in Charles Garside, Jr., The Origins of Calvin's Theology of Music: 1536 1543 (Philadelphia: The American Philosophical Society, 1979).

in shaping the moral tone of the state."[51] The real issue is not the influence of Plato, but whether Calvin's use of Plato enables him to see the implications of biblical teaching more clearly or not. Calvin clearly felt it did. The power inherent in music meant that it had to be handled carefully:

> And in truth we know by experience that singing has great force and vigour to move and inflame the hearts of men to invoke and praise God with a more vehement and ardent zeal. Care must always be taken that the song be neither light nor frivolous; but that it have weight and majesty (as St Augustine says), and also, there is a great difference between music which one makes to entertain men at table and in their houses, and the Psalms which are sung in the Church in the presence of God and his angels.[52]

Indeed the tunes of the Genevan Psalter show a remarkable range of emotion carefully reflecting the emotions of the Psalms for which they were composed.[53]

Conclusion

For Calvin true worship must wed inward sincerity to outward faithfulness to God's Word. Worship must be outwardly obedient to God's inspired direction and also flow from the heart: "...it is not sufficient to utter the praises of God with our tongues, if they do not proceed from the heart...."[54] In true worship the believer exercises faith and repentance as he meets with God and grows

---

51. Calvin, *Commentary on 1 Corinthians,* 289.
52. Calvin, "Preface" to Genevan Psalter, 3.
53. The tunes of the Genevan Psalter with English versifications of the Psalms are available in *Book of Praise*, Anglo Genevan Psalter, (Winnipeg, Manitoba, Canada: Premier Printing, Ltd., 1987). For a good discussion of the development of the Genevan Psalter, see Pierre Pidoux, "The History of the Origin of the Genevan Psalter," Reformed Music Journal I (1989), 4 6, 32 35, 64 68.
54. Calvin, *Commentary on Psalms,* 1:126. Later in the same volume, Calvin wrote, "It were, indeed, an object much to be desired, that men of all conditions in the world would, with one accord, join in holy melody to the Lord. But as the chief and most essential part of this harmony proceeds from a sincere and pure affection of heart, none will ever, in a right manner, celebrate the glory of God except the man who worships him under the influence of holy fear," (380).

in grace.[55] As Hughes Oliphant Old stated, "The outward form of worship and the inward adoration of the heart must remain firmly joined together.[56]

Calvin's labor to relate the inward and outward dimensions of worship properly flowed out of his theology as a whole. Reformed Christianity for him was an integrated whole. His doctrine of sin made him deeply suspicious of human instincts and human desires in the matter of worship. His doctrine of grace led him to expect God to be sovereign in directing worship. He would have insisted that those who think that they can preserve Reformed systematic theology while abandoning a Reformed theology of worship are wrong.[57] Rather, he would suggest that where theology stresses the sovereign power and work of God, where the priority of his action and the regulative authority of his Word are recognized, there a form of worship very like Calvin's own will emerge. The church today needs to listen anew to Calvin on worship so that its worship will not be man centered, but God centered and God directed.

---

55. Calvin, "On the Necessity," Selected Works, 1:153f: "It is easy to use the words faith and repentance, but the things are most difficult to perform. He, therefore, who makes the worship of God consist in these, by no means loosens the reins of discipline, but compels men to the course which they are most afraid to take."

56. Hughes Oliphant Old, "John Calvin and the Prophetic Criticism of Worship," in *John Calvin and the Church*, ed. Timothy George, (Louisville:: Westminster Press, 1990), 237.

57. Ibid., 234f: Old notes "a completely different concern in liturgical reform on the part of Calvin from the more popular concerns of our day. Calvin's theology of worship is consistent with his strong doctrine of grace. In the ministry of the Word, prayer, and sacraments, God himself reaches out to his people in redeeming and sanctifying power."

Chapter 3

The Purpose of Worship

Joseph A. Pipa, Jr

In order to use a thing properly, you need to understand something of its nature and purpose. Perhaps some of you remember the funny stories that were circulating when computer manufacturers began to put CD drives in their computers. Some people were actually calling the technical advisers at the computer companies and complaining about the cup holder not working. After all, it looked like a cup holder. If one did not know what a CD was, one easily would think the device was a cup holder. Of course, when one placed a cup in it, it would break. The user broke it trying to use it for something that it was not made to do. He did not understand its nature and purpose, and thus he could not use it properly. This principle holds true for all kinds of things whether mechanical or mental; if we do not understand the nature and purpose of the thing, we really cannot use it properly.

Certainly, this principle holds true for worship. Among the reasons we are in the midst of what some have called the "worship wars," is that the church has lost sight of the nature and purpose of worship. Many can no longer correctly answer the questions "What is the purpose of worship; what are we to be doing and why?" If we are to reform worship, we must correctly answer these questions.

What better place to seek the answer to these questions than the Psalms and what better place to begin than Psalm 100. This

Psalm (sung to the familiar tune of Louis Bourgeois) is a favorite of the church. Because he composed the tune specifically for Psalm 100, it is called the "Old Hundredth." It is known best today as the traditional tune for the Doxology. The Psalm is the climax of a group of Psalms that begin with Psalm 93. These Psalms anticipate the beauty and loveliness of the Lord Jesus Christ; they speak of the Messianic king who rules over all the heavens and earth. They exude confidence in the expansion of the kingdom of God. One prominent feature of these Psalms is their focus on worship. This Psalm is the fitting climax of the whole as it summons us into the presence of the Lord in order to worship Him.

As I said, Psalm 100 is an appropriate place to seek the answer to our questions about the nature and purpose of worship. You will note from its title that Psalm 100 is a liturgical Psalm: a Psalm for thanksgiving or, as some translations suggest, for the thanks offering. Clearly it was used in the worship of God, perhaps in connection with bringing sacrifices to God at the temple.

God teaches in this Psalm that because of who He is and what He does, we are to assemble in His presence for the service of corporate worship. The Psalm is divided into two parts (vv. 1-3 and 4, 5). Each part contains a call to worship and gives a foundation or basis for that call. From this dual call to worship, we will develop three points: (1) the duty of worship; (2) the purpose of worship; and (3) the ground or the basis of worship.

The Duty of Worship

We begin by considering what the Psalmist says about the duty of worship. The Psalmist begins by summoning us to come to God in worship: "Shout joyfully to the LORD all the earth. Serve the LORD with gladness; come before Him with joyful singing…. Enter His gates with thanksgiving and His courts with praise. Give thanks to Him; bless his name."[1] God summons us into His presence to worship Him. Of course we are to worship God in all of life, and all that we do is to be done for His glory and honor. As the Shorter

---

1. Unless otherwise noted I am using the New American Standard Version.

Catechism teaches, "Man's chief end is to glorify God, and to enjoy Him forever" (WSC 1). Paul reminds us in Romans 12:1, 2 because of the marvelous grace of God, we are to present ourselves as living sacrifices to God.

But obviously God is calling us to something more. Note that the call to worship is corporate in nature. All the commands are in the plural: "You all shout joyfully to the LORD all the earth"; "You all serve the LORD with gladness," "You all come before Him." God is calling His people corporately, as the church of the Lord Jesus Christ, to worship Him.

The corporate nature of this worship is further demonstrated by the place of worship; it is the temple: "Enter His gates with thanksgiving, His courts with praise." God summons us to meet with His people at the Place he has appointed for corporate worship.[2] Indeed we are to worship Him, in all that we do. We are to worship Him privately and in our families, but above all we have this responsibility to worship Him in a corporate capacity.

As we reflect on the duty of worship, notice that the Psalmist addresses this commandment to the whole world. The Psalmist says, "Shout joyfully to the LORD all the earth." The phrase "all the earth," could be translated, "all the land." If thus interpreted, it would be a commandment to God's covenant people. But when we consider the commandment in the context of Psalms 93 through 100, we understand that the Psalmist addresses the nations of the world: all people, men and women, boys and girls of the world, are to worship the Lord God. Take for example Psalm 96: "Sing to the LORD. Bless His name. Proclaim good tidings of His salvation from day to day. Tell of His glory among the nations. Ascribe to the LORD, O families of the peoples"; or Psalm 97:1: "The LORD reigns; let the earth rejoice; let the many islands be glad." Not only does Israel not have islands, but the Old Testament often used the term "island" to refer to the Gentiles. Naturally, since these Psalms focus on the Messianic reign and glory of the Lord Jesus Christ, they call on the nations of

---

2. In the Old Testament God appointed the temple as the central place of worship, but in the New Testament he instructs his people to worship Him in the public assemblies of his church as they exist throughout the world.

the earth to worship God. Every individual who has or is or shall live on the face of this planet has the responsibility to worship God, for all are made in His image and thus are to glorify Him and pay homage unto Him.

God made the entire creation for His glory, and the creation in its entirety glorifies Him. These Psalms call on the trees, the fields, the streams, and the oceans to praise God. One of my favorite things to do in spring is to open the door early in the morning around 5:00 or 5:30, and hear the raucous singing of the birds. And what are they doing? They are glorifying God. They are praising their creator. And as the trees begin to bud and the flowers bloom, they are glorifying God. Why? Because they are doing that for which God has created them. Adam and Eve were the crown of creation and they not only were to glorify God in their actions, but they were also to glorify God by offering intelligent worship to Him. As the crown of the creation, they were the choir directors of all the rest. They were to reflect on the glory of God in creation and compose praise for Sabbath worship. When Adam rebelled against God, he refused to honor God according to His Word. As his descendants, you and I were born dead in our sins and trespasses; we refuse to give honor and homage to God. Man is the only creature made in God's image; the one who has the capacity to think God's thoughts after him. And what does he do? Paul says in Romans 1:21-23 that the natural man suppresses the revelation of God and gives His glory to gross creatures; to anything regardless of how foolish. Man will worship a blade of grass rather than to give glory to God. As Calvin said, our hearts are idol factories. The chronicle of history is man's futile attempt to ignore God. The refusal to worship God is the most serious and gross offense of all mankind and of every individual. This rebellion reaches its nadir in man's refusal to honor God as God, to come to Him in Christ Jesus.

Reader, if you are not a Christian, this is your greatest offense. You might be a very self-righteous person. You might have a fine little checklist and can say more or less with the Apostle Paul that, with respect to the outward acts of the law, you are blameless (Phil. 3:6). You are not a gross sinner. You are not a fornicator or an adulterer or a robber or a murderer, but you know what your worst sin is? Your most reprehensible act of rebellion against God is your refusal to come to Him in Christ Jesus and to worship Him according to His Word. For this offense you shall be judged more severely than Sodom and Gomorrah. But the Bible holds out hope to you. There are many places in the Scripture that give warrant for sinners to come to Christ, not the least of which are these Psalms.

These Psalms, for example 96 and 98, set Christ before us. He is the King of Jehovah. He is the one who comes to rule and to judge. He has come to judge His People, to vindicate and deliver His church. He is now a King and Judge ruling over all people. The Psalmist anticipates His coming and in light of His coming, he calls the nations to shout joyfully unto the LORD and come before Him. Christ has come. He is the One who is being exalted now in the praises of His church from the rising to the setting of the sun. From one end of earth to the other praise is offered to Christ in heaven. The peoples of the earth worship God because the Lord Jesus Christ suffered and died, was buried, is raised from the dead, and is exalted on His throne. He rules over all the nations and calls them to worship.

Do you not hear God saying to you, my friend, "Come before Me. Come unto Me with praise."? And how do you do that? You do that in Christ Jesus. You do that by submitting to God according to the gospel, by repentance and faith. Submit to Him. Heed now His call. But heed it now, "Lest He become angry, and you perish in the way" (Ps. 2:12a). While you live, while Christ tarries, repent and believe in Him.

But as God summons all people to worship Him, He particularly speaks to us, His covenant people. For after addressing all the earth, He addresses us, saying, "Come before Him with joyful singing. Know that the LORD himself is God. It is He who made us and not we ourselves. We are His people and the sheep of His pasture" (100:2b, 3). Indeed, all have the responsibility to worship God, but you and I whom Christ has redeemed, we have the great obligation and privilege to join heart and voice in the corporate worship of our Savior; for it is unto that end that He has redeemed us. The great purpose in evangelism and missions is that the nations might be brought to worship the triune God in Christ Jesus.

Jesus said to the Samaritan woman, "God is a Spirit and He is seeking a people to worship Him in spirit and in truth," (John 4:23, 24). And how is God seeking people to worship Him? As He redeems them, as He brings them with their children into the covenant community, into the church that worships Him, He is gathering a people to worship Him in spirit and in truth. Earlier Moses revealed the same truth to Pharaoh: "'The God of the Hebrews has met with us. Please, let us go a three days' journey into the wilderness that we may sacrifice to the Lord our God" (Exod. 5:3). Some wonder if this was just a trick, an excuse to get them out of Egypt? Was it not God's purpose to free them from their slavery? Yes, but why? He would deliver them to have a people who worshipped Him. God says, "I want this people to be My unique possession, My kingdom of priests, to worship Me (Exod. 19:6) and so let them go. And if you will not let them go, I will deliver them by My own strong hand."

For this end God has saved us. Corporate worship, therefore, is the special activity and the peculiar duty of God's covenant people.[3] It is our distinguishing mark as Christians. We are the people who have been redeemed and instructed that we may worship God. Worship, therefore, is your duty. But your duty is your glorious privilege. May you revel in it and delight in this great purpose of redemption.

Purpose of Worship

Having laid the foundation of the duty, which in fact is a privilege, we look in the second place at the purpose of our worship. The Psalmist summarizes the purpose of worship under the concept of coming into the presence of God in order to serve Him with worship. Let us reverse those two and note first thing that we are to serve God with acts of worship. The Psalmist says "serve the LORD with gladness" (v. 2).

In the Bible (both in the Hebrew and the Greek) there are

---

3. David McKay, *The Bond of Love* (Fearn, Scotland: Christian Focus Publications, 2001), 228, 229.

three primary groups of words for the act of worship. There is the broad term (often translated "worship" that signifies bowing down, paying homage and obeisance. There is the bridge term that refers to the specific acts that we perform in worship (the particular acts of worship such as those performed by the Levites). And there are the words "serve" and "service." That reminds us that our worship is work or labor. These words both in the Greek and in the Hebrew describe the service of a slave. The Psalmist teaches that worship is work. Often this word "serve" is joined with the broader term for worship, as in the second commandment, "not to worship them or serve them." We join the two terms when we speak of "worship services." The term "serve" reminds us that corporate worship is an act of service performed by God's children. Worship therefore, is work and we need to understand it is work. You ought to approach worship as you would any serious job. You need to think about it, study it, and train yourself to do it with skill. Moreover, keep in mind that the great purpose of worship is to offer this service to God.

But the most precious part of this service is the place where we perform this work. We worship in the special presence of God. God directs is people to gather at His temple: "Enter His gates with thanksgiving, His courts with praise" (v. 4). In the Old Covenant God was enthroned in His temple. There He visibly manifested Himself enthroned on the mercy seat in the midst of His people. Since God dwelt there, the temple was the center of His worship. The life and worship of God's people in all their villages and cities, in their synagogues, was connected to the temple. The daily, monthly, and festival sacrifices with the priestly ministry were the hub of the life of God's people. The temple was the place God manifested His special presence.

But where or rather who is our temple? The one who said, "Destroy this temple and in three days I will rebuild it." The Lord Jesus Christ is our temple and He is our priest. He has entered into the Holy of Holies on our behalf and the veil has torn apart so that we as the sons and daughters of God, as the priests of God, have free access in Christ into the throne room of heaven. If Christ's work is the fulfillment of the temple, how do we enter His courts? Where do we come before God, when we worship? In a mysterious manner, because of union with Christ, we are lifted up into heaven. R.B. Kuiper wrote of this transaction: "How lofty a conception of corporate worship Scripture presents! When God's people assemble for worship they enter into the place where God dwells. God meets them, and they meet God. They find themselves face to face with none other than God Himself. Their worship is an intimate transaction between them and their God."[4] When we gather with God's people in a local congregation on the Lord's Day and the elders exercise the keys of the kingdom through the call to worship, we assemble in a unique way in the presence of Christ. We are transported into the throne room of heaven. We come into the presence of the King Jehovah. We are in the presence of His awesome, holy angels. We are in the presence of the souls of just men made perfect. In corporate worship we enjoy God's special presence.

Some of you have to worship in small and unattractive places – strip centers, houses, or church buildings that you cannot afford to keep up. You would like to be able to serve your God in a way that is more aesthetically pleasing, but you do not have the resources. Remember, because Christ has come, our worship is not tied to a physical place. We worship in the Spirit. And by the Spirit of Christ we are taken up into the throne room. Regardless of the physical place we are in the presence of God, before the great throne, reveling and glorying in our God.

Well how do we serve God in His glorious presence? What is our purpose? Our service consists of three things. In the first place it is clear from the Psalm that to serve the Lord in His glorious presence is to offer to Him praise, thanksgiving, and adoration with great joy and exuberance. "Shout joyfully to the LORD. Come before Him with joyful singing. Enter His gates with thanksgiving, His courts with praise. Give thanks to Him and bless his name." When we serve

---

4. R. B. Kuiper, *The Glorious Body of Christ* (London: The Banner of Truth Trust, 1967), 347. See also Frank J. Smith, "What is Worship?" in *Worship in the Presence of God*, eds. Frank J. Smith and David Lachman (Greenville, SC: GPTS Press, 1992), 11ff.

God in our worship we are to praise Him, adore Him, bless His name, thank Him, and describe His greatness, beauty, splendor, and glory. And we are to do these things with exuberance. Shout joyfully. Come with gladness.

Too often for too many Reformed worship today is boring, not because we do not do the right things, but because our hearts are unengaged and we are not coming into the Lord's presence with joy and exuberance. Let us rekindle the vision. Remember you worship in God's special presence. This reality is the thing that will make worship special.

The second aspect of our service is communion with God. The concept of communion is too often lost today. I commend to you the book by Jeremiah Burroughs, *Gospel Worship*. The main thrust of that book is teaching us how to commune with God in corporate worship. As we come into His special presence, we come to gaze on Him; we come to reflect on who He is and what we are in relationship to Him. "Come before Him. Know that the LORD Himself is God." We are to come into His presence with this experimental grasp, this experimental knowledge of God. We enter not only to offer our worship, but also to enjoy sweet communion. As we come into His presence, we gaze on His loveliness. And how do we do so? How does He show us His loveliness? He reveals Himself to us in the parts of worship in which He shows us Himself and speaks to us. As Mr Johnson writes later in this book, when our worship is full of Scripture, we will see the glory of God. He reveals Himself to us in the Word read, recited in our creeds and preached. When God speaks and we respond in praise, prayer, and song, communion occurs. Communion is a two-way communication. We see Him in His loveliness and hear Him saying, "I am your God, and you are My People." When we come to partake of the Lord's Supper, He says to us, "You are mine. I have forgiven you of your sins. Walk boldly in Me." Our hearts run out to Him in response to the manifestations of his gracious love and favor, and through corporate worship a genuine communion occurs between the worshiper and the triune God. That is glorious, is it not? I trust you know what I am talking about.

Think about those times you have seen the beauty and loveliness of God in corporate worship in ways that you had not imagined possible. As you took communion and suddenly the Spirit overwhelmed you with the beauty of Christ and what He has done for you or the enormity of your sin and how wonderful it is that it has all been taken away. You responded in love and gratitude. That is communion and it takes place in corporate worship.

This leads to the third purpose edification, which is really an outworking of communion. We refer to the things we do in worship as means of grace. The Larger Catechism 154 defines the means of grace as "The outward and ordinary means whereby Christ communicates to his church the benefits of his mediation, are all his ordinances; especially the word, sacraments, and prayer; all which are made effectual to the elect for their salvation". God uses these things to sanctify us. We are to use the Word and pray in private and with our families, but as Clarkson says, there is much greater blessing attached to using these ordinances corporately.[5] Moreover, there are many things that we do corporately that we may not do in private such as participate in the sacraments and hear the preaching of God's Word. So in our communion with God He not only reveals Himself to us, but also is working in us. He is communicating grace to us from the great reservoir of Christ; namely, the grace of sanctification, mortification, and increased conformity to the image of the Lord Jesus Christ. Thus as we serve God in worship, He edifies us.

As we think about the purposes of worship there are two important lessons. First, our worship must be God centered and not man centered. Is this truth not obvious? If we are to come into His special presence with the service of our worship, if we are to fasten attention on Him, to adore and praise Him, and to commune with Him, then worship must be God centered. Here is one of the places where the Church has gone astray today, and we are confused about worship because we approach worship asking, "What am I going to get out of it?" "What kind of buzz am I going to have?" "Am I going

---

5. David Clarkson, "Public Worship to be Preferred Before Private" in *The Works of David Clarkson* (reprint, Edinburgh: The Banner of Truth Trust, 1988), 3:187ff.

to leave selfaffirmed, feeling good about myself?" "Am I going to be moved?" We are coming for all the wrong reasons and are asking all the wrong questions. We are using the CD player for a cup holder. Our question ought to be, "What glory will abound to God?" "How will His name be blessed and His loveliness portrayed?"

When our worship is God centered a wonderful thing happens. We acknowledge that worship is not to be emotionless. And as we fix our attention on God and seek His glory and commune with Him, we will be moved to the depth of our being. We will be exuberant. We will rejoice with trembling. We will serve the LORD with fear. We shall indeed be moved in the very depths of our being because we sought Him. Is not this analogous of a marriage relationship? If in your marriage relationship you seek your own satisfaction, well being, and fulfillment, then your marriage is going to be a wreck. But if in the marriage relationship you are seeking the well being and satisfaction of your spouse, you are going to be fulfilled. Worship works on a similar plane. When we forget ourselves and seek Him, He will be honored and we will be blessed.

The second lesson we learn from the purpose of worship is that it is by nature covenantal and not evangelistic. Again the church is making the mistake of turning corporate worship into an evangelistic enterprise. This change of focus explains why so many are departing from the principles detailed in this book. Christians wrongly are defining what is done in worship in terms of bringing the unconverted in, making the unconverted comfortable so they will be saved. Admittedly their motives are good; they desire to see the lost converted. But I ask the very simple question; if an unconverted person comes to your worship service and leaves comfortable or feeling good, who has not been present? God. No unconverted person can come into the presence of God in the way the Psalmist describes it and feel good or fulfilled. No, the Lion of Judah will have torn and probed his conscience. As Paul says, he will fall down before the Lord; his heart made naked and bare before God (1 Cor. 14:24, 25). The Word of God suggests that people will be saved as we focus on God in our worship. We are so foolish to take that which is God's and profane it and adulterate it, attempting to package it for the world.

As I was finishing this chapter, I had the privilege of ministering in Israel. While there I stayed with one of the families in the congregation. The first night I was there they invited me to attend a birthday party for one of their children. I had a good time, but you can imagine that I did not quite fit in. I did not understand Modern Hebrew, so I did not always understand what was going on nor could I sing the songs. Some of their games were strange to me as was some of the food. Imagine as the family thinks about these cultural problems, they start changing the birthday party to suit me. That would have been great for me, but by the time they finished, it would not have been a party for their child.

When we change God's glorious and holy celebration into an outreach enterprise, He is no longer the center of attention. He is no longer honored and glorified in our worship. My friends, if we are going to worship well and correctly, we must recover these purposes of worship and their attendant principles. We must understand that we serve the Lord in His special presence and we serve Him by adoring him and giving thanks unto Him, praising Him, and communing with Him. As we do so, He changes us. Thus our worship will become increasingly God centered and covenantal.

These principles do not give us an excuse to ignore the visitor that is unfamiliar with our worship. He will not understand what we are doing, thus it is important for us to explain what we are doing, to relate what we do so they will understand. To go back to the Israeli birthday party, a member of the family sat with me to translate and explain the games. They made me comfortable without changing the focus of the party. When I preached in Israel I needed a translator. It is good to have a translator for those who visit our worship service. The one who leads worship can do that. Others can sit with visitors and explain what is being done. But by all means structure the service for God and not men.

Foundation of Worship

Having seen the duty and the purpose of worship, we examine in the third place the foundation or the basis of worship. The Psalmist teaches that the exuberant worship he describes flows out of a keen, personal knowledge of God. Since He is to be the focus of our worship, our response to him will grow out of the reality of who He is. Thus the Psalmist anchors his call to worship in God; namely His names, works, and attributes. As we learn of Him by these means, we respond to Him. The Psalmist begins by reminding us of just who this God is: "Know that the LORD, He is God" (v. 3). There is but one true God, and He is Jehovah.

By the title, "God", He teaches that He is the mighty, all powerful divine being, who created the heavens, the earth, and all that is in them. His personal name is LORD (Jehovah or Yahweh). He revealed His name to Moses at Mount Sinai through the burning bush. A bush burned and was not consumed, revealing "I am who I am." This name reminds us that our God is self existent and eternal. He is sovereign. He needs nothing else. He is the fullness of all within Himself and yet He is the covenant God. This God who does not need us has reached down to take us to Himself. He has delivered us from our bondage and entered into a covenant relationship with us. And of course you know that this Jehovah is the Lord Jesus Christ, the one who became man, that as the God Man He might obey, suffer, and die to deliver us from the wrath and condemnation of God. By His resurrection we are justified that we might then live forever as the sons and daughters of God. Our God is Jehovah. A rich revelation that we take for granted. For many of us, these names have become commonplace. We read "Lord" or "God" and simply rush on. But you understand every time the name of God is used in Scripture, it is used with the special intent and purpose of what God is revealing to us in that context. I am as guilty as anybody, but we take God's name in vain when we simply rush through these passages and do not stop to observe, "Now, how is God revealing Himself here?"

Being reminded that our God is Jehovah, the triune creator and redeemer, we meditate on His work. The Psalmist says that, as we know Him as God, we remember "It is He who has made us and not we ourselves; we are His people and the sheep of His pasture." The Psalmist reminds us that our God is the creator. He is the physical creator and He is the spiritual creator. And although in this Psalm the spiritual aspect is predominant, in the context of this group of

Psalms, the Psalmist has been celebrating the fact that our God is the creator of all things. In Psalm 96:5, "For all the gods of the people are idols, but the LORD made the heavens." He is the creator, and we are to meditate on His mighty work of creation and all that it reveals to us about Jehovah God. He planned it all and then according to His own good pleasure spoke into existence all that is. What power! Let there be, and there was. This God is our God. Do you not love Him as creator and delight in His power? It is the Lord your God who has made you.

The Psalmist, however, deals more with our redemption: "For He made us His people and the sheep of His pasture." He took us who were enemies, the bastard children of Satan, and made us His sons and daughters. He is to us a tender shepherd. He leads us. The Psalmist says He shepherds us even unto death (Ps. 48:14). What love! From Eternity He has chosen us and in the fullness of time He sent His Son to redeem us and His Spirit to call us. Do we deserve it? Was there anything in us to incline His saving favor toward us? No! It was but His love, which leads us to the last thing the Psalmist shows us about God, His attributes.

We know God through His name, His works, and His attributes. The Psalmist gives three reasons to worship God. "For the LORD is good; His lovingkindness is everlasting, His faithfulness to all generations" (v. 5) God is good. Some people have complained that the Shorter Catechism definition about God does not identify God's love or grace as an attribute. But it does, when it talks about His goodness. God's goodness is His tender love, His benevolence toward His people. The term often is joined with the lovingkindness of God. God's lovingkindness is His covenant love and tender mercy by which He deals with us not according to the just desserts of our sin, but rather in mercy. Think on the goodness of God. One example is Christ's dealing with Peter during His trial. As Peter denies His Lord the third time and the rooster crowed, the Savior turned and looked at Peter. That was not a look of condemnation. It was a look of goodness and compassion. He had told Peter, "Satan wants you, but I have prayed for you, and you will be kept." That look. Oh, it broke Peter's heart. Can you imagine? Here's the Savior in the midst of increased agony, the dark cloud of the cross, feeling the growing weight of the wrath of God and eternal condemnation. In the midst of all that, Peter is on His heart. He turned and looked at Peter as He so often turns and looks on you and me, not in condemnation, but in goodness and lovingkindness, drawing us back and restoring us.

The Psalmist also declares His faithfulness. He is true, true to Himself and true to His Word. His word thus is true and perfect; it does not fail; in Christ Jesus every promise is Yes (2 Cor. 1:20). And all of God's threats shall be fulfilled in Him as well. All that He has promised you in the covenant and all that He has sworn to be on your behalf He faithfully fulfills.

Thus as we think about God we respond in worship. Why do we come into His presence with joyful shouting? We worship Him because of who He is. How wonderful and gracious and mighty and powerful and sovereign and tender He is.

One of the reasons, therefore, our worship totters on the edge of irrelevance is because we do not come into God's presence aware of who He is. We rush into God's presence just as we rush into work or into school. But if we are to worship God well with exuberant hearts, we must prepare ourselves by meditating experimentally on God, not just who He is, but who He is and what He is in our own lives. We not only meditate on His great works, but also on how those works reveal who He is and what He does for us as well as what He does objectively (Ps. 66:5, 6, 16).

As we prepare for worship we are to meditate until our hearts are in a ready frame to join with others in social worship. One of the reasons God calls us to careful observance of the Lord's Day is that we might have time to prepare ourselves to come to worship and then we return home to savor the experience. We love to savor life's experiences that are rich and precious. But, unfortunately we rush into God's presence, we rush home, and we rush into other activities. And we lose the fruit of our worship, because we have not savored it. We have not lulled it over on our tongues and retasted it and meditated on it and thought about how great it was. But God has given us a day so that we can worship Him; worship Him well and enjoy Him and His worship.

Therefore, because of who God is and what He does we are to come into His presence with the service of corporate worship. As we are gripped by the nature and purpose of worship, we then will be compelled to enjoy this privilege and enter into it wholeheartedly. We minimize the privilege of worship. We often fail to grasp or to continue to focus on this glorious privilege that God gives us to come by Christ Jesus into His presence. There is no better privilege that belongs to us, no better work that we do for God, but we often denigrate worship.

Some of you attend churches that do not have evening worship, while others of you may neglect the second service. Why in the world, if all these privileges are attached to worship, would we omit evening worship? Perhaps one cannot dogmatically assert from Scripture the necessity of a second service; it is surely implied both in Psalm 92 and in pattern of the morning and evening sacrifice. Although I cannot make a dogmatic case, I can make a pragmatic one. When we come into worship and go up into heaven in God's presence, when the Word of God is preached by the lawfully ordained man of God and Christ Himself is speaking to us, why would we want to be anywhere else? Why would we neglect the privilege of doing this twice on the Lord's Day?

Some of you prefer to spend time at home on Sunday nights with your children to catechize them. I had a friend who said, "I do not come to the evening service, because I am spending time with my children and catechizing them." You ought to catechize your children, but why catechize them when Christ is speaking down the street and manifesting His presence? Some of us dread worship. You wake up on Sunday morning – "Oh, no, it's Sunday, and I've got to go to church." We need to be gripped with the beauty and glory of the privilege that is ours to enter into His courts with thanksgiving.

Moreover, let us become zealous and jealous that God's people will again discover the fullness of worship. God is most glorified in Biblical corporate worship. Let us pray and labor for the reformation of worship. Let us support those churches committed to such worship.

When we rightly understand the nature and purpose of worship, we will worship better. We will understand the need of Biblically regulated worship; we will seek God centered worship. May God grant to you and me the continued growth in grace to worship Him with skill, in the way He spells it out here.

Chapter 4

The History of Worship in Presbyterian Churches

Morton H. Smith

History is not the standard by which the Church does what it does, the Scriptures alone provide the Church her *principia theologiae* (source of theology) and, therewith, her basis of practice. Historically, however, the Church has recognized the Biblical importance of observing the past (history) and learning from God's work in history through His Church. God's exhortation to His Church to "remember" should leave us unable to be either antagonistic or indifferent toward history. Thus, it is imperative that the Church often review her past and this is certainly true in regard to her worship of the Triune God. In this overview of "The History of Worship in Presbyterian Churches," we shall briefly survey the Reformed Churches of Europe, and then turn our attention to a more extensive consideration of worship in the American Church.

The Reformed Churches of Europe
The Protestant Reformation was an effort on the part of the Reformers to return to the Bible, both for its doctrines and its practices in worship. Roman Catholic scholar Carlos M. N. Eire, in his *War Against the Idols*, maintains that the "central focus of Reformed Protestantism was its interpretation of worship."[1] For Zwingli and

1. Carlos M. N. Eire, *War Against the Idols: The Reformation of Worship from Erasmus to Calvin* (Cambridge: Cambridge University Press, 1989), 2.

his successors, the Reformation was not so much concerned with finding a just God, as taught by Luther, but rather in turning away from idolatry to the true God. This meant that true worship was a basic motif of the Reformed Reformation.

Heinrich Bullinger, Zwingli's successor at Zurich, Martin Bucer at Strasburg, William Farel in Neuchatel and later John Calvin in Geneva all emphasized the pre-eminence of true worship. Calvin lists the two defining elements of Christianity as "a knowledge first, of the mode in which God is duly worshipped; and secondly, of the source from which salvation is to be obtained."[2] Furthermore, as Eire explains, "Calvin defines the place of worship as none of his predecessors had done before.... Worship, he says, is the central concern of Christians. It is not some peripheral matter, but "the whole substance" of the Christian faith.... One may even argue that it becomes the fundamental defining characteristic of Calvinism."[3]

As we know, the Reformers were divided on the issue of worship. The Lutheran Reformation allowed whatever was not forbidden in the Scripture to be practiced in its worship. Generally speaking, this is the modern day position of the evangelical churches. The Reformed Churches, on the other hand, adopted the regulative principle, to the effect that we include in worship only what is explicitly taught in Scripture, or which can by good and necessary consequence be deduced from it.

Calvin had a fairly well developed liturgy, which broadly speaking has been followed by the continental Churches. His liturgy centered on the preaching of the Word. Of particular interest is the question of whether Calvin held to singing only the Psalms. It is true that many of the Reformed limited their singing to the Psalms alone. The Synod of Dordt was stricter than the French Reformed Church, not allowing the use of hymns. Calvin's liturgy at both Strasburg and Geneva included the singing of the Law, and sometimes the Creed or other hymns, as

---

2. John Calvin, *The Necessity of Reforming the Church* (reprint, Dallas: Presbyterian Heritage Press, 1995), 15.
3. Eire, "War Against the Idols", 232, 233, as cited in Terry Johnson, "Introduction to Worship," in Premise III (Jan. 31, 1996): 7.

well as the Psalms.[4] One hymn from the Strasburg Liturgy, "I greet Thee, who my sure Redeemer art," is often ascribed to Calvin.

James Hastings Nichols indicates that there were two primary reasons for the adoption of the Psalter. First, it provided a comprehensive and complete body of liturgical song. "The Reformed had, in one leap, acquired a complete liturgical system," argues Nichols, "which then could not be gradually changed by adding hymns, but must be challenged as a system."[5] The second reason was that Calvin held that "the Old Testament and the Psalms were to be read christologically and as prophetic of the life of the church."[6] Thus the sixteenth century congregations saw allusions to their life in the Psalms. The French Reformed, or Huguenots, sang the Psalms as they went to their deaths as martyrs. Their executioners tried to gag them, but when the cords burned through, the psalm would come forth from the smoke again. They sang them as they went into battle. The Huguenots were so distinguished, as well as inspired and encouraged, for singing the Psalms that in 1661 the Psalm singing was forbidden throughout France by the Roman Catholic authorities. In addition to the Psalms, the French Church sang a hymn of thanksgiving following the Lord's Supper. The Ten Commandments were also set to music and sung during the worship service, as was the Apostle's Creed.

Knox's Reformation of Scotland

Kevin Reed, in his treatment of "John Knox and the Reformation of Worship in the Scottish Revolution," says, "In the battle to reform Scotland, John Knox sent forth a call for purity of worship. Indeed, the struggle between true and false worship was the central conflict of the Scottish Reformation."[7] Knox was committed to the regulative principle of worship as taught in Deuteronomy 4 and 12, which

---

4. Bard Thompson, *Liturgies of the Western Church* (Cleveland and New York: Meridian Books, World Publishing Co., 1962), 159-215.

5. James Hastings Nichols, *Corporate Worship in the Reformed Tradition* (Philadel-phia: Westminster Press, 1968), 36-37.

6. Ibid., 37.

7. David Lachman and Frank J. Smith, eds., *Worship in the Presence of God* (Greenville, SC: Greenville Seminary Press, 1992), 295.

teaches that it is unlawful to add to or take away from the worship that God has instituted in His Word. When Knox returned from exile in 1559, he called for a reform in worship in Scotland. His greatest tool for reformation was his fearless preaching of the Word of God. He called for a cleansing of the churches much like Jesus had cleansed the Temple. Reed says of the results of this reform, "Scotland emerged from the struggle as the beneficiary of a thorough Reformation. Throughout the land, the Papal Mass was abolished, as well as other 'monuments of idolatry.' These 'monuments' included religious images, the ritual trimmings of the Papal ceremonies, ecclesiastical holidays, and other implements of superstition."[8]

Douglas Bannerman points out that under Knox, the Church of Scotland used Knox's liturgy, which included more than exclusive Psalms. He made a case for the return to a voluntary Reformed liturgy for the Scottish Churches.[9] He also indicates that the Scottish Psalter was particularly beloved by the Scots. "This Scottish Psalter, he wrote, " forms a wonderful bond of union and sympathy among Scotsmen all the world over. It is in fact a national liturgy of praise and prayer in the best sense of the word."[10] Furthermore, writes Bannerman,

Inseparably linked in this respect with the Psalter, are those fifteen or twenty noble hymns which, rising by their native virtue above the mass of the "Paraphrases," have for nearly a hundred and fifty years held a place in Scotland except in the Highlands second only to that of the Psalms. I refer to such hymns as "O God of Bethel," "Where high the heavenly temple stands," "'Twas on that night," "Hark, how the adoring hosts above," "How bright these glorious spirits shine." These were first printed by permission of the General Assembly in 1745, and had won their place in Scottish worship, along with the Psalms, for generations before a separate hymn book was adopted by any Presbyterian Church in Scotland.[11]

---

8. Ibid., 317.

9. D.Douglas Bannerman, *Worship, Order, and Polity* (Edinburgh: Andrew Elliot, 1894), 30-82.

10. Ibid., 39.

11. Ibid., 39, n. 2.

The Puritans and Worship

The Puritans of the Elizabethan period were not originally anti liturgical. They sought to have the liturgy of the Continental Reformed Churches (specifically the Middleburg Liturgy from the Netherlands) approved in England. The Queen and the Parliament rejected it. It was the Separatists, under the leadership of Robert Browne and Henry Barrow, who began the opposition to forms as such in worship, their basic concept being that worship should be under the direct guidance of the Holy Spirit. Thus all forms of prayer, even the Lord's Prayer, were viewed as binding the worshipper and not allowing for the free influence of the Spirit. It was the Separatists who migrated to New England, and established the Congregational Church with its simple worship in the 1620s and 1630s.

The Westminster Assembly, which convened over a century after the Reformation had begun, produced the finest of the Reformed confessional statements of faith and practice. Their position was that of the Puritans. Dr Gregg Singer says of their work:

> Because Calvinism gave the highest expression of Biblical truth yet set forth from the Scripture for the life of the Church, the various forms of worship adopted by the Reformed Churches have likewise reflected the strength of this doctrinal foundation. This development of creed and worship received its highest expression in the work of the Westminster Assembly. Its achievements stand as a sharp rebuke not only to modern liberals, but also to many evangelicals in the Church today who seek to free themselves from the Biblical modes of worship in favor of those new schemes which they feel are adapted to the needs of the present day and are somehow more able to capture the attention of those who have become the slavish victims of modern cultural life. This is particularly true as this culture is expressed in the music of the day. Against all these unBiblical deviations the Westminster Assembly spoke with a Biblical authority and clarity, which we must not ignore or neglect. We are the custodians of the work and achievements of the Reformation in all its aspects. We have an inheritance that is truly Biblical and we are its stewards. We dare not surrender any part of it.[12]

12. Singer, "Reformation Creeds and Worship," in *Worship in the Presence of God.*, Lachman and Smith, ed., 294.

This Assembly produced the Westminster Directory for Worship in addition to the Westminster Confession and Catechisms. The Confession and Catechisms clearly taught the regulative principle, both in the treatment of the Second Commandment, and in Chapter XXI "Of Religious Worship, and The Sabbath Day." In this chapter, elements of "ordinary religious worship" are listed, namely, prayer, the reading of Scriptures, preaching and conscionable hearing of the Word, singing of psalms, administration and worthy receiving of the sacraments. In addition to these, religious oaths, vows, solemn fastings, and thanksgivings are proper elements on special occasions. Whether these were intended to be an exhaustive list of the elements has been debated. Additional elements such as confessing the faith, confession of sins, and the receiving of offerings are generally included in most Presbyterian Churches today. In the instruction regarding the Sabbath day, the Shorter Catechism appears clearly to reject the Church calendar. "The Fourth commandment requireth the keeping holy to God such set times as he hath appointed in his Word: expressly one whole day in seven to be a holy Sabbath."[13]

Regarding the Sabbath, the Westminster divines held that the entire day was to be set aside for public and private exercises of worship. Dr Singer comments on this teaching about the Sabbath:

It is to be kept holy unto the Lord, and for this purpose Christians were to prepare their hearts for its proper observance. On this day they must not engage in their usual work or their usual conversation or manner of life, not even in their thoughts. Christians are to refrain from their usual means of recreation and center their attention on the Word of God throughout the course of the day, while they are attending the worship services and at home.[14]

In addition to these confessional Standards, the Assembly also adopted *The Directory for Worship*, about which Nichols says: "It is also the indispensable base point from which to grasp the development of

---

13. Shorter Catechism Question 58.
14. Singer, "Reformation Creeds and Worship," 293.

the worship of the English speaking Presbyterian, Congregationalists, and Baptists for the three centuries since that day."[15]

Among the particular emphases of the *Directory* was the pre-eminence accorded the weekly Sabbath and also the exclusion of the church calendar, which some of the earlier Reformers had followed. In this Sabbath worship, priority was given to the reading and exposition of Scripture. "Preaching of the Word," explains Nichols, "was viewed as 'the power of God unto salvation.' It presupposed 'the illumination of God's Spirit, and other gifts of edification which (together with reading and studying of the Word)' a minister 'ought still to seek by prayer and a humble heart.'"[16]

One of the changes that the *Directory* brought was the shift of daily prayers from the church to the home. The Church of England holds morning and afternoon prayer services in the Church, but family worship was a hallmark of Reformed Christians, both on the Continent and in Great Britain. This was possible because there had been a great increase in literacy on the part of the members of the congregations. The heads of families were expected to conduct family prayers twice each day, together with catechizing of the children on the Sabbath. There was a great increase in the production and use of catechisms for the instruction of the children in this period, the loss of which is greatly to be lamented.

The Directory set forth a more simple form of worship, without a set liturgy. Suggestions regarding prayers were given, but no set prayers such as the Church of England had. Like the *Confession*, the *Directory* seems to condone only the singing of Psalms. Nevertheless, Douglas Bannerman has argued that the earliest references to the worship of the Christian Church after the Biblical period refer to the singing of hymns.

> In them [the Psalms], as in the praises of heaven heard by the Apostle in his vision in Patmos, "the song of Moses, the servant of God," was joined with "the song of the Lamb.'" It is true, indeed, that the first mention of praise in Christian worship, beyond the

---

15. Nichols, *Corporate Worship*, 98.
16. Ibid., 101.

pages of the New Testament, is of "a hymn to Christ as God," the "Gloria in Excelsis" and "The Sanctus" occur in some of the oldest known liturgies; and the "Te Deum" in its earliest forms follows not long after.[17]

Presbyterian Churches in the American Colonial Period

In considering Reformed worship and the American Colonial Period, we shall restrict our consideration to what might be called "mainline" Presbyterian Churches in the United States. In this group we include both the Northern and Southern Presbyterian Churches and those groups which have separated from them in the twentieth century.

One of the earliest references to worship in the American Presbyterian Church is found in a letter from 1716 by the Rev. James Anderson, to the Principal of Glasgow College, Glasgow, Scotland, in which he mentions that the Scottish Directory was followed.[18] Because American Presbyterians came from various roots in Great Britain, there were some differences regarding worship among the churches during the Colonial period. The Synod of 1729 adopted the *Westminster Confession* and *Catechisms*, without any stated scruples or exceptions regarding the regulative principle of worship which, as shown above, is found in several places in these Standards. *The Directory for Worship*, which was not specifically mentioned in the Adopting Act, was commended by the Synod to the Church in the following words:

> The Synod do unanimously acknowledge and declare that they judge the *Directory for Worship*, Discipline and Government of the Church commonly annexed to the *Westminster Confession* to be agreeable in substance to the word of God, and founded thereupon, and therefore do earnestly recommend the same to all their Members to be by them observed as near as Circumstances will allow, and Christian prudence direct.[19]

---

17. Bannerman, *Worship, Order and Polity of the Presbyterian Church*, 22-23.

18. Maurice W. Armstrong, Lefferts A. Loetscher, Charles A. Anderson, editors, *The Presbyterian Enterprise, Sources of American Presbyterian History* (Philadelphia: The Westminster Press, 1956), 19-20.

19. "Minutes of the Presbyterian Church in America", 1706-1788 (hereafter Minutes), Guy S. Klett, ed. (Philadelphia: Presbyterian Historical Society, 1976), 105.

The 1736 Synod, in interpreting the action of 1729, listed *The Directory* along with the *Westminster Confession* and *Catechisms* as adopted "without the least variation or alteration."[20]

With its adoption of the Westminster Standards and the *Directory for Worship*, the American Presbyterian Church appears to have been committed to the simple non liturgical Puritan service. The central element of this worship was the preaching of the Word. The singing of the Psalms was the only part of the worship in which the congregation vocally participated. In theory, the Church of this period sang only the Psalms, though there is some evidence that individual congregations were already beginning to sing some hymns. It is the opinion of Julius Melton that the change from exclusive Psalms came largely as a result of the Great Awakening in the eighteenth century and of the revivals of the nineteenth century. He cites the fact that this matter disturbed the First Presbyterian Church of New York City in the 1750s.[21] One of the issues considered was the question of whether the Session could introduce a new version of the Psalms without the congregation's consent. Synod in 1753 said: "It being further Moved to the Synod, whether a Church Session hath Power to introduce a new Version of the Psalms into the Congregation to which they belong without the Consent of the Majority of sd

---

20. "Minutes," 141. "That the Synod do declare that inasmuch as we understand that many persons of our persuasion, both more lately and former, have been offended with some expressions or distinctions in the first or preliminary act of our Synod for adopting the Westminster Confession and Catechisms, etc; that in order to remove said offense and all jealousies that have arisen or may arise in any of our people's minds on occasion of said distinctions and expressions, the Synod doth declare that the Synod have adopted and still do adhere to the *Westminster Confession*, *Catechisms*, and *Directory*, without the least variation or alteration, and without any regard to said distinctions. And we do further declare this was our meaning and true intent in our first adopting of the said Confession, as may particularly appear by our adopting act, which is as followeth (Here appears the Adopting Act of the afternoon session, without the preliminary act of the morning.) And we do hope and desire that this our Synodical declaration and explanation may satisfy all our people as to our firm attachment to our good old received doctrines contained in the said Confession, without the least variation or alteration, and that they will lay aside all jealousies, that have been entertained through occasion of the above hinted expressions and declarations as groundless. This overture approved nemine contra-dicente."
21. Julius Melton, *Presbyterian Worship in America* (Louisville, KY: Westminster/John Knox, 1967, 1984), 11, 12.

Congregation: It was voted in the negative *Nemine Contradicente.*"[22]

The Synod again dealt with Watts' Psalms in 1756. It said: "Yet as the sd Psalms are orthodox and no particular Version is of divine Authority, and that the Using them is earnestly desired by a great Majority of sd Congregation, Contrary to the view we had of the Case the Last Year; The Synod, for the Sake of their Peace, do permit the use of sd Version unto them: And determine that this Judgment Shall be finally decisive as to this Affair."[23]

Paul Conkin asserts that it was Samuel Davies, a mildly New Side minister, often called the Apostle to Virginia, who pressed the use of Watt's Psalms and Hymns in the Presbyterian Church.[24]

> The most influential advocate for Watts was Samuel Davies, the father of southern Presbyterianism. He helped form several congregations in the area around Richmond, led a revival in the 1750s, took the lead in proselytizing among blacks, loved hymn singing, and even wrote one enduring hymn. He used hymns at the ordination of John Todd in 1752. Todd became a pastor of a church at which half the members were blacks. Davies rejoiced at the musical abilities of slaves, tried to teach those in his congregations how to read, and requested copies of Watt's hymn book from Britain to circulate among his appreciative "Negroes".... At Princeton, hymn singing was normal after Davies became president. Before him, Jonathan Edwards had welcomed a mixture of hymns and psalms in worship.[25]

The influence of the New Side men was found elsewhere as well. In Rockbridge County, Virginia, which was settled by Scotch Irish who were largely Presbyterian, the issue of exclusive Psalmody caused divisions in several congregations. For example, both the Timber Ridge and the New Providence Churches lost members to

---

22. "Minutes," 288.
23. "Minutes of Synod," 311.
24. By "mildly New Side" we mean to emphasis his interest in Biblical revivals while distancing Davies from the more radical extra-ecclesiastical antics of some prominent first generation New Side ministers.
25. Paul K. Conkin, *The Uneasy Center, Reformed Christianity in Antebellum America* (Chapel Hill & London: University of North Carolina Press, 1995), 205.

the Associate Reformed Presbyterians, who continued to use only the Psalms until after World War II.[26]

In 1787 the Synod said:

> In respect to the psalmody, the Synod have allowed the use of the Imitation of the Psalms of David for many years, to such Congregations as choose them, and still allow the same; but they are far from disapproving of Rouse's version commonly called the old Psalms, in those who were in the use of them and chose them; but are of opinion that either may be used by the Churches as each Congregation may judge most for their peace and edification; and therefore highly disapprove of public, severe and unchristian censures being passed upon either of the systems of psalmody; and recommend it to all Ministers in those parts of the Church, to be more tender and charitable on their heads.[27]

The foregoing indicates that the American Presbyterian Church was divided in the eighteenth Century over the version of the Psalms to be sung. Watts' Psalms of David Imitated in the Language of the New Testament was clearly a paraphrase of the Psalms, and was viewed as a departure from Rouse's more careful attempt to preserve the text of the Psalms.

Presbyterian Churches in the National Period
The forming of the first American General Assembly in 1789 gave rise to a review of the various constitutional documents.

---

26. Taylor Sanders, *A Journey in Faith*: The History of Timber Ridge Presbyterian Church (Lexington, VA: Timber Ridge Presbyterian Church, 1999), 91-92. "Watts' simple words spoke to revival-prone children of the Revolutionary generation, and the popularity of his music spread, bolstered by the Synod ruling in 1756 that "no particular version" was sanctioned by God's authority. The Seceder congregations, however, maintained that for true followers of Calvin and the Westminster divines, only the psalms, which were divinely ordained, should be sung and only in Rouse's metrical versions. No doubt many former Old Siders agreed. The disagreement was a sharp one. Many Assembly congregations preserved harmony by using each version one half of the time; old Psalters containing both versions side by side reflect this compromise. Other local congregations argued and eventually divided over the issue. During the 1760s, Presbytery had lost to the Seceders the South Mountain congregation that became the core of Old Providence Associate Reformed Presbyterian Church."
27. "Minutes," 625.

Changes were made to the *Confession* and *Catechisms* to remove any suggestion of the authority of the civil magistrate over the Church. A committee was appointed to revise the *Directory for Worship*, and subsequently the Synod revised the *Directory*. Among the "irregularities" in American Presbyterian worship at this time noted by the Committee were:

I. Persons going out and in, during divine services....

II. Another evil ... is, that many, in some of our Congregations, do not join in singing the praises of God....

III. There is a want of devotion, awfully apparent in our Congregations, during the time of public prayer. Some are gazing about, some turning their back to the Minister, and others putting themselves into different attitudes of ease....

IV. As the reading of the holy Scriptures is a very important part of divine worship, it is much to be lamented, that this should be neglected in any of our Congregations....

V. There are also some things amiss, while the Minister is preaching. None ought to stand up; much less turn their back ... to indulge in sleep, whispering or laughing.[28]

The original Westminster Directory reads as follows regarding the singing of praise to God: "It is the duty of Christians to praise God publickly, by singing of psalms together in the congregation, and also privately in the family."[29] The revised form of this paragraph in the American form of the Directory reads: "It is the duty of Christians to praise God, by singing psalms, or hymns publicly in the church, as also privately in the family."[30] Thus we see that the Presbyterian Church as it established its first Assembly revised its Directory for Worship to allow for hymns to be sung, though it did

---

28. Melton, *Presbyterian Worship*, 19.
29. *The Directory for the Public Worship of God*, "Of Singing of Psalms."
30. The Revised form of the Directory as adopted by the Synod of 1788. Chapt. IV, Sect. I.

not change the Confession, which may account for the fact that further action by the Assembly was taken in 1802.

Conkin, who surveyed not only Presbyterian worship but the broader picture of the American Protestant churches, says:

> By 1800, despite a few reactionary holdouts, hymn singing had largely replaced the use of psalms in American worship. In most Protestant services, hymns became the only major part of worship that involved overt congregational participation (of course, silently and intellectually, worshipers were supposed to participate in sermons and ministerial prayers).[31]

This may be an overstatement when applied to the Presbyterians. It is true that some congregations were singing hymns by 1800, but hymns had not replaced the singing of the Psalms exclusively. The controversy over this issue was still simmering in the Presbyterian Church. In addition to the above change in the Directory for Worship, the Assembly of 1802 explicitly allowed the use of uninspired hymns as well as the Psalter for singing in public worship.

> Whereas, The version of the Psalms made by Dr Watts, has heretofore been allowed in the Congregations under the care of the General Assembly, it is now thought expedient that the Hymns of Dr. Watts be also allowed; and they are accordingly hereby allowed in such Congregations as may think it expedient to use them in public and social worship; and whereas, the Rev. Dr Timothy Dwight by order of the General Association of Connecticut, has revised the version of the Psalms made by Dr Watts, and versified a number omitted by him, and has also made a selection of Hymns from various authors, which, together with the Psalms, were intended to furnish a system of psalmody for the use of Churches and families, which system has been revised and recommended by a joint committee of the General Assembly and the General Association of Connecticut heretofore appointed, as well as examined and approved by a committee of this present Assembly; the said system is hereby cheerfully allowed

---

31. Ibid., 206.

in such Congregations and Churches as may think it for edification
to adopt and use the same.[32]

The 1806 Assembly stated that it "did not intend that Churches
under their care should use only the Psalms and Hymns specified
in this resolution."[33] In the same resolution the Assembly warned
families or congregations against using hymns containing erroneous
doctrine or trivial matter. A Psalter hymnal was produced by the
Assembly in 1830, and upgraded in 1843.

Mention has been made of only Watts to this point, but it should
be observed that the ministry of the Wesleys, both in Great Britain
and in America, contributed greatly to the use of hymns. Nichols
described their influence thus: "John Wesley had been much affected
by Moravian congregational hymn singing and hoped to emulate it.
The hymns of Charles Wesley in fact became the greatest literary
achievement of the Evangelical movement, ranked by some critics
with the Book of Common Prayer, and the psalms themselves."[34]

The revised *Directory for Worship* adopted in 1788 assumed the
regulative principle found in the *Westminster Confession* and *Catechisms*
as its underlying philosophy of worship. The new directory followed
that of Westminster in not giving detailed instructions for the
conduct of worship. As the Church moved into the nineteenth
century, it was affected by its close contact with the New England
Congregationalists which gave rise to New School thought. This

---

32. Samuel J. Baird, "A Collection of the Acts, Deliverances and Testimonies of the
Supreme Judicatory of the Presbyterian Church, from its Origin in America to the Present Time; with Notes and Documents, Explanatory and Historical: Constituting A Complete Illustration of Her Polity, Faith, and History" (Philadelphia: Presbyterian Board of
Publication, 1855), 209.

33. Ibid.,209.

34. Ibid., 127-128. The same influence may explain the position of the Southern Church
concerning Psalms and hymns. In 1861, the first General Assembly of the Southern
Presbyterian Church appointed a committee on hymnody. Six years later the Church
published its first hymnbook, *Psalms and Hymns for the Worship of God*. This book included
150 Psalms (most of them being from Watt's *Psalms of David Imitated*), and 697 hymns. Two
hundred eighty of these were by either Isaac Watts or Charles Wesley. This book included
only words without tunes, and it was replaced by a Psalm and Hymnbook with tunes in
1873. The latter book included a number of the popular hymns of the period and relatively
few psalms.

ultimately brought the division of the Church in 1837. There were distinct differences between the Old and New School Churches regarding worship.

Samuel Miller of Princeton Seminary was the chief exponent of the Old School view of worship. He maintained the Puritan ideal of worship, which included the rejection of prescribed liturgies, holy days, godparents, the sign of the cross at baptism, confirmation, kneeling at the Lord's Supper, private communion services, bowing at the name of Jesus, and reading the Apocryphal books in worship. This reflects the principle that the New Testament, and not the Old, should guide us in worship. Furthermore, he chronicled the rise of liturgies as evidence against their normative place in Presbyterian worship.

> The result, then, is that liturgics were unknown in the primitive church; that, as piety declined, the clergy began to need external aids for conducting the public devotions of their congregations; that this matter, however, continued for several centuries to be managed by each pastor for himself; that in the exercise of this individual discretion, frequent blunders occurred, through the gross ignorance of the clergy, and sometimes blunders of a very unhappy kind; and that liturgies did not finally obtain universal prevalence until the church had sunk into a state of darkness and corruption, which all protestants acknowledge to have been deplorable.[35]

Miller argued for what he considered to be the primitive, apostolic simplicity of worship. He said, "In Scotland the advocates of primitive simplicity prevailed, and established in their national Church the same mode of worship which we believe existed in the apostolic age, and which now obtains in the Presbyterian Church in that country, and in the United States."[36]

Miller personally urged that the congregation stand during public prayers, and always stood during prayer, even when the congregation

35. Samuel Miller, "On the Use of Liturgies," Biblical Repertory and Theological Review, New Series, II (July 1830): 403.
36. Samuel Miller, "Presbyterianism, the Truly Primitive and Apostolic Constitution of the Church of Christ" (Philadelphia: Presbyterian Board of Publication, 1835), 67.

remained seated. In this he was in accord with the action of the 1849 General Assembly of Old School Church, which said,

> While the posture of standing in public prayer, and that of kneeling in private prayer, are indicated by examples in Scripture, and the general practice of the ancient Christian Church, the posture of sitting during public prayer is nowhere mentioned, and by no usage allowed; but on the contrary, was universally regarded by the early Church as heathenish and irreverent; and is still, even in the customs of modern and western nations, an attitude obviously wanting in the due expression of reverence: therefore this General Assembly resolve, that the practice in question be considered grievously improper, whenever the infirmities of the worshipper do not render it necessary; and that Ministers be required to reprove it with earnest and persevering admonition. [This was reiterated in 1857.][37]

Concerning the Lord's Supper as part of the worship of the church, Miller believed it should be observed at least quarterly, and without the extended services before and after which had developed in Scotland. The question of the frequency of the Lord's Supper has existed from Calvin's era to the present. Calvin desired weekly Communion, whereas many in Scotland moved to only once a year (as some, like Jay Adams, continue to prefer today). Most of our Churches observe either quarterly or monthly Communion.

Worship and Revivalism

The 19th century was marked by revivals. There had been an awakening that centered around Hampden Sydney College in Virginia during the last decade of the eighteenth century. James McGready (1758–1817) visited Hampden Sydney during this period and sought to carry the revivals to North Carolina. He subsequently moved to Kentucky, where he was involved in the Kentucky revivals, which tended to excesses.

On the frontier, the camp meeting grew up around the special communion seasons. People gathered from a whole region. A week

---

37. Baird, *A Collection of the Acts, Deliverances, and Testimonies*, 205.

of preaching services was held, culminating in the observance of the Lord's Supper. Because unbelievers were present, these services were often designed to reach the lost. They thus were not primarily designed to worship God, but rather to affect the unregenerate attendees. A number of Presbyterians were supportive of these revivals, although others became very critical of them because of the increase in excessive, odd physical activities. After failed attempts to bring order to Cumberland Presbytery, the Synod of Kentucky suspended a group of ministers for their contra-Confessional beliefs. In 1810, the suspended ministers reconstituted themselves as the independent Cumberland Presbytery, which served as the seed presbytery for the Cumberland Presbyterian Church (1829). Barton Stone and many others also separated, largely from Presbyterian sources at the Cane Ridge (Kentucky) services in 1801; their separation included the rejection of all creeds and a claim to being the true Church of Christ, or Christian Church.

Because both unbeliever and believer alike could join in the numerous services preceding the Communion, quite understandably, the preachers in the midst of these folk with whom the church rarely had contact were under considerable pressure of conscience to reach them. Concern to win the "lost" gradually caused a shift of emphasis from the sacrament to the admonitory and evangelistic sermon. The seasons of sacramental preparation was transformed into revivalistic camp meetings.

Julius Melton provides a vivid description of the revivalistic practices of the camp meetings when he writes:

> For one thing, preaching to the unconverted became quite spirited. Passion to save souls called forth from McGready "the fierceness of his invectives," "the hideousness of his visage and the thunder of his tones."
>
> Quite out of keeping with Presbyterian tradition, worship at times took on a charismatic and even disorderly flavor. "Different hymns were sung at the same time, each to its appropriate tune"; the singing was "very loud," and accompanied by "violent motions of the body" combining to destroy all melody. "Several would also pray at once; sometimes two, sometimes ten or twelve,

and sometimes almost all the serious people." And all the while "praying, singing, groaning, and shouting" were heard all around, from various small and large gatherings of people. Other unusual practices in such worship were the "Holy Laugh" and exhortations by women. "The Millennium was supposed to have commenced," wrote an early historian of Kentucky Presbyterianism, "and the ordinary means of grace were superseded, as rather embarrassing the new and free outpouring of the Spirit."[38]

Eventually the camp meetings developed into the "protracted meeting," where services were held at a particular church for a week or more, with intensive evangelistic preaching. To the North, revivalism was adopted as a method for evangelism under the leadership of Charles G. Finney. Though he had been a New School Presbyterian for a time before moving to the Congregational Church, he approached worship as a pragmatist, without any regard for the regulative principle of worship. Melton analyzes Finney's approach thus:

> More than just eagerness and Arminianism undergirded the "new measures" introduced into services of the church. In his Lectures on Revivals of Religion, delivered in 1835 while he was still a Presbyterian, Charles G. Finney revealed a well worked out theory of worship. In essence, Finney's theory was the opposite of Samuel Miller's. He held that the church possessed no scriptural directives for worship. When he looked to early Christianity, all he found was that it sought to "make known the gospel in the most effectual way." This was the church's criterion. Choosing and creating measures was left to the discretion of the church. But so individualistic was Finney's view of the "church" that he could and did say elsewhere that this was left to the discretion of the minister.
>
> Finney claimed the support of church history as he cited prominent examples of changes in "measures": changes in clerical dress, in psalmody, in style of preaching. He adduced a list of men prominent in introducing innovations: the Apostles, the Reformers,

---

38. Melton, *Presbyterian Worship*, 45; Robert Davidson, *History of the Presbyterian Church in the State of Kentucky* (New York: Robert Carter, 1847), 132.

Wesley, Whitefield, Jonathan Edwards and himself. Over and over he ridiculed Presbyterian divines who acted as though they had a "Thus saith the Lord" for their traditional ways of worship and evangelism.[39]

Sad to say, one can see Finney's loose view of worship pervading much of the contemporary evangelical Church. At the time, however, there was a strong reaction to Finney's "new measures" as an "overthrow of scriptural measures formerly used – namely, praying without ceasing for the outpouring of the Holy Spirit and unwearied preaching of the gospel."[40]

The Move Away from Simplicity

Among the developments in America during the mid nineteenth century was the building of gothic style churches, professedly to develop a more worshipful place for services. Thomas E. Peck of Union Seminary in Virginia criticized this trend:

> Whence the gross departures from Presbyterian and primitive simplicity in our meetinghouses...? Why have we gone back to the Middle Ages...? Is there anything in the history of the old cathedrals, designed in sin, founded in inequity cemented with the tears and blood of the living temples of Christ, the monuments of idolatry and tyranny, dark and gloomy, chilly and fear inspiring, to commend them to us who rejoice in the liberty and light of the gospel?... Why do we abuse the papists, and then imitate them?[41]

This move toward Gothic architecture may well have been an aspect of the impact of Romanticism upon the people in the Church at that time.

Along with this change in architecture came the introduction of organs and choirs into Presbyterian churches. A movement for the introduction of liturgies in Presbyterian churches also arose. It is

---

39. Melton, *Presbyterian Worship*, 5 3-54.
40. Ibid., 54. Here Melton is quoting William M. Engles.
41. Thomas E. Peck, "Rationalism and Traditionalism," Miscellanies, 3 vols. (Rich-mond: The Presbyterian Committee of Publication, 1895-97; reprint, *Writings of Thomas Peck*, Edinburgh: The Banner of Truth Trust, 1999), 1: 299.

interesting to observe that the New School, under the leadership of Albert Barnes of Philadelphia, opposed this movement. This was due in part to their close ties to the revival movement, which stressed informality in worship. On the other hand, A. A. Hodge at Princeton and James W. Alexander, pastor of an Old School Church in New York, favored the possibility of developing Reformed liturgy. In 1855 Charles Baird, whose father had served in Europe during a good deal of his ministry, published a book entitled *Eutaxia*, or *the Presbyterian Liturgies: Historical Sketches*. In this work Baird presented a number of liturgies from Continental Reformed Churches, including Calvin's and Knox's, which predated the Puritan period. Baird himself maintained the Old School criteria of Scripture and primitive Christian practice. He proposed the voluntary use of liturgy, not a mandated form. Douglas Bannerman adopted a similar position in Scotland, advocating the voluntary liturgy.

At Princeton, one generation after Samuel Miller denounced formal liturgies, A. A. Hodge (1877) published a manual of forms for special occasions (such as weddings and funerals) through the Presbyterian Board of Publication. Two years later, Herrick Johnson of McCormick Seminary published a similar manual with the Board. Though published by the denominational Board, neither of these had the endorsement of the denomination. Samuel Hopkins, a Congregational leader in New School thought, published a general manual entitled, *A General Liturgy and Book of Common Prayer* (1883), also without denominational authority.

As alluded to above, during this time there was a growing attraction to instrumental music in worship. Calvin had opposed instruments as being a distraction from the words being sung. None of the Reformed Confessions had sanctioned the use of instrumental music. Chalmers in Scotland, Spurgeon in England, Thornwell, Dabney and Girardeau in the Southern Presbyterian Church in America, all opposed instrumental music.[42] Despite the opposition of these leaders, popular sentiment inclined toward the use of

---

42. For a book length argument by an American theologian against the intrusion of musical instrumentation upon corporate worship see John L. Girardeau, *Instrumental Music in the Public Worship of The Church* (Richmond: Whittet & Shepperson, Printers, 1888).

instruments. An organ was installed at the historic Presbyterian Church of Columbia, South Carolina in 1866. Organs were installed in Petersburg, Virginia in 1870 and in the First Church of Lynchburg by 1872. By 1890 there was an organ at the College Church at Hampden-Sydney College and by 1892 at the Union Seminary Chapel. The use of choirs and soloists was also coming into vogue at this time.

The issue of the use of organs was the cause of a good deal of contention during the nineteenth century. Conkin says:

> Early in the nineteenth century American Protestants rarely sang with organs or pianos. For most, this was primarily a matter of cost or lack of any tradition. Roman Catholics, Lutherans and most Episcopalians never had qualms about organs and procured them as soon as they could afford them.... Congregationalists, Presbyterians and Calvinist Baptists usually had doubts about organs or overtly opposed them. Their opposition had been uniform in the seventeenth century, was pervasive in the eighteenth, and gradually relaxed in the nineteenth. The issue divided local congregations but rarely whole denominations. The story of change is one tied to regions and to local congregations. By 1900, the only holdouts for a cappella singing were the small Covenanter sects and a major faction within the restoration movement, the present Churches of Christ.[43]

From the literature of the period and the minutes of presbytery, synod, and Assembly records the American Presbyterian church moved away from its historical positions on instrumental music, as well as choirs without the benefit of careful, theological scrutiny.

It was, perhaps surprisingly, the Southern Presbyterian Church, which in 1893 adopted the first revision of the *Directory* for Worship as adopted by the first General Assembly. This revision included the following additions to the 1788 Directory: added the Holy Spirit to the list of matters for which to give thanks; inserted a list of concerns for prayer, including the missionary movement; advised standing as the proper posture for prayer; added the offerings as a specific

---

43. Conkin, *The Uneasy Center*, 206-207.

act of worship. New chapters were added on the "Sabbath School" and "Prayer Meetings." An appendix included forms for a marriage service and two forms for funeral services. These forms were clearly designated as optional, but came to be widely used in the Church. The Presbyterian Church in America (PCA) has such optional forms appended to its Directory, adapted from the Southern Presbyterian Book of Church Order and from the Orthodox Presbyterian Book of Church Order.

American Presbyterian Worship in the Twentieth Century
In the North, the Church Service Society was established on March 2, 1897. This society was made up of a select group of ministers and laymen of the Northern Presbyterian Church. Henry van Dyke, pastor of the Brick Presbyterian Church of New York City, was the leader of the Society. His father had been involved in a movement toward a more liturgical service of worship for the Presbyterian Church. He (the father) openly rejected the regulative principle of worship – that nothing is to be permitted in our worship which is not expressly commanded or sanctioned in Scripture – asserting "that it was based on a false and legalistic view of Scripture and led to a hypocritical twisting of Scripture to support established customs."[44] The Society surveyed the variety then existing among Presbyterian Churches and also the teaching regarding worship at Presbyterian seminaries. The Synod of New York appointed its own Committee to conduct a similar survey within its churches. It produced what it called typical Presbyterian worship service in New York in 1902, as follows:

> Organ voluntary (50% of worshippers arrive late)
> Doxology or call to worship (people standing)
> Invocation (people standing)
> Anthem (people seated)
> Responsive reading of Psalter (used in 50 % of churches)
> "A Gloria may then be sung" (used in 10% of churches)
> The Lesson (10% of churches read regularly from both Testaments)
> Hymn

---

44. Melton, *Presbyterian Worship*, 120.

General Prayer
Offertory and announcements
Reception of offering with prayer
Hymn (people standing)
Sermon
Prayer
Hymn (people standing)
Benediction[45]

In 1906 the Northern General Assembly authorized the Board of Publications to publish the first edition of *The Book of Common Worship*. Its use was voluntary only. An effort was made to defend each feature in the service from the Scripture, and excerpts were taken from the 1789 *Directory for Worship*.

As elements and circumstances of worship began to filter into the Presbyterian branch of the Church from other traditions, it is not surprising that the "church calendar" began to attract followers. It should be observed that the *Second Helvetic Confession* (1561) contained the following:

> Moreover, if the Churches do religiously celebrate the memory of the Lord's nativity, circumcision, passion, resurrection, and of His ascension into heaven, and the sending of the Holy Spirit upon His disciples, according to Christian liberty, we do very well approve of it. But as for festival days, ordained for men or saints departed, we cannot allow them. For indeed, festival days must be referred to the first table of the law, and belong peculiarly unto God....[46]

The General Assembly of the Church of Scotland approved the *Second Helvetic Confession* in 1566 with an official exception to its view of special festivals. This was some eighty years prior to Westminster, which we have already cited as approving the "keeping pure and entire one whole day in seven."

The beginnings of the use of the church calendar in the American Presbyterian Church are found in *The Book of Common Worship*, first

---

45. Ibid., 125-126.
46. Second Helvetic Confession, as found in Joel R. Beeke and Sinclair Ferguson, eds., Reformed Confessions Harmonized (Grand Rapids: Baker Book House, 1999), 208.

published in 1906, with references to Good Friday, Easter, Advent, and Christmas. Corporate participation in worship was instituted in unison prayer of confession, responses, responsive readings, the Gloria, and the Lord's Prayer.

In 1932 the Northern Church revised the *Book of Common Worship*. This revision showed an increased emphasis on the calendar, including prayers for Lent, Palm Sunday, Pentecost and All Saints Day. The Southern Presbyterian Committee on Publications printed this edition, with approval. There were two other editions, in 1946 and 1955.

Regarding the Church calendar, in 1899 the Southern Presbyterian Church said,

> There is no warrant in the Scriptures for the observance of Christmas and Easter as holy days, but rather the contrary (see Gal. iv. 9-11; Col. ii. 16-21), and such observance is contrary to the principles of the Reformed faith, conducive to will worship, and not in harmony with the simplicity of the gospel of Jesus Christ.[47]

Nevertheless, one of the instruments used to change the views of the Church on worship was Sunday school material, which included both liturgical guides and references to Christmas and Easter. The Southern Assembly repeatedly attempted to stop this teaching until about 1920.

Dr Walter Lingle (1868–1956), a Southern Presbyterian minister, wrote in 1951 about the changes in worship which had occurred during his lifetime. E. T. Thompson says of him:

> In his youth he noted that services were conducted with Puritan simplicity. All that went before the sermon was frequently referred to as the 'preliminary exercises.' Some churches were still opposed to instrumental music in the church. In many churches a paid church choir was looked upon as an abomination. Now, he noted, more

---

47. Minutes of the General Assembly of 1899, 430, also in "A Digest of the Acts and Proceedings of the General Assembly of the Presbyterian Church in the United States", revised down to and including Acts of the General Assembly of 1922, G. F. Nicolassen, compiler, (Richmond: Presbyterian Committee of Publications, 1922), 847.

emphasis was placed upon worship and maybe a little less on the sermon. Many of the newer churches were being constructed with a view to making the architecture an aid to worship. Members of the choir wore vestments, and many of the ministers were wearing the Genevan gown with tabs, which the Professor of Systematic Theology in his student days had contemptuously dismissed as "rags of popery." Church services had become more elaborate. Responsive readings, the Lord's Prayer, and the Apostle's Creed had been brought into the services and there was more and better music. The people were given a larger part in the services.[48]

Thompson continues with the statement that "these and other trends continued in the decades that followed."[49] The Church continued to develop more liturgical worship. In 1965 the Southern General Assembly approved adding the four Sundays of Advent, Epiphany, and the beginning of Lent to the Church calendar. The traditional colors for the various seasons were approved, and ministers in various parts of the Church began "to garb themselves in the appropriate colors white, green, red, violet, purple and black."[50]

In 1927 the Southern Presbyterian Church published *The Presbyterian Hymnal*, "The Blue Book." After a generation it was deemed less than satisfactory, and thus the PCUS initiated a joint project, which resulted in the publication of *The Hymnbook* in 1955. Five Presbyterian and Reformed Churches joined in this project. This book contained some 600 hymns, Psalms, and choral responses.

The 1960s saw further experimentation in worship which included contemporary worship – including jazz, folk music, the idea of celebration, the use of lights, flashing pictures, and more. An article in the Presbyterian Journal described an experimental worship service that took place at Montreat, NC, on August 4, 1968, sponsored by the denominational agencies, under the title of "New Days! New Ways?"

---

48. Walter Lingle quoted from the "Presbyterian Outlook", (February 19, 1951) by Ernest Trice Thompson, *Presbyterians in the South*, 1890-1972 (Richmond: John Knox Press, 1973) 3: 482-483.
49. E. T. Thompson, *Presbyterians in the South*, 3: 483.
50. Ibid.

Objective of the whole effort is to shake up the admittedly jaded average churchgoer and set his spine tingling with a wild cacophony of color, sound and movement called (for want of a better name) a "worship experience."

Somehow as we sat there in Montreat the Sunday of the "New Ways?" conference, we couldn't help wondering if there was really any essential difference between the agony and ecstasy unfolding before our battered senses, and the wild festivities which met Moses when he came down from the mountain with the tablets of stone in his hand.

Those people in the wilderness had wanted something real to relate to. They had sacrificed their gold to get it and they were having a soul satisfying celebration in the best religious sense of the times – when Moses came upon them with the wrath of God.

It may have been a "relevant" celebration to them honestly conceived and humanly interpreted, but to God it was idolatrous sacrilege.

Isn't the essence of sacrilege a reveling of the human spirit in the things that bring in human delight – calling the experience the worship of God? Wasn't Cain rejected by God essentially for choosing to worship God as it pleased him?

Sunday night in Montreat, while the audience went on a wild foot stomping, hand clapping spree around tables from which sports-shirted dignitaries served pieces of French bread and offered sips of grape juice, we sat frozen with disbelief at the scene.

The rafters were ringing with "The Battle Hymn of the Republic," while an instrumental jazz combo provided the accompaniment. The audience was dancing its way to the tables for "communion."

....They were prostituting the Lord in His own House and we did not intend to be any part of it.[51]

In May, 1973, Aiken Taylor stated "that the 'modern craze over expressing the faith via dances, psychedelic art forms and liturgical drama' was 'indefensible,' because these new forms 'are a modern

---

51. G. Aiken Taylor, "Worth Asking: What is Sacrilege?", Presbyterian Journal (August 21, 1968), 16, as cited by Frank J. Smith, The History of the Presbyterian Church in America, The Silver Anniversary Edition (Lawrenceville, GA: Presbyterian Scholars Press, 1999), 493-494.

version of the ancient tendency to allegorize the faith out of all practical existence.'"[52]

This author remembers hearing that the University Church in Charlottesville, Virginia served cracker jacks and Pepsi cola for the Communion service. Complaints were filed with the General Assembly, but after a heated debate, the Assembly commended the Boards for their "creative leadership in communicating the Gospel in our time."[53]

The preaching of this period also showed a marked change. Previously sermons had laid emphasis on doctrine, while the latter part of the 20th century saw a greater emphasis on ethical preaching. Psychological preaching addressed to the inner needs of men was also becoming popular.

With such things going on in the denomination, along with open denial of the gospel in many places, is there any wonder that the conservative wing of the Church felt it was time for a separation from the Southern Presbyterian Church? This took place in 1973.

The Separated Churches – OPC and PCA

During the twentieth century, both the Northern and Southern Presbyterian Churches were brought under the control of liberal bureaucratic elements within the respective denominations. A separation was forced in the North in 1936 with the trial of J. G. Machen, which resulted in the formation of the Orthodox Presbyterian Church, and subsequently of the Bible Presbyterian Church. Neither of these denominations made any innovative changes in worship. In 1973 the Presbyterian Church in America separated from the Southern Presbyterian Church or PCUS. The 1933 version of the *Book of Church Order* was proposed to the PCA. The Form of Government and the Rules for Discipline were adopted in a normal fashion. However, when it came to the *Directory for Worship*, the Third General Assembly adopted the following "Temporary Statement:" "*The Directory for Worship* is an approved guide and should be taken seriously as the mind of the Church agreeable to the Standards.

---

52. Ibid., 497.
53. Minutes of the 109th General Assembly, PCUS, 1969, 109.

However, it does not have the force of law and is not to be considered obligatory in all its parts."[54]

This was an unprecedented action. No previous Presbyterian denomination had adopted a part of its Constitution in such provisional way. The sixteenth General Assembly was presented a full reworking of the Directory, but after lengthy discussion determined to retain the present *Directory* "in its present status."[55] The twenty-eighth General Assembly declined to rescind the "prefatory statement to the Directory,"[56] with the result that a wide variety of worship is now practiced in the PCA, including everything from what is called "traditional Presbyterian worship" to all sorts of varieties of "contemporary worship." It has been the cause for division within local congregations and continuing debate across the denomination.

In addition to general looseness in the worship practices of PCA churches, there are some serious proposals about worship espoused by individuals within these circles. Professor John Frame of Reformed Seminary in Orlando has published a work entitled *Worship in Spirit and Truth*, in which he rejects the historic understanding of the regulative principle of worship, and seeks to reinterpret it according to modern principles of Biblical interpretation. The result is, in effect, the abandonment of the Presbyterian and Puritan principle which includes in worship only that which is taught in the Bible, for the Lutheran principle which allows inclusion of what is not forbidden by Scripture. Although this is not the place to thoroughly analyze his work, it may be said that he has tended to make assertions which he has not demonstrated to be based upon sound exegesis. Frame allows for the validity of dance and drama as proper parts of worship. Though this view is clearly a departure from the historic and accepted understanding of the *Confession*, *Catechisms*, and the *Directory for Worship*, it has been broadly circulated in the Church as though it represented a proper understanding of these documents. Consequently, many in the PCA have followed him uncritically, and thus have departed from the clear teaching of the Standards.

---

54. Minutes of the General Assembly, PCA, 1975, 82.
55. Minutes of the General Assembly, PCA, 1988, 169.
56. Minutes of the General Assembly, PCA, 2000, 87-89.

The differences in views regarding worship within the PCA, some of which reflect the same views held by Frame, came to the fore at the fourteenth General Assembly. The evening services of "worship" at the General Assembly proved to be so objectionable to a number of the Assembly, that some fifty commissioners entered a formal protest against the "impropriety of incorporating non-Reformed worship principles and practices into these services in such a predominant way that the clear distinctives of our Reformed worship, as set out in *Book of Church Order*, chapters 47 and 49, were obscured, if not excluded."[57] At the seventeenth General Assembly another protest was filed by some seventy-nine commissioners regarding the sermon preached that was clearly Arminian in its approach to evangelism.[58] A second protest was entered against the use of drama at the Sunday morning worship service.[59] This same Assembly failed to uphold the Confessional view of the Sabbath. The eighteenth General Assembly saw 126 commissioners protesting the Concert of Prayer service.[60] The next Assembly was confronted by a ballet performance as part of the Sunday evening service of holy worship, and a "patriotic" service, including the pledge of allegiance and the "Battle Hymn of the Republic." Again a protest was filed.[61]

Due to the reframing of Presbyterian principles, the PCA is marked by a looseness of principle and strikingly broad diversity of practice in public worship. A historian of the PCA, Frank J. Smith, has observed that "in practice, the PCA is not committed to uniformity in public worship."[62]

A second line deviating from the historic understanding of the regulative principle may be found in the writings of James Jordan (independent) and Peter Leithart (an ordained member of the PCA). They argue that the Davidic tabernacle and the Temple of the Old Testament, instead of the OT synagogue, is the model for Christian

57. Minutes of the General Assembly, PCA, 1986, 141.
58. Minutes of the General Assembly, PCA, 1989, 125f.
59. Ibid., 174f.
60. Minutes of the General Assembly, PCA, 1990, 166-168
61. Minutes of the General Assembly, PCA, 1991, 136, 169-70, 207f.
62. Ibid., 519.

worship.[63] This teaching has resulted in a highly liturgical approach to worship, including the use of clerical garb, chanting, and more. Here also the Lutheran principle of allowing what is not forbidden in Scripture underlies their approach.

Conclusion

In this survey of the worship practices of the Presbyterian Churches since the Reformation, we have seen that historically, Presbyterian commitment to the regulative principle has been firmly settled; nevertheless, there have been and continue to be differences as to how the principle is to be applied. Generally speaking, the history of Presbyterian worship has been marked by the centrality of preaching the Word. Formal liturgies have been used to varying degrees, as well as uninspired hymns. Calvin and the Continental Churches included liturgies, and some of the early Reformed Churches used hymns as well as the Psalms. In reaction to the liturgy forcibly imposed by the Anglican Church, the Puritans discarded any liturgy. The Westminster Assembly, which represents the pinnacle of the Reformed view with its adherence to the regulative principle of worship, endorsed the use of Psalms, but the Presbyterian Churches that have adopted the Westminster Standards have shown considerable variety in their interpretation of the Standards' statements on the Psalms, and in the use of hymns.

Perhaps the most serious challenges to the regulative principle of worship are those being put forward within conservative Presbyterian circles today. Those who hold to the historic position regarding the regulative principle of worship ought to accept the challenge and carefully re-examine the Biblical teaching on this subject to determine whether the historic interpretation is the true view. If, on the one hand, the historic interpretation cannot be defended from Scripture, then we should advocate adjustments to the Standards to make them more Biblical. If, on the other hand, the historic interpretation is the proper Biblical position, then it is

---

63. Peter J. Leithart, *From Silence to Song* (Moscow, Idaho: Canon Press, 2003) is representative of this type of argument.

incumbent upon us to answer the challenges and to insist that the Church return to her Standards.

Let me conclude with a statement regarding worship made by William Childs Robinson in face of the challenge of the liberal controlled PCUS.

The acceptable way of worshiping the true God is instituted by Himself, and so limited by His own revealed will, that He may not be worshiped according to the imaginations and devices of men," states the Westminster Confession of faith. Nor is He to be worshiped in any way other than that prescribed by Holy Scriptures. As the Larger Catechism specifics, God forbids "corrupting the worship of God, adding to it, or taking from it, whether invented, and taken up of ourselves, or received from the traditions of others, though under the title of antiquity, custom, devotion, good intent, or any other pretense whatsoever." When the constitution of our Church is followed, every worship service in each congregation witnesses to the reign of Christ the King. On the other hand, when that worship is used to express the imaginations of any group, however *well intentioned*, the Church is no longer His kingdom. Instead, it becomes only a representative democracy.[64]

---

64. William Childs Robinson, "True Worship Acclaims Him King," Presbyterian Journal, 23 July 1969, 13.

Chapter 5

The Psalms and Contemporary Worship

W. Robert Godfrey

The last thirty years or so have seen the most dramatic and speedy changes in Protestant worship in any time since the Protestant Reformation. It may be one of the signs of modernity that whatever happens, happens quickly and seems to pass from one place to another quickly; and surely the principal mark and symbol of that change is the change in the music of the church. The development of what has come to be called contemporary Christian music has become an amazingly widespread phenomenon. It has spread through very different denominations, from conservative to liberal, from Pentecostal to Reformed. It has invaded the precincts of some liturgical churches as well as free churches. My wife teaches at a Reformed Christian high school, and she says all that they hear in chapel now is contemporary Christian music; and if she raises any questions, she is immediately labeled as one out of touch with young people and insensitive to the needs of evangelism. Even where contemporary Christian music has not completely swept the old hymnody and Psalmody away, we are often confronted with what has become known as blended worship, where you have a little bit of this, and a little bit of that, and in my judgment not much of anything.

Now while those of us who have reservations about contemporary Christian music can poke fun at it, and I may not always be able to resist the temptation to do that, nonetheless, its pervasive character and its numbers of strong supporters mean we need to give to it a careful and serious examination. We can not just define contemporary Christian music as four notes, three words, two hours. Ridicule, however personally satisfying, is not usually a way to convince other people of our position. We need to think carefully about this phenomenon because it has become so influential and so very widespread.

We ought to begin by removing from the table certain false issues that sometimes are brought up and yet are not really at the heart of what we need to think about today. We do not oppose contemporary Christian worship because it is contemporary. There is nothing in our Reformed or Christian commitment that says we cannot support melodies that are written in our own time if they are good and appropriate melodies. We have never taken the position that the old is good just because it is old. We have never taken the position that the music of the church cannot in some ways be reformed and improved. So the issue with contemporary Christian music is not that it is contemporary. It is not that it has been written in the twentieth or twenty-first century, although it is interesting how much contemporary music seems now slightly dated and sounding more like the 1970s than the twenty-first century.

Furthermore, we should not reject contemporary Christian music simply because it is unfamiliar. I do believe that for most of us who are non musicians what we principally like in music is what is familiar. I think most church musicians do not take that into account adequately in their planning. Non musicians like what is familiar. Musicians like to be experimental. They like to find new things. They like to move into new areas. Most of us come wanting to sing a tune we already know because we have trouble with a tune we do not know. But unfamiliarity in and of itself is not an adequate argument against something new or different. We probably sing a lot of bad tunes that we are very familiar with and like, even though musically they could not be defended.

We also cannot object that we should not sing contemporary Christian music because some of the lyrics are heretical. Now I am not advocating heretical lyrics. I am only making the point that heretical lyrics are no more a problem in contemporary Christian music than they are in some forms of historic hymnody. The only songs you can sing and be sure *a priori* that they are not heretical are Psalms.

Some time ago I was at a conference for twenty year-olds in California. (We have very specific ministries in California). The conference was on the importance of theology. It was quite a good conference, but we closed singing a troubling contemporary song. The refrain of the song was, "Father, you are God alone, and we know You through the Son." I stopped singing in the middle of the song. My wife leaned over and said, "So, what's wrong with this one"? And I said, "It is Arian." If the Father alone is God, then the Son is not God; and really, at a theology conference it is not very good to be singing an Arian song. I was told by others in the conference, "Well, surely the composer or the author did not intend that." And I said, "No, he probably did not intend that. But whatever he intended, what he said was Arian, and we ought not to sing that." But such a problem could as easily arise in a traditional hymn. So that is not the issue before us.

Also the issue is not whether we sing off the wall or not. We may like song books because we more easily have musical notes that we can see. Nonetheless exactly where the words and music appear is not the issue.

Origins of Contemporary Christian Music
What are the real issues that we need to look at as we consider contemporary Christian music? The first issue is to take a hard look at the origins of this music. Establishing its origin does not necessarily prove whether it is right or wrong, but it should clarify for us something of the theology and piety that inspired it. Music is not neutral. Music expresses both in lyrics and in tune something of the orientation of the composer and author as to what the truth of religion is and how we ought to practice it.

Sometimes we feel that contemporary Christian music is a complete revolution in the life and music of the church, that it is a completely new phenomenon, sort of dropped out of heaven or sprung full armed from the head of Zeus. But most of the time in history we do not have radical changes like that. Rather we have historic continuity. If we step back a minute and really look at the character of contemporary music, what we will find is that it is just a new stage in the evolution of revivalist hymnody. Revivalist hymnody, that came to be more and more prevalent in the nineteenth century and early twentieth century, was music that was more upbeat, more lively, and more enthusiastic. It also often had a declining level of theological content in the texts of the hymns.

Let me, in the interest of trying to offend everyone, mention a mid nineteenth century hymn probably familiar to many of you: the hymn "He Leadeth Me," written in 1862. Now think for a minute, as we tend to complain about the repetitious character of contemporary Christian music, about the text of "He Leadeth Me." "He leadeth me, O blessed thought, O words with heavenly comfort fraught. What e'er I do, where e'er I be, still 'tis God's hand that leadeth me. He leadeth me, He leadeth me, by His own hand He leadeth me. His faithful follower I would be, for by His hand He leadeth me." We are "led" six times in the first stanza. Now, whether we really want to be overly critical of "He Leadeth Me" or not, we have to see that if you look at the text and then compare it with some contemporary texts, there is not a huge change that has taken place. I would argue that the origin of contemporary Christian music is very much to be found in the evolving character of the revivalist hymnody of this country.

If there is a somewhat dramatic shift that took place in music leading to contemporary Christian music, that shift probably took place with the rise of Pentecostalism. The Pentecostal movement in its drive for religious experience and religious energy and religious excitement did indeed think in new ways about music and sought to take the revivalist tradition of hymnody and make it even more exciting, even more engaging. We can see such developments in the work and music of Aimee Semple McPherson. Although born in western Ontario, Canada, she came to fame and prominence in southern California. She was a pioneer in many of the notions of music and worship that have become widespread beyond Pentecostalism in our time.[1] In the 1920s Mcpherson had a praise band at her church. She wrote choruses that were sung in her church. (When she got criticized by the press, she wrote a chorus that went, "You may talk about me just as much as you please. I'll talk about you down on my knees. I'm not going to grieve my Lord anymore.") She was also a pioneer with the cantatas that she wrote. You can still occasionally go to Angelus Temple and hear the "Bells of Bethlehem" composed by Sister Aimee Semple McPherson. She also pioneered with drama. She had "illustrated sermons" on the stage.

What originated as a natural expression of the life, theology, and piety of the Pentecostal movement in the 1920s has become generalized far beyond Pentecostal circles. These origins should give us pause to ask, "If this kind of music is good for Pentecostal churches, is it good for non Pentecostal churches"? Can you take the piety of one group that has emerged rather naturally and spontaneously out of the theological and religious life of that group and just superimpose it on another? I do not think you can, but that is what is happening far and wide in our time.

If we look even more deeply, we could say that this new music reflects something of the continuing influence of nineteenth century romanticism on modern world views. We hear a lot about post modernism. In my judgment post modernism is just another stage in the development of romanticism in Western civilization. It is a movement away from rationality towards experience and particularly to mind transcending experience. This romanticism has shaped much of this new musical development.

Character of Contemporary Christian Music
Having looked at the origins of contemporary Christian music, let us next look at its character. Of course it is not all the same, and we have to beware of generalizing. There is really a wide range of things to be found in contemporary Christian music. Still, it does seem to

---

1. See Edith L. Blumhofer, *Aimee Semple McPherson*, (Grand Rapids: William B. Eerdmans Publishing Co., 1993).

me that we can say there are certain issues that seem common to most of it. First, it often promotes itself as being a more intelligible form of music than traditional hymnody. What that really seems to mean is that contemporary Christian music is form of music to which there is immediate access. It does not take any reflection. It does not take any study. It does not take any effort. You can just immediately enter into this music.

Now, when I occasionally have been in churches or meetings where this music has been sung, it is often flashed on the wall without notes. I usually stand and do not sing. Then people say, "Why aren't you singing"? I respond, "I do not know the tunes." They look just baffled at me. They react that way because they sense that you don't need to know the tunes to sing them. The tunes are usually predictable and immediately available. (Still I usually do not know them.) Proponents of contemporary Christian music often seem to confuse intelligibility with a desire for immediate experience.

Let us think about the intelligibility of the hymn "He Leadeth Me." In that hymn we have the word "fraught." I do not know how many of us really know what fraught means. We hardly ever use fraught in normal language. So there are language issues that are legitimate; but we cannot take an issue like intelligibility and just make it abstract. Intelligible to whom? How simple does it have to become? Does it have to be intelligible to the two year-old in church? Does it have to be intelligible to the person with Alzheimer's disease? Well, these are extremes, but where is the cutoff point? If someone walks in from the street completely unaware of anything Christian, must the hymnody of the church be fully intelligible to that person? We must not think about intelligibility abstractly. We need always to be biblical in our thinking. How intelligible is the Bible? It must be our standard of intelligibility. The Bible has some difficult concepts and some difficult words. It sometimes requires a certain measure of study to understand. We have to be careful with contemporary Christian music's claim to be intelligible when what it may really be after is immediate accessibility and heightened experience.

Second, contemporary Christian worship often commends itself for being simple. In response its critics ask, is it simple or is it shallow? Many contemporary songs – not all, but in my experience a preponderance of them – have the feeling of having been dashed off. One wonders if the poet spent more than five minutes stringing together some rather familiar phrases of Christian piety. They do not have a sense of development. They do not have a sense of being carefully crafted most of the time. They often leave us with the feeling they are not so much simple as shallow.

Third, contemporary Christian music presents itself as being an expression of genuine emotion. My fear, however, is that it tends to be emotionally shallow and often rather sentimental. As a reaction to sentimentality, for example, I refuse to sing love songs to Jesus. Now I do not know if that makes me strange or unduly difficult and critical. But in the minds of most Americans a "love song" has a particular orientation and focus. You sing love songs in a romantic relationship. To sing love songs to Jesus seems to me an uncomfortable mixing of categories and notions that is fundamentally distracting and unhelpful. Even songs about Jesus being my best friend distress me. Such language seems to take us away from biblical images to using categories of our dominant culture that are problematic.

Purpose of Contemporary Christian Music
Having looked at the character of the new music, next we could ask the purpose of contemporary Christian music. For many of its defenders its purpose is to energize the life of the church, to make the church more evangelistically successful, to reach out. But I fear that in fact too often contemporary worship and music is not the door into the church but the door out of the church. It is interesting that George Barna, who has beaten the drum for decades about the importance of the church growth movement, now finds in his polling that after twenty, thirty, forty years of intensive church growth in America, church attendance is in decline in America. Such results should not be surprising. Where God and his worship have been trivialized, people in time stop worshiping. They get the message that worship is not really important.

Most of us know of churches that have adopted more contemporary music and worship. What do we find happening?

Very soon the evening service is gone; and in many, many cases attendance begins to decline. Of course, those are not the stories that get written up in the church growth magazines. In the same way Pentecostal magazines do not carry the stories of the many who were not healed. They carry only the stories of those who were healed. Nobody has a vested interest in recording all the failures. But just from my own experience, over and over again in California, I have seen church planting efforts, which have carefully followed church growth methods, fail, causing great spiritual damage and great financial cost to the churches. But there is not much recording of that reality.

There is a minister in the Christian Reformed Church – the Reverend David Snapper – who did a Doctor of Ministries project in which he studied Christian Reformed Church plants over a given period of time a decade or so ago. He compared church plants that had followed church growth principles with church plants that had followed a more traditional approach to church planting. What he found was that the traditional approach was much more successful than the church growth approach in the CRC.

The statistics produced by church growth advocates like George Barna are showing us that the church is not growing in America. Now why is that? Barna would say that it is because not enough of us are following church growth principles. If people would go to conferences at Willow Creek, the church would be growing, which is a lot like saying, "If you just have enough faith, you'll be healed." So the purpose is noble – grow the church, invigorate the church. But the underlying notion of what it takes to grow the church and invigorate the church is very troubling.

We can illustrate what is troubling about this music by looking at a brief essay by a church growth advocate. Charles Kraft, who taught at Fuller Seminary, wrote in "Christianity Today" (April 7, 1989) an article defending contemporary Christian music and expressing why he thought it had an important purpose for the church. He wrote: "True worship usually takes a lot of singing to create an atmosphere of praise and worship." Notice his conviction that music creates an atmosphere that is critical to worship. You cannot have worship without the right atmosphere being created.

Kraft wants experience, not rationality, to characterize worship. One of the problems he sees in the church is traditionalism bent on transmitting information. He writes, "Our worship services revolve around an informational sermon preceded by a token number of informational hymns." At this point we can see that he has not understood historic Reformed worship. Good Reformed sermons are not about information. They are about God speaking to His people. When God speaks to His people, part of his communication is information. God has information we need. But it is not just information. It is God speaking to our hearts as well as to our minds. It is God speaking that our lives might be changed. It is God speaking that we might be drawn to faith in Jesus Christ. But I suspect Kraft probably had experienced a number of evangelical churches where the sermon seemed to be a glorified Bible School lesson whose purpose seemed to be passing on informational tidbits about the meaning of a Scriptural text. But that is not good preaching. That is not the standard that we want to hold up.

Kraft goes on to complain, "We sing hymns so chock full of rational content and information that they are unmemorizable." That observation is really strange. One thing that can be said for traditional hymns is that they have been well memorized over the years. But his complaint is that they are too full of rational content and information. So what is the solution Kraft proposes? What is the real purpose of the new music? He writes, "Let's stop being enslaved to the present rationalistic, intellect centered approach to church that characterizes much of evangelicals. Let's get above the mind and just experience God." He continues, "And it is the new music sung with eyes closed for 10, 15, or 20 minutes at a time that makes that experience possible." What experience? What kind of experience do you get if you sing for twenty minutes with your eyes closed?

Kraft's approach to experience is a religious point of view, but it is not a Christian one. It is really a Hindu one. Go read F.M. Forrester's novel *A Passage to India* and his description of Hindu worship there. What is at the center of it? The escape from time and reason and mind, to experience for a moment the eternal, the transcending of self and individuality, to dissolve in the one. There is a mystical tradition in Christianity something like that, but it is really not Christianity at all. It is a desire to escape from being a creature. It is a desire to escape from being a creature who has been given certain faculties and qualities by God, one of which is our mind. If Kraft is correct, then this new music is really very dangerous. It is in its effect a movement in a pantheistic direction. That is probably not what most people who advocate it intend. It is probably not what most people who advocate it have ever thought about, but it seems to be the underlying reality driving this music. And so in a sense this new music has become a new sacrament. It becomes the way that God ministers grace to us. It is in the experience, the ecstasy of music or the catharsis of music, that somehow we experience grace.

If we have been in twenty minutes of singing with our eyes closed, we may feel exalted, we may feel wonderful, we may feel that we are close to God. But I am haunted by the words of Robert Dabney who, facing what he saw was a dangerous trend in revivalistic music in the nineteenth century, said, "Millions of souls are in hell because they were unable to distinguish the elevation of animal feelings from general, genuine religious affections."[2] And that is an extremely significant observation. It is easy to manipulate emotions so that people think they have had a profound experience; and if it takes place in the context of religious language, they will think it is a profound religious experience. But is it? Or is it only emotional manipulation? The intent may not be manipulation, but that seems to be the effect. Aimee Semple McPherson knew all about it. I do not think she was a cynical manipulator, but she stood in the tradition of Charles Grandison Finney who said, "There must be excitement sufficient to wake up the dormant moral powers...."[3] Now, of course, as Calvinists, we do not think souls without regenerating grace have any moral powers, dormant or otherwise.

2. Ernest Trice Thompson, *Presbyterians in the South* (Richmond: John Knox, 1973), 2:430; R. L. Dabney, "A Review of Instrumental Music in the Public Worship of the Church, by Dr. John L. Girardeau," *The Presbyterian Quarterly* 3 (July 1889): 462-69.
3. Charles Finney, *Revival Lectures*, (reprint, Old Tappan, New Jersey: Revell, n.d)., 4.

But if a preacher does think man has free will, then it is not much of a step to say, "How can I move this free will? How can I get him to exercise his free will"? By excitement, Finney said. And the whole revivalist tradition since Finney has followed that advice.

The excitement is not always foot stomping. It can be more subtle. For example, Aimee Semple McPherson in the 1920s conducted a big crusade in Denver. She had a crowd of thousands in an auditorium, and she introduced the song "My Faith Looks up to Thee," a traditional hymn. She had everyone sing the first verse. Then she had the fifty to sixty year-olds sing the second verse, the sixty to seventy year-olds sing the third verse, and the eighty year-olds, sing the last verse. The last verse reads, "And when death's cold, sullen stream shall o'er me roll." And one of the observers said that when you heard just that handful of octogenarian voices singing that chorus, a mood had been created.[4] For Aimee it was not a matter of manipulation, but a matter of preparation for her to come preach about death and about life in Christ. But it was intentionally mood controlling, because she believed that there needed to be some kind of excitement, some kind of emotional connection if people were to be moved. But, you see, this does not fit our theology. It cannot be our piety. People are not saved by excitement.

Evaluation of Contemporary Christian Music

If we are confronted with this new musical sacrament, how are we to evaluate it? What standard are we going to use? I think sometimes we are tempted to react with the standard of, "I don't like it. I'm old and I'm not going to learn anything new." I increasingly feel that way. I just do not like it. But that is not an adequate standard of evaluation.

What standard then can we use to evaluate what has been coming out of this contemporary Christian music movement? The standard we ought to use is the Bible. We use the Bible as a standard of truth in many areas of life, indeed in all areas of life to which the Bible speaks. We evaluate sermons and prayers by the Bible. We ought

---

4. Blumhofer, *Aimee Semple McPherson*, 229.

to recognize that there is a particular appropriateness to using the Bible as our standard when it comes to music because the Bible has a whole book of songs. But it is curious the number of people who seem not to feel any great compulsion to judge our singing or our praise by the Bible, aside from avoiding heretical statements. God has not given us a book of prayers in the Bible. He has not given us a book of sermons in the Bible. But He has given us a book of songs. Now I am not certain why He did that. My best supposition is that He saw the human propensity to run amuck when it comes to song precisely because the emotions aroused by song are so significant. And so He gave us a book of Psalms. It seems to me that Reformed people should all agree that the Psalter has to be the standard and the measure of our praise. We may debate whether it is the exclusive source of our praise, but I do not see how we can avoid as Reformed people agreeing with the proposition that the Psalter must be the standard by which our praise is measured. If God has given us by inspiration 150 songs, those 150 songs must surely be adequate to give us indications of what kind of song pleases Him.

We should, therefore, look into the Psalter at some of the same issues we raised in relation to contemporary Christian music. First, what is the origin of the Psalter? The origin of the Psalter is that it comes from God. That is a good beginning place. It comes through ancient poets by the inspiration of His Holy Spirit. Second, what is the purpose of the Psalter? In Hebrew the Psalter is titled "The Book of Praises." It is the book that God has given us of praises that please Him. It is the book to give voice to our praise. Its purpose is to help direct our speaking to God. Our worship is meeting with God in a dialogue where He speaks to us and we speak to Him. He speaks in sermon, in Scripture reading, in benediction, and sacrament. We speak to Him in prayer and in praise. The Psalter's purpose is to give us models of how we are to speak to Him.

Third, what is the character of the Psalter? What do we find in the Psalter? If you have your Bibles, you might want to look at Psalm 146. I am going to try to illustrate some of the points I am making out of Psalm 146. One of the great values of the Psalter is that it gives us an indication of the kind of balance of elements that we ought to have in our praise. It presents an inspired balance. Sometimes we have debates in terms of contemporary Christian music: how subjective should praise be, and how objective should it be? How much should I talk about me, and how much should I talk about God? How much should I talk about my experience, and how much should I talk about redemptive history? What is the proper balance there? We need to look at the Psalter to answer these questions. What we find in the Psalter is an interesting balance and an interesting movement back and forth from the subjective to the objective, from the objective to the subjective. It talks both about God and about us. It is my praise of God. I am in the Psalm and God is in the Psalm.

Look at how Psalm 146 begins: "Praise the LORD," a call to praise. The Psalm continues: "Praise the LORD, O my soul. I will praise the LORD all of my life. I will sing praise to my God as long as I live." Here is a focus on my religious experience, on my religious activity, on what I am going to do in relationship to God. Here is the subjective element, and yet it is soon linked in the Psalm to objective statements about God. Notice verse 6 – "He is the maker of heaven and earth, the sea and everything in them. He is the LORD who remains faithful forever." Then it goes on to a listing of specific activities of our God for His people. You can see the Psalm here is balancing the subjective with the objective, and it does it sometimes in ways that are very surprising to us. Both elements are balanced in the Psalter in a remarkably helpful way. The danger of a lot of contemporary music is that it is too subjective. On the other hand sometimes traditionalists say, "We need hymns that teach theology." The Psalter does not tell us that the function of praise is primarily to teach theology. Rather its function is to show the interrelationship of God and His people.

Another balance we find in the Psalter is between the individual and the communal. How much of worship is a matter of my individual heart and response to God, and how much of my worship is my being a part of a community? We have some forms of Christianity that are radically individualistic and talk only about the individual, and you have hymnody that reflects that. You also have some forms of Christianity that are radically communitarian and only talk about the community. You have hymnody that reflects that. But the Psalter gives us an inspired balance of both. Again, in verse 1 the emphasis is on the individual – "I will praise the LORD all my life. I will sing praise to God as long as I live." But the communal is also very much present. Notice verse 10: "The LORD reigns forever, your God, O Zion, for all generations." From all of Zion and all of its generations comes this praise to God. The Psalm balances the individual and the communal. Now I am not saying the balance is the same in every Psalm. There is variety in the Psalter, and there ought to be variety in our praise. But the Psalm helps us to see how these things are held together.

There is an interesting balance between what is taught and what is not taught. Those who argue that we ought not to sing Psalms exclusively often say, "the Psalter is not adequate to the New Covenant. It does not tell us everything that is in the New Covenant. We do not have the name of Jesus in the Psalter." But the Psalter on that standard is not adequate to the Old Covenant either. If you had only the book of Psalms, there is an awful lot of Israel's history and religious life that you could not reconstruct. We would not know anything about the prophets. We would know very little about the Sabbath. Much of the sacrificial system would be unknown. There is much history we would not know. So we have to be careful when we say, "The Psalter does not tell us everything." No one element of the worship service can tell us everything in a worship service. So the Psalms challenge our thinking by what they do not teach. They are not primarily didactic in character. They are not intended to tell us everything that is in the Old Covenant or in the New Covenant, but are intended to give us praise to the God of the Old Covenant and the New Covenant. The Psalter serves the New Covenant because it gives us the new song of redemption as well as the old song of creation. Both songs have to be sung to God in His praise. But the new song is already in the Psalter. The Psalter itself says so.

Not only are there interesting elements of God's truth that are not taught in the Psalter, but there are also interesting elements that are taught in the Psalter but are characteristically neglected in our hymnody. Let me look at just a few of those things as we find them in Psalm 146. Think about those verses 3 and 4: "Do not put your trust in princes, in mortal men who cannot save. When their spirit departs, they return to the ground; on that very day their plans come to nothing." "Do not put your trust in princes," the inspired Psalmist implores us. How often do we sing in our hymns about the unreliability of the powers and forces of this world? Notice the Psalm does not say that princes are bad people. It does not warn against trusting in wicked princes. Rather, it is saying, do not put your ultimate trust in any prince because even the best of princes die. The reason princes are not a reliable source of help is because they are mortal, because they are transient, because they pass away. Is that a theme that is picked up much in our hymnody? I do not think so.

You also have a reflection on creation in Psalm 146:6. "God is the maker of heaven and earth, the sea and everything in them." There are some hymns that touch on creation, but I think creation is a much more prominent theme in the Psalter than it is in most of our hymnody. How do we know that God is reliable? We know that God is reliable because He made the heavens and earth and everything in them. We must never move away from that great confession. If He made everything we see in creation, then how could we doubt that He is in control of everything and can accomplish everything according to the counsel of His will?

Also notice what we find in Psalm 146:9 about God and the wicked: "He frustrates the ways of the wicked." In every Psalm, I think, except two, there is some explicit reference to the wicked as those who stand against God. The Psalter is full of an antithesis between the righteous and the wicked, between those who are in covenant with God and those who have rejected the covenant of God. It is a constant reminder to the people of God that we are either with God or we are against God. We are either living outside of His covenant and apart from His saving grace or we are living within His covenant and under His saving grace. But how frequently does that antithesis get expressed in our hymnody?

We also see references to God's covenant in Psalm 146:5: "Blessed is he whose help is in the God of Jacob." Then over at the end of verse 6: "The LORD who remains forever faithful." God is forever faithful to His covenant people. How often is the covenant of God exalted in our hymnody? I am not saying it is never there, but I am saying that it is one of many relatively neglected topics.

Then look at the wonderful specificity of the mercies of the Lord highlighted in this Psalm. How does God help His people? How does He bless the man who trusts in Him? How does He remain forever faithful to us? We are told in Psalm 146:7-9: "He upholds the cause of the oppressed and gives food to the hungry." How many of our hymns talk about the oppressed and the hungry? "He sets prisoners free and gives sight to the blind." How many of our hymns talk about prisoners and the blind? "He lifts up those bowed down. He loves the righteous." Most of us, of course, do not even dare think of ourselves as righteous. We have become hyper-humble. But God's grace does make a difference in us. When we are measured against the standard of the world, there is a difference and we are righteous.

When we think of these specific blessings of the Lord to the oppressed, to the hungry, to the prisoner, to the blind, to the bowed down, to the righteous, to the alien, to the fatherless, to the widow, who comes to mind? Where do we see the Lord blessing such people? We see the Lord working this way pre-eminently in our Lord Jesus Christ. He is the one who came as Messiah to help all of those who are weary and burdened and to save them. Is Jesus Christ in this Psalm? I do not know who else would be. Jesus is the Lord who is ever faithful. Jesus is the Lord who lifts up the bowed down and the oppressed and cares for the alien and the prisoner and the fatherless and the widow – and he frustrates the ways of the wicked. In this one Psalm we see a marvel of balance and of perception and of depth that we do not find in most of the kind of music, the kind of singing, the kind of reflection that we have in contemporary Christian music – and also in much traditional hymnody. The Psalter is a model here that we need to know, that we need to stand by, that we need to follow.

The Psalter is sometimes hard to read because it is so carefully crafted. One of the joys of studying the Psalms is the constant discovery of new things in the way the poet crafted the Psalms. For example, one of the things that is important to keep in mind is that in many Psalms the real meaning of the Psalm, the real heart of the Psalm, is at the center of the Psalm. We usually look at introductions and conclusions as the real key to what most writings are about. We learned that in school. In school you often did not need to read the whole book if you read the introduction and the conclusion. But you miss the heart of a Psalm if you do that because often the essence of the Psalm is at the very center of the Psalm. In Psalm 146, what is the heart of the Psalm? It is not quite as obvious in this Psalm as it is in many; but if you count the lines of Hebrew poetry, at the center of the Psalm we find the words "who remains faithful forever," (v. 6). Why do we praise the Lord? Because He remains faithful forever. That truth helps open up the whole of the Psalm. Why can we not trust princes? They do not remain faithful forever. They die. How do we know God will remain faithful forever? He is the creator of heaven and earth. How does God remain faithful forever? He helps the oppressed. And then how do we respond to that faithfulness? We acknowledge "the Lord reigns forever, your God, O Zion, to all generations." It is wonderful. Think about how God is faithful forever and worthy of our praise.

This careful, crafted quality to the Psalter stands in such marked contrast with the dashed off character of so much hymnody and contemporary music. We have to ask, if God inspired His poets in the Old Covenant to give such effort to the careful composition of His praise, how dare we praise God carelessly, running together random phrases in reference to God, with no development of thought? Such songs provide little real help for His people.

Another thing we find in the Psalter that I think is so important is the full range of human emotions. We live in a happy time. If you are a Christian, you have to be happy, and the function of the church is to make you happy. So the only legitimate emotion becomes the emotion of joy. Now joy is an important emotion. It is a proper response to the wonderful saving work of God. It is a wonderful experience of who God is, and our lives should be filled with joy and with thanksgiving. But the truth is that joy is not the only experience of the people of God. We also find Psalms in which the Psalmist speaks of some anger and frustration with God, because the people of God are angry and frustrated sometimes. We may not want to admit it. We may try to hide it. But the fact is that sometimes life is so frustrating that we get angry. It is a blessing to know God has given us words with which to express that frustration. He does not just say, "Well, if you had enough faith, you would never be angry or frustrated." He also gives us words to express sorrow and lament and grief over our sin and over the condition of the world. As He gives us words to express our confidence in Him, so He gives us words to appeal to Him for relief and for help.

A friend of mine who is a minister went to visit a distant relative who had been for some time in a nursing home and had been somewhat neglected by her family. She asked him to read Psalm 88 to her. Do you know Psalm 88? Psalm 88 is the bleakest Psalm in the Psalter. "O LORD, the God who saves me," the first verse, is the only positive word in the whole Psalm. The Psalmist begins with faith and proceeds with the lament of a lonely, tormented heart: "O God, the God who saves me. Day and night I cry out to You. My prayer comes before You; turn Your ear to my cry. For my soul is full of trouble, and my life draws near the grave. I am counted among those who go down to the pit. I am like a man without strength." God gave these words to an old lady in a nursing home so that she could know that her experience and suffering was not unique amongst the people of God. He gave voice to her life so that she could talk to Him. It is an amazing gift.

Among the questions that often come up about using the Psalter, one is: "We have inspired poems in the Psalter, but what about tunes"? And my short answer to that is, "God has not given us tunes, and yet He has commanded us to sing. Therefore, obviously He intends that we should create tunes to support the words with which we need to sing." What should be the character of those tunes? Obviously there are two basic criteria for tunes. First, they should be singable. By and large contemporary Christian music does all right with that criterion. Good tunes for Christian singing should be easily – maybe not immediately – but easily singable by the congregation. Second, good tunes should support the text. They ought to express the range of emotions that the text carries. If it is a sad song, it ought to be a sad tune. If it is a joyful Psalm, it ought to be a joyful tune. But the tune must above all else support the text and carry the text in singing.

Another critical issue in our time is the proper instruments to support our praise. One of the great dangers of our time is that instrumentation overwhelms the singing so that what you hear is the instrument and not the singing. We have to be honest here and say that can happen with an organ as well as with a drum. It is not just drums and guitars that can overwhelm singing. An organ can overwhelm singing. (I will not quote the statement of Robert Dabney when he said that of all the musical instruments ever created the organ is most uniquely suited to support Roman Catholic piety.[5])

Most of our problems with musical style and tunes could be solved if we said, "We ought to sing tunes that could be sung *a capella*." Now we do not have time to get into the issue of whether they should be sung *a capella*. But I think that much in the music wars is about instrumentation. I certainly know that when most organists play a praise song on the organ, it ceases to be a praise song and sounds remarkably like a traditional hymn.

Conclusion

What is the great issue with contemporary Christian worship? The great issue is this: since music is one of the most effective ways in which our souls are moved and in which our minds are informed, what is the character and context of the music that is moving our souls and informing our minds? We had a funeral recently in our congregation for one of the matriarchs of the church. Two of her granddaughters spoke at the funeral, and they talked about their grandmother. They said, "We used to play a game with Grandma growing up. We would open the Psalter and read a verse out of the Psalm. And Grandma could always tell us what Psalm it was from. And sometimes we would try to trick her. We would read half a

---

5. Thompson, *Presbyterians in the South,* 2:429ff.

verse from one Psalm and half a verse from another, and she could always tell us which two Psalms it was from."This was a woman who sang Psalms predominantly through her life and had hid the Psalter in her heart. Was that a blessing? Was that a good thing? Or would she have been better off just singing Alleluia eleven times? It is not a close call.

We are impoverishing our souls by not using one of the best ways of learning the Word of God, namely by singing it. And, again, putting aside the issue of exclusive Psalmody versus inclusive Psalmody, for Reformed people not to treasure the Psalms and love the Psalms and learn the Psalms and sing the Psalms is a major tragedy for us spiritually. We will have their contents in our heads so that in the moment of distress when we feel abandoned by God, we will know that there is Psalm 88 to which we can turn for expressing to God our sense of abandonment.

The best strategy for us is not to spend a great deal of time criticizing contemporary Christian music. The best strategy for us is to spend our time learning the Psalter, singing the Psalms, and rejoicing in the Word that God has given us. If we become really acquainted with the Psalter and are able to quote it and use it appropriately, there will be something contagious about its spiritual power. You know, we strict Calvinists are often known as God's grumpy people. Let us not be the grumpy people. Let us be the people characterized by love for the Word of God reflected in the way the Psalter gives voice to our praise.

Chapter 6

Reformed Liturgy

Joseph A. Pipa, Jr

There is a form of worship, shaped by Scripture and consistent with the Reformed tradition, that is richer than many of us are experiencing. There are aspects of liturgy and posture, practiced in the past by Reformed churches, which we are neglecting today. In this chapter we will explore these two aspects of liturgy and posture.

Liturgy

Some have a knee jerk reaction to the concept of liturgy, relating it to High Church Anglicanism, with its imposed, brief prayers and congregational responses. In fact all worshiping congregations use a liturgy. The term is derived from one of the three primary Greek terms for worship the noun *leitourgia* and its verb *leitourgeo*, which translate the Hebrews term *sharath*. These words deal with the specific acts involved in worshiping God. For example, in the Old Testament the word describes the work of the priests and Levites. Luke uses the Greek term in Acts 13:2 to describe the scene where the Holy Spirit directed the church to set aside Barnabas and Saul for missions: "And while they were ministering to the Lord and fasting, the Holy Spirit said...."The verb translated "ministering" is the term *leitourgeo*.

Baird suggests that there are four types of ritual.[1] "The first is imposed ritual, responsive in its character, and prescribed to the

---

1. Charles W. Baird, *The Presbyterian Liturgies*: Historical Sketches (1855, 1856; reprint, Grand Rapids: Baker Book House, 1957), 8,9.

minister and people for their common use." Such is the liturgical practice of the various Anglican and Episcopal congregations.

Second, "discretionary ritual, not responsive, and supplied to the minister alone, for his guidance as to the matter and manner of worship; leaving freedom of variation, as to the latter, according to his judgment." Strasbourg, Geneva, and Scotland practiced this form of ritual.

Third, *"rubrical* provision, consisting of directions without examples; indicting the subjects, but omitting the language of prayer." This pattern is found in the *Westminster Directory of Worship* and shaped the early practice of Scottish and American Presbyterianism.

Fourth, "is that of *entire freedom*, as respects both subject and language, leaving all to the option of the minister." This was the practice of many of the Puritan Independents and has become the practice of evangelicals and a large majority of Scottish and American Presbyterians.

Historically, Reformed and Presbyterian churches eschewed both the first and fourth types of ritual, but today many of our most conservative Presbyterian congregations practice a worship that little reflects the earlier reformed practices or the *Directory for the Public Worship of God*. Terry Johnson chronicles the development of liturgy in Presbyterian Churches:

1. 1562–1645, Genevan styled, moderately liturgical worship of *Knox's Book of Common Order* (1562) prevailed, using as fixed forms the Lord's Prayer, Apostles' Creed, and Ten Commandments.

2. 1685–1855, non liturgical worship was in the ascendancy [sic.], purportedly governed by the Westminster Assembly's *Directory for the Public Worship of God* (1645), but in practice moving beyond it is its complete absence of fixed forms.

3. 1855–1960s, moderately liturgical worship again became commonplace. Its revival was sparked by the publication of Charles W. Baird's *Eutaxia* (1855), calling for restored liturgical use of the Lord's Prayer, Apostles' Creed, and Ten Commandments. To these often were added the Gloria Patri

and/or the Doxology. What many identify as 'traditional' Presbyterian worship was in fact regarded as an innovation as recently as the mid to late nineteenth century.[2]

There are, however, no grounds for the rejection of either a "discretionary ritual" or a "rubrical provision." Baird concludes: "*That the principles of Presbyterianism in no wise conflict with the discretionary use of written forms*; and secondly, *That the practice of Presbyterian churches abundantly warrants the adoption and the use of such forms.*"[3]

Some confuse the issue of liturgy with the regulative principle. But we are not discussing what one offers to God in worship, rather how one organizes worship. In other words, we are talking about forms of worship and not the elements. The distinction is made quite clear in the preface to the *Westminster Directory of Worship*:

Wherein our care hath been to hold forth such things as are of divine institution in every ordinance; and other things we have endeavoured to set forth according to the rules of Christian prudence, agreeable to the general rules of the word of God; our meaning therein being only, that the general heads, the sense and scope of the prayers, and other parts of publick worship, being known to all, there may be a consent of all the churches in those things that contain the substance of the service and worship of God; and the ministers may be hereby directed, in their administrations, to keep like soundness in doctrine and prayer, and may, if need be have some help and furniture, and yet so as they become not hereby slothful and negligent in stirring up the gifts of Christ in them; but that each one, by meditation, by taking heed to himself, and the flock of God committed to him, and by wise observing of the ways of Divine Providence may be careful to furnish his heart and tongue with further or other materials of prayer and exhortation, as shall be needful upon all occasions.[4]

---

2. Terry Johnson, *Leading in Worship* (Oak Ridge,TN: The Covenant Foundation, 1996), 7. Unfortunately although there is a more common use of the Creed, the Gloria, and the Doxology, a large number of conservative Presbyterian churches do not use the Ten Commandments with a public confession and declaration of pardon and use a woefully ordered liturgy.

3. Baird, *The Presbyterian Liturgies*, 9.

4. "The Directory for the Publick Worship of God," *The Westminster Confession of Faith*

Since some today are confusing "elements," "circumstances," and "forms," before discussing the forms of liturgy, we need to be clear in our definitions. T. David Gordon gives the following definitions: "'Elements' of worship are those things which the Bible teaches to be essential to worship; the elements of worship are those things which constitute worship to be worship." "'Circumstances' of worship are those considerations regarding how, when, where and in what amount to perform the elements." "'Forms' of worship are the precise *contents* of a particular element."[5]

Let us look more fully at "circumstances" and "forms." First, what does the *Westminster Confession of Faith* mean by circumstances of worship? Circumstances are those things that enable us to perform the acts of worship (time, place, order, arrangement of pews and pulpit, sound system, etc.). The elders may order them according to the general customs of the time and place and according to the general principles of the Word of God. The Puritans derived the concept of circumstances from 1 Corinthians 14:40, "But let all things be done properly and in an orderly manner." They worked out the principle in WCF I.6: "that there are some circumstances concerning the worship of God, and the government of the Church, common to human actions and societies, which are to be ordered by the light of nature, and Christian prudence, according to the general rules of the Word, which are always to be observed."

As noted in the definition above, circumstances have to do with things that enable us to worship. Note that the English word "circumstance" implies something that is peripheral. "Thus, a 'circumstance' is something that is 'around' something, but not part of its essence."[6] Circumstances are those things that enable us to perform the elements of worship in an orderly manner. They are "common to human actions and societies, which are to be ordered by the light of nature" (W.F.C. 1.6). Whenever a body of people

(Inverness, Scotland: The Publications Committee of the Free Presbyterian Church of Scotland, 1985), 374.
5. T. David Gordon, unpublished paper, "Presbyterian Worship: Its Distinguishing Principle."
6. Gordon, "Presbyterian Worship: Its Distinguishing Principle."

meets in a public gathering certain details must be worked out with respect to time, place, how long, and so on. Worship must be regulated similarly.

Jeremiah Burroughs expands on the concept "common to human actions and societies, which are to be governed by the light of nature:"

> It's true that there are some things in the worship of God that are natural and civil helps, and there we do not need to have a command. For instance, when we come to worship God the congregation meets. They must have a convenient place to keep the air and weather from them. Note this is only a natural help, and so far as I use the place of worship as a natural help, I need have no command. But if I will put anything in a place beyond what it has in its own nature, there I must look for a command, for if I account one place more holy than another, or think that God should accept worship in one place rather than another, this is to raise it above what it is in its own nature.[7]

A thing that is circumstantial must be used according to its nature (a building serves as a shelter whether for worship or any other purpose) enabling us to worship God.

John Owen expands on the point that the use of something in the religious acts of worship must not be contrary to its natural use:

> Circumstances are either such as follow actions as actions, or such as are arbitrarily superadded and adjoined by command unto actions, which do not of their own accord nor naturally nor necessarily attend them. Now religious actions in the worship of God are actions still. Their religious relation doth not destroy their natural being. Those circumstances, then, which do attend such actions as actions not determined by divine institution, may be ordered, disposed of, and regulated by the prudence of men.

---

7. Jeremiah Burroughs, *Gospel Worship* (1648; reprint, Ligonier, PA: Soli Deo Gloria Publications, 1990), 14. See James Henley Thornwell. The Collected Writings of James Henley Thornwell (1875; reprint, Edinburgh: The Banner of Truth Trust, 1986), IV:247; James Bannerman, Church of Christ (1869; reprint, Edinburgh: The Banner of Truth Trust, 1960), I:355-357.

For instance, prayer is a part of God's worship. Public prayer is so, as appointed by him. This, as it is an action to be performed by man, cannot be done without the assignment of time, and place, and sundry other things, if order and conveniency be attended to. These are circumstances that attend all actions of that nature, to be performed by a community, whether they relate to the worship of God or no. These men may, according as they see good, regulate and change as there is occasion; I mean, they may do so who are acknowledged to have power in such things....

Owen also helps us to understand the abuse of the concept of "circumstances" in worship:

There are also some things, which some men call circumstances, also, that no way belong of themselves to the actions whereof they are said to be the circumstances, nor do attend them, but are imposed on them, or annexed unto them, by the arbitrary authority of those who take upon them to give order and rules in such cases: such as to pray before an image or towards the east, or to use this or that form of prayer in such gospel administration, and no other. These are not circumstances attending the nature of the thing itself, but are arbitrarily superadded to the things that they are appointed to accompany. Whatever men may call such additions, they are no less parts of the whole wherein they serve than the things themselves whereunto they are adjoined. The schoolmen tell us that that which is made so the condition of an action, that without it the action is not to be done, is not a circumstance of it. But such an adjunct as is a necessary part.[8]

We can illustrate the true nature of "circumstance" by considering the use of candles. If the electricity goes out and the elders determined to use candles to light the building, such use would be a circumstance, because that it is the natural use of a candle. On the other hand, when one gives some liturgical value to a candle (candlelight service or advent candles) one is not using them in their natural way and thus they are not circumstances, but rather imposed additions to worship.

---

8. John Owen, *The Works of John Owen,* ed. William H. Goold (reprint, London: The Banner of Truth Trust, 1966), XV:35, 36.

The *Westminster Confession of Faith* lays down some principles to guide in the use of "circumstance." First, according to the Confession, since the meetings are for the worship of God and the edification of the people of God, they are to be ordered by "Christian prudence." In other words, the Church officers must act wisely for the ends determined. For example, in rural agricultural areas the second service was often in the afternoon so that the farmers would be able to return in the evening to feed their livestock or milk their cows. When a denomination, however, establishes a congregation in a large metropolitan area, where there are no farms, it would be not wise to keep the service in the afternoon. In a non agricultural context, where transportation is readily available, an evening service might be wiser than an afternoon one.

Second, the Confession also teaches that the regulation of the circumstances must be "according to the general rules of the Word." In other words, whatever circumstances are implemented, they must be consistent with Scripture and for the fulfillment of scriptural duties.

Third, we note that the officers of the church may not arbitrarily legislate circumstances. George Gillespie, one of the Scottish commissioners to the Westminster Assembly, offered three principles to guide Church officers as they legislate circumstances. First, the matter must truly be a circumstance of worship: "It (any matter legitimate for the church to legislate) must be only a circumstance of Divine worship, and no substantial part of it; no sacred, significant, and efficacious ceremony."[9] It must not be an element in worship offered to God, but a thing to enable us to fulfill the element. The great Scottish theologian, James Bannerman, expands:

> There is plainly a wide and real difference between those matters that may be necessary or proper about Church worship, and those other matters that may be necessary and proper in worship; or, to adopt the old distinction, between matters *circa* and matters *in*

9. George Gillespie, "A Dispute Against The English Popish Ceremonies," in *The Works of George Gillespie,* (reprint, Edmonton, AB Canada: Still Waters Revival Books, 1991), 1:130.

sacris, Church worship is itself an express and positive appointment of God; and the various parts or elements of worship, including the rites and ceremonies that enter into it, are no less positive Divine appointments. But there are circumstances connected with a Divine solemnity no less than with human solemnities, that do not belong to its essence, and form no necessary part of it. There are circumstances of time and place and form, necessary for the order and decency of the service of the Church, as much as for the service or actions of any civil or voluntary society; and these, though connected with, are no portion of, Divine worship. When worship is to be performed on the Sabbath, for example, – where it is to be dispensed – how long the service is to continue, – are points necessary to be regulated in regard to the action of the Church as much as in regard to the action of a mere private and human society; and yet they constitute no part of the worship of God.[10]

Gillespie's second principle was "[It] must be one of such things as were not determinable by Scripture…. The case being thus put, as it is, we say truly of those several and changeable circumstances which are left to the determination of the church, that, being almost infinite, they were not particularly determinable in Scripture; for the particular definition of those occurring circumstances which were to be rightly ordered in the works of God's service to the end of the world, and that ever according to the exigency of every present occasion and different use case, should have filled the whole world with books."[11] In other words, because things circumstantial to worship change from time to time and place to place, the Scriptures are silent about them.

Bannerman further expands:

Within the limits of what strictly and properly belongs to public worship, the directory of Scripture is both sufficient and of exclusive authority; and the service of the Church is a matter of positive enactment, suited for and binding upon all times and all

---

10. Bannerman, *Church of Christ*, I:355, 356.
11. Gillespie, *A Dispute*, 131.

nations. But beyond the limits of what strictly and properly belongs to Divine worship, there are circumstances that must vary with times and nations; and for that very reason they are circumstances not regulated in Scripture, but left to be ordered by the dictates of natural reason, such as would be sufficient to determine them in the case of any other society than the Church. In addition to the test of their being merely circumstances and not substantials of worship, they are also to be distinguished by the mark that from their very nature they are 'not determinable from Scripture.'[12]

Gillespie's third principle was "If the church prescribe anything lawfully, so that she prescribe no more than she hath power given her to prescribe, her ordinance must be accompanied with some good reason and warrant given for the satisfaction of tender consciences."[13] The point of this last condition, in other words, is that, even with the first two conditions met, it is not an "anything goes" situation. In the case of a merely circumstantial matter, about which Scripture is silent, the officers are not free to do, or to permit, just anything they wish; they must demonstrate a sound reason. When the church adapts practices from the surrounding culture it must do so with great caution and confidence that such things are not inimical to God's worship. Again listen to Bannerman:

> This third mark is necessary, in order that the canon of Church order under consideration may not be interpreted so widely as to admit of the indefinite multiplication of rules and rubrics, even in matters that stand the two other tests already mentioned, – that is to say, in matters merely circumstantial, and not determinable form Scripture. Even in the instance of such, there must be a sufficient reason, either in the necessity of the act, or in the manifest Christian expediency of it, to justify the Church in adding to her canons of order, and limiting by these the Christian liberty of her members. There must be sufficient reason, in the way of securing decency or preventing disorder, to warrant the Church in enacting regulations even in the circumstances of worship as contradistinguished from its ceremonies. Without some necessity laid upon it, and

12. Bannerman, *Church of Christ,* I:356.
13. Gillespie, *A Dispute,* 131.

a sufficient reason to state for its procedure, the Church has no warrant to encroach upon the liberty of its members.... Even in matters lawful and indifferent, not belonging to Divine worship itself, but to the circumstance of it, the Church is bound to show a necessity or a sufficient reason for its enactments.[14]

We may conclude this section by listing some of the more obvious "circumstances" of worship: where we worship; what time of day we worship; how long is the service; how long the sermon; how many prayers and hymns; the selection of hymn tunes; whether we use musical accompaniment; what type of accompaniment; the use of a bulletin or a hymnal.

The second area in which God grants some liberty in worship is in the use of "forms." The concept of "form" is found in the Larger Catechism 186: "The whole Word of God is of use to direct us in the duty of prayer; but the special rule of direction is that form of prayer which our Savior Christ taught his disciples, commonly called the Lord's Prayer" (see Shorter Catechism 99). The concept of "form" is found in the *Directory of Worship* of the Presbyterian Church in America:

> The Lord Jesus Christ has prescribed no fixed forms for public worship but, in the interest of life and power in worship, has given His Church a large measure of liberty in this matter. It may not be forgotten, however, that there is true liberty only where the rules of God's Word are observed and the Spirit of the Lord is, that all things must be done decently and in order, and that God's people should serve Him with reverence and in the beauty of holiness (47-6, cf. 52-4; 63-3).

Forms consist of the precise content of an element, the liturgical structure of the elements, and the postures used in the acts of worship (e.g., which song or Psalm to be sung, whether to use common prayer or free prayer, how to structure our worship, and what postures to adopt). Of course, the content of our prayers must be in accord with the truth of Scripture; if we sing hymns in addition

---

14. Bannerman, *Church of Christ*, I:356, 357.

to Psalms, they must be faithful to Scripture; and our preaching must focus exclusively on the truth of Scripture. Moreover, we shall see that forms are suggested, though not required by Scripture. This commitment to liberty in forms gave rise to the concept of a *Directory of Worship* rather than a *Book of Common Prayer*, but as we shall see, the Bible is not opposed to a rubrical liturgy. Whatever we do, though, must be consistent with a proper understanding of the principles of circumstances and forms.

One of the great struggles for the Puritans was the imposed worship of the *Book of Common Prayer*. As the exiles returned from Geneva and Zurich, they had high hopes that Elizabeth I would support their efforts for a more thoroughgoing reform of the Church. She quickly dashed their hopes to pieces. In 1559, in order to unify the Church, she asked Parliament to pass two pieces of legislation: The Act of Supremacy and the Act of Uniformity. The Act of Supremacy was the same Act that her father had implemented in 1534 when he broke with the Roman Catholic Church. This Act declared the monarch to be the head of the church. Elizabeth's Act of Supremacy insured the hierarchy of the Episcopalian form of government. The Act of Uniformity required all ministers to conduct all the services with the liturgy and words of the 1552 Prayer Book. Although the content of this book was more scriptural than the one before it, it still contained vestiges of Romanism. In connection with the use of the *Prayer Book*, ministers were required to wear the liturgical, symbolic, ministerial garments called vestments. This Act also established the 42 Articles as the doctrinal standard of the Church (in 1563 they would be changed to the 39 Articles). The Puritans really did not have a problem with the doctrinal statement, but the remainder of The Act of Uniformity as well as the Act of Supremacy, created great problems for them. It is in this context that Puritanism developed.

According to Haller, "Elizabeth to their dismay did not reform the church but only swept rubbish behind the door. The Puritan movement may be said to have sprung out of the shock of great disappointment."[15] Those who were dissatisfied eventually became

---

15. William Haller, *The Rise of Puritanism* (Philadelphia; University of Pennsylvania Press,

known as Puritans. In his history of the Puritans, Neal discussed six general principles that united the Puritan opposition.[16] Two of these principles dealt directly with worship. The fifth was that the Puritans contended that the Church did not have the right to legislate in things neither commanded nor forbidden in Scripture:

> But the Puritans insisted, that those things which Christ had left indifferent ought not to be made necessary by any human laws, but that we are to stand fast in the liberty wherewith Christ has made us free; and farther, that such rites and ceremonies as had been abused to idolatry, and manifestly tended to lead men back to Popery and superstition, were no longer indifferent, but to be rejected as unlawful.[17]

The sixth dealt with Church authority. Although the Bishops and the Puritans agreed that there ought to be uniformity in the worship enforced by the civil magistrate, the Bishops believed that it was the Queen's prerogative to order such worship, while the Puritans believed that such uniformity ought to be enacted by the church.

With respect to the *Book of Common Prayer* the Puritans were also opposed to the imposed use of prayers, the brevity of the prayers, and multitude of congregational responses.

The majority of the Puritans were not opposed to some common prayer, although some of the radical Puritans were. At the Westminster Assembly the Puritans replaced the *Book of Common Prayer* with a *Directory of Worship*. As noted above, a directory lays down guidelines and leaves a certain freedom as to how one expresses oneself: the selection of hymns and psalms, the number of prayers and their content, the content of the sermon, and the order of the service.

As we begin to study the liturgy, let us briefly review the elements that the Reformers and Puritans believed the Bible required. At the outset, let us note that the Scriptures are clear about the acts God requires in worship and that there are relatively few areas of

---

1972), 8.

16. Daniel Neal, *History of Puritans* (Minneapolis: Klock & Klock, 1979), 1:100-103.

17. Ibid., 102.

disagreement. Furthermore, whatever difficulties we encounter should not lead to the agnosticism expressed by Professor Frame: "Unfortunately, it is virtually impossible to prove anything is divinely required specifically for official services."[18] Bannerman reaches the opposite conclusion:

> The Scriptures are the only rule for worship, as truly as they are the only rule for the Church in any other department of her duties. And the Scriptures are sufficient for that purpose; for they contain a directory for worship, either expressly inculcated, or justly to be inferred from its statements sufficient for the guidance of the Church in every necessary part of worship.[19]

Admittedly even those seriously committed to the regulative principle will differ with respect to some aspects such as the use of non inspired hymns, choirs, or musical instruments. In the areas of difference, we are to be patient and humble as we continue to seek the mind of God.

What then are the elements derived from the Scriptures by the Regulative Principle of worship? The *Westminster Confession of Faith* lists them in XXI.III & V:

> Prayer, with thanksgiving, being one special part of religious worship, is by God required of all men; ... The reading of the Scriptures with godly fear; the sound preaching, and conscionable hearing of the word, in obedience unto God, with understanding, faith, and reverence; singing of psalms with grace in the heart; as also the due administration and worthy receiving of the sacraments instituted by Christ; are all parts of the ordinary religious worship of God: besides religious oaths and vows, solemn fastings, and thanksgivings upon special occasions, which are, in their several times and seasons, to be used in a holy and religious manner.

To these the Directory of Worship adds the Invocation, Benediction, the repetition of the Lord's Prayer, and in some form the offering. We ought to note that until the middle of the nineteenth century

---

18. John Frame, *Worship in Spirit and Truth* (Phillipsburg, NJ: P & R Publishing, 1996), 44.
19. Bannerman, *Church of Christ*, I:368.

Presbyterians did not use choirs, non lyrical music, or other forms of special music. In 1867 the Old School Northern Assembly said, "the introduction of choirs or musical instruments can be justified only as they serve this end (to inspire and express devotion) and aid or accompany sacred song; and no display of artistic skill, no delicacy of vocal training, no measure of musical ability, compensates for the violation, or even neglect, of the proprieties of divine worship." They further said, "that the Scriptures nowhere recognize the service of song as to be performed by the few on behalf of the many."[20]

As we consider the ordering of worship, we should ask whether there are principles "set forth according to the rules of Christian prudence, agreeable to the general rules of the word of God" that we may apply?

Let us lay the foundation for our discussion by considering the three questions that Terry Johnson puts to us. Are all forms equally suited to express Presbyterian convictions? Is the emotive power of forms being taken seriously enough? Are the forms of the Reformed tradition being taken seriously enough?[21] We agree with Johnson that not all forms are suited for communicating Reformed piety and worship. He says, "Reformed theology once did and must continue to generate its own forms or it will vanish from the face of the earth, first neglected, then forgotten."[22]

Second, forms do communicate emotionally. Children raised under a specific form (Episcopalian, Charismatic, Baptist) will grow up attached to that form and, if they move, will usually end up in a non Presbyterian church. The French Huguenots are a good example. When they came to the United States in the nineteenth century many joined the Episcopal church rather than the Presbyterian. According to Johnson, Girardeau attributed this new allegiance to "the power of forms: the worship of the American Episcopal church was more like that of the French Reformed church than that of the utterly non liturgical worship of seventeenth to nineteenth century Anglo-Saxon Presbyterians."[23] Johnson concludes that we may lose

---

20. Quoted by Gordon from *Presbyterian Digest*, ed. Wm. E. Moore, 1873, 653.
21. Johnson, *Leading in Worship*, 1-3.
22. Ibid., 2.

a whole generation of young people, if we do not achieve a greater uniformity in worship that is Reformed in form. Is this not one reason so many of our Presbyterian congregations have lost their young adults to broadly evangelical congregations? Since they were taught to worship like broad evangelicals, why not join them?

Third, Johnson points out that we are not taking seriously the forms of our Reformed tradition. On the one hand some are turning to a form of worship more akin to the imposed liturgy of Anglicanism, while on the other hand, some to a charismatic free for all. My purpose is to direct your attention to some of the forgotten forms of the Reformed tradition.

Before looking at the liturgical forms, we need to ask "Is it valid to speak of a traditional reformed approach to liturgy?" Although the Bible does not spell out an order of worship, it gives us some clear criteria. The first criterion is that biblical worship ought to be *covenantal* in structure.[24] As we know the Covenant has two parties: God the initiating party and man the responding; we could say God's part and man's. This is not to say that our part is equal to God's. Vandooren says, "Although, in a certain sense, the covenant of grace is *bilateral*, in that there is now a 'back and forth' relationship between the LORD and us, in general, and also in the liturgy, in its origin this Covenant is bestowed upon us as a 'testament,' a free and sovereign gift. 'Love came from one side,' while we were yet enemies. The LORD took, and still takes, the initiative. Thus the covenant, in its origin, was *unilateral*, and it always remains that way. We are always on the receiving end. Even when we give to our God, we give what we have first received."[25]

With this caveat in mind we still may think of our covenant relationship as a two-way street and we are to reflect this relationship in our worship. "As a result," explains Vandooren, "the various 'elements' of Reformed liturgy can be divided into two groups, i.e.,

---

23. Ibid.; For a full treatment of the historical position of Presbyterians on musical instrumentation in worship, see John L. Girardeau., Instrumental Music in the Public Worship of the Church (Richmond: Whittet and Shepperson, 1888).

24. G. Vandooren, *The Beauty of Reformed Liturgy* (Winnipeg: Premier Publishing, 1992), 15.

25. Ibid., 15.

first those elements that come from the Lord, such as His blessing, His Word, etc.; secondly, those that come from us, His people, such as praise and prayer and offerings, but most of all the sacrifice of a repentant and thankful heart."[26] Rayburn calls this covenantally structured liturgy the "divine human dialogue."[27]

This pattern, moreover, is illustrated in the tabernacle/temple. The outward court with the laver and the altar of sacrifice was the place of the congregation. The Most Holy Place was the part of the tabernacle/temple in which God dwelt in the midst of the people and the High Priest entered only once a year. In the Holy Place the priests served daily as mediators representing God to the people and the people to God.[28] The work of the priests depicts the two-way street of worship. In the fulfillment of the New Covenant, Christ has entered the Most Holy Place once for all and dwells with the Father in heaven. The congregation as priest has free access through Him, while He through the word, preaching, and sacraments speaks to them. Vandooren calls this the vertical sanctuary, since Christ has ascended on high. He says, "In this vertical sanctuary there is still – but now in fulfillment – the covenantal 'two-way traffic,' ...There is a movement from heaven to earth, when God blesses His people, proclaims His law, speaks His word (including the sacraments). There is also a movement from earth to heaven, when the congregation prays, confesses, sings, brings offerings of gratitude (also listening to Scripture and the sermon)."[29] Vandooren concludes:

> It now should be clear to all that our Reformed, or covenantal, liturgy consists of several elements which must be divided into two groups. Some Latin words are used for this distinction. There are elements *a parte Dei* (from God's part or side); they are: 1. the benedictions, 2. the Ten Words (the Ten Commandments), 3. public reading of the Scriptures, 4. proclamation of the word.

---

26. Ibid., 15.
27. Robert Rayburn, *O Come, Let Us Worship* (Grand Rapids: Baker Book House, 1980), 165.
28. Vandooren, *The Beauty of Reformed Liturgy*, 17.
29. Ibid., 19.

Other elements are a *parte homini*, from the side of man, of the congregation, such as: 1. The votum, 2. Creed, 3. Prayers, 4. Offertory, 5. singing the praise of the LORD.

There are, of course, also the sacraments ... they, and especially Holy Supper, are a 'two-way' business. Also in the preaching there is or should be two-way traffic. Listening, 'hearing the Word,' is a very important activity on the part of the assembled holy nation.[30]

If we designate God's part "A" and our part "B," we should be able to observe an alternation between them in the flow of a worship service: "A," "B", "A," "B." I am not suggesting that every "A" is followed immediately by a "B" and vice versa, but there is a flow of dialogue.

The second criterion is what Johnson calls the gospel cycles.[31]

1 A cycle of praise (call/invocation hymn/Gloria Patri/Creed)
2 A cycle of confession (Law of God/confession of sin/ assurance of pardon)
3 A cycle employing the means of grace (intercessory prayers/ sacraments/Scripture reading/sermon)
4 A cycle of thanksgiving and blessing (concluding hymn/ collection/benediction)

He notes that this is the pattern of Isaiah 6, the Lord's Prayer, and the Gospel. The order is not prescribed, but what he calls "Gospel logic," combining form and freedom.[32] Some churches will divide their service into major parts: service (or liturgy) of praise; service of confession; service of the Word; service of response. Within these divisions one should still observe the covenantal dialogue.

A third criterion in determining if there really is a biblically-determined, reformed liturgy is the practice of the Church. Rayburn writes,

> The importance of the corporateness of worship is also emphasized by the doctrine of the church universal, the body of Christ which is made up of all believers of the past, present, and future. It was not

---

30. Ibid., 20
31. Johnson, *Leading in Worship*, 15.
32. Ibid.,15

our action but that of Christ which first constituted the church; and since it is his body, responding to his initiative in worship, a sense of the universal and corporate is always necessary if worship is to be authentically Christian. Because this is true, traditional forms in the liturgy of the church have great value when they are properly used and understood for what they are by the worshipers. Of course, there is danger in the use of traditional components in a worship service. To focus attention on forms of prayer or upon hymns, which come out of the ancient church, might arouse an excitement and interest which will draw the attention of the worshiper away from the living God, who is the object of worship and who alone makes forms meaningful. However, tradition should never be discarded out of hand by the believers in any age. It does aid in the communication of a sense of the universal and corporate nature of the church.[33]

The awareness of the Church's practice not only keeps touch with the tradition, but also it helps shape worship. As Johnson points out, this was Calvin's method:

The Reformers claimed to be doing nothing more or less than reviving the worship instituted by the Apostles. Calvin's liturgy claims to provide a 'Form of Church Prayers… According to the Custom of the Ancient Church.' As Hughes O. Old has demonstrated in his important (but neglected) study, *The Patristic Roots of Reformed Worship*, the Reformers based their reformation of worship primarily upon the exegesis of Scripture. Theirs, however, was not a naïve Biblicism. They also valued the Church Fathers as witnesses to how scripture was understood by those closest to the Apostles. For them, as Old argues, 'the writings of the Fathers were read as witnesses to the purer forms of worship of the ancient church should be ours.'[34]

Johnson notes a number of elements that the Reformers reintroduced on the basis of their study: invocation and/or call to

---

33. Rayburn, *O Come, Let Us Worship*, 32.
34. Johnson, *Leading in Worship*, 6; Hughes Oliphant Old, *The Patristic Roots of Reformed Worship* (Zurich: Theologischer Verlag, 1970).

worship; Scripture reading and preaching by *lectio selecta*; prayer of illumination; reading of the law of God and confession of sin; prayer of intercession; congregational singing; recitation of the creed; and the benediction.[35]

By looking at Justin Martyr's liturgy (about AD 140) we can see the parallels with the early Reformation orders:

THE LITURGY OF THE WORD
> Lections from the prophets, and the Epistles and Gospel (called memoirs of the Apostles)
> Instruction and exhortation based upon the Lections
> Common prayers, apparently in litany form
> Psalms and hymns also probably had a place

THE LITURGY OF THE UPPER ROOM
> Kiss of Peace
> Offertory: Collection of gifts for poor
>> Bringing in the elements
> Prayer of consecration:
>> Thanksgiving for creation, providence, and redemption
>> Memorial of Passion (later known as Anamnesis)
>> Oblation of gifts with self oblation
>> Invocation of the Word and Holy Spirit to bless the gifts of bread and wine (later known as the Epiclesis)
>> Intercessions
>> People's Amen
> Fraction
> Communion
> Dismissal

By applying these three criteria, we are able to understand how the Reformed Church developed its liturgy and how we may do so as well. We have inherited from the Reformed and Presbyterian Churches two types of liturgy: rubrical and discretionary. For the rubrical we will look at Calvin's Strasbourg and Geneva liturgies and Knox's Scottish.

---

35. Ibid., 6.

Stras. French, 1540	Geneva, 1542	Knox's Scottish Rite:
The Liturgy of the Word	**The Liturgy of the Word**	**The Liturgy of the Word**
Scripture Sentence: Psalm cxxiv. 8	Scripture Sentence: Psalm cxxiv. 8	
Confession of sins	Confession of sins	Confession of Sins
Scriptural words of pardon	Prayer for pardon	Prayer for pardon
Absolution		
Metrical Decalogue Sung with Kyrie elesion (Gr.) after each law	Metrical Psalm	Psalm in metre
Collect for illumination	Collect for illumination	Prayer for illumination
Lection	Lection	Scripture Lection
Sermon	Sermon	Sermon
The Liturgy of the Upper Room	**The Liturgy of the Upper Room**	**The Liturgy of the Upper Room**
Collection of alms	Collection of alms	Collection of alms
Intercessions	Intercessions	Thanksgiving and Intercessions
Lord's Prayer in long paraphrase	Lord's Prayer in long paraphrase	Lord's Prayer
Preparation of elements while Apostles' Creed sung	Preparation of elements while Apostles' Creed sung	Apostles' Creed (prose version)
Consecration Prayer	Exhortation	Offertory: preparation or presentation of elements while a
Lord's Prayer	Words of Institution	psalm in metre is sung
Words of Institution		Words of Institution
Exhortation		Exhortation
		Prayer of Consecration:
		Adoration
		Thanksgiving for creation and redemption
		Anamnesis
		Doxology
Fraction	Fraction	Fraction
		Ministers' communion
Delivery	Delivery	Delivery
Communion, while psalm sung	Communion while Psalm or hymn sung	People's communion, while celebrant reads "the whole history of the Passion"
Post-Communion collect	Post-communion collect	Post-communion thanksgiving Psalm ciii in metre
Nunc Dimitis in metre	Aaronic Blessing	Aaronic or Apostolic Blessing
Aaronic Blessing	Dismissal	

These orders reflect the pattern of Justin Martyr's liturgy, they are faithful to Scripture, they are patterned on a covenantal dialogue, and they reflect gospel logic. Moreover, even though they did not observe the Lord's Supper weekly, they were structured with the Lord's Supper in view.

The *Directory for the Publick Worship of God* is an example of the discretionary liturgy. The purpose of the *Directory* was to serve as a discretionary guide for ministers in preparing and leading worship. Nichols writes, "It is not a service book to be placed in the hands of all literate worshipers, but a manual for the discretionary use of ministers. And even for ministers the suggested prayers are supplied as examples only and require some verbal transpositions (readily made, to be sure) if they were to be used as set forms."[36]

The Directory was organized on the pattern of the worship of Strasbourg/Geneva/Scottish orders:[37]

A Directory for the Public Worship of God
London 1644

Call to Worship
Prayer of Approach:
    Adoration
    Supplication
    Illumination
Metrical Psalm
O.T. Lection (one chapter)
(Metrical Psalm)

N.T. Lection (one chapter)
Prayer of Confession and Intercession
SERMON
General Prayer and Lord's Prayer

Liturgy of the Upper Room
Exhortation
Warning and Invitation
Words of Institution
Prayer of Thanksgiving/Blessing
Fraction
Delivery
Exhortation
Prayer of Thanksgiving

---

36. James Hastings Nichols, *Corporate Worship in the Reformed Tradition* (Philadelphia: Westminster Press, 1968), 99.
37. Ibid., 99, 100.

Collection of Alms
(Psalm)
Blessing (Aaronic or Apostolic)

The *Directory* incorporates and combines some of the best elements of the earlier liturgies. Since it is the source of most contemporary, conservative Presbyterian orders and its direction, particularly in prayer, are pastorally rich, I will discuss it in greater detail. The *Directory* suggests that the service begin with a call to worship and a prayer of adoration and invocation: "The congregation being assembled, the minister, after solemn calling on them to the worshiping of the great name of God, is to begin with prayer."[38]

Prayer was to include all the aspects of prayers and subject matter found in Scripture, particularly derived from the Lord's Prayer and in 1 Timothy 2:1ff.: invocation or adoration, confession of sin, supplications, prayers, intercessions, and thanksgiving.

The *Directory* placed the prayer of Adoration and Invocation at the beginning of the service. The prayer of Confession and Remission along with petitions for Sanctification was offered before the sermon. This prayer included as well petitions for the spread of the gospel, the prosperity of the church, and blessing on civil rulers, pastors, and the universities. The minister would pray as well in this prayer that the people would properly sanctify the Sabbath and that God would make them profitable hearers of the Word preached. This prayer concluded with petitions for God's blessing on the preaching of the Word.

The prayer after the sermon included thanksgiving for God's spiritual and temporal blessings: "To give thanks for the great love of God, in sending his Son Jesus Christ unto us; for the communication of his Holy Spirit; for the light and liberty for the glorious gospel, and the rich and heavenly blessings revealed therein; as, namely, election, vocation, adoption, justification, sanctification, and hope of glory; ... for the covenant; and for many temporal blessings."[39] The minister was to pray as well for the advance of the gospel among the people and the

---

38. *The Directory for the Public Worship of God*, 375.
39. Ibid., 381.

fruit of the sermon: "To pray for the continuance of the gospel, and all ordinances thereof, in their purity, power, and liberty: to run the chief and most useful heads of the sermon into some few petitions; and to pray that it may abide in the heart, and bring forth fruit."[40]

The minister was to conclude this prayer with their eye on heaven and the acceptance of their worship for Christ's sake: "To pray for preparation for death and judgment, and a watching for the coming of our Lord Jesus Christ: to entreat of God the forgiveness of the iniquities of our holy things, and the acceptation of our spiritual sacrifice, through the merit and mediation of our great High Priest and Saviour the Lord Jesus Christ."[41]

The Directory also recommended the use of the Lord's Prayer at this point: "And because the prayer which Christ taught his disciples is not only a pattern of prayer, but itself a most comprehensive prayer, we recommend it also to be used in the prayers of the church."[42]

The minister was to use great discretion in the subject matter of his prayer. For example he may move petitions of thanksgiving before the sermon and some of the petitions recommended before the sermon afterwards: "We judge this to be a convenient order, in the ordinary public prayer; yet so, as the minister may defer (as in prudence he shall think meet) some part of these petitions till after his sermon, or offer up to God some of the thanksgivings hereafter appointed, in his prayer before his sermon."[43] He should also include special matters at hand as well as appropriate petitions in connection with the sacraments and thanksgivings or fasts. The great principle is summarized: "every minister is herein to apply himself in his prayer, before or after sermon, to those occasions: but, for the manner, he is left to his liberty, as God shall direct and enable him in piety and wisdom to discharge his duty."[44]

The nature of the *Directory*, as well as this instruction, demonstrates the commitment to free prayer. One of the primary objections of

40. Ibid., 382.
41. Ibid., 382.
42. Ibid., 382.
43. Ibid., 379.
44. Ibid., 382.

the Puritans to the *Book of Common Prayer* was its requirement to read all prayers. The Puritans believed that this requirement was contrary to the gifts and calling of the minister and quenched the Holy Spirit. Horton Davies states the issue thus: "In summing up the opposing views on prayer, it may be said that the Puritans favoured long prayers said by the minister either from a book or extemporarily, to which the people added "amen" whilst the Anglicans preferred many short prayers, some of them being responsive in character, all of them being set forms."[45]

John Owen summarized well the Puritan position:

> It remaineth, then, to consider how the persons appointed by him unto the administration of these holy things in his assemblies, and so to the discharge of the whole public worship of God, should be enabled there unto, so as the end by him aimed at, of the edification of his disciples and the glory of God, might be attained. Two ways there are whereby this may be done: First, By such spiritual abilities for the discharge and performance of this whole work as will answer the mind of Christ therein, and so serve for the end proposed. Secondly, By the prescription of a form of words whose reading and pronunciation in these administrations should outwardly serve as to all the ends of the prayer and thanksgiving required in them, which they do contain. It is evident that our Saviour fixed on the former way; .... [46]

Davies points out many of the Puritans were not opposed to the use of some common (read) prayers (some of the more radical independents were opposed to any use of common prayer). All the Puritans, though, were opposed to the mandatory use of common prayer and the exclusive use of such.

On the other hand the Puritans did not favor careless, extemporary prayer. They taught that the minister should carefully

---

45. Horton Davies, *The Worship of the English Puritans* (1948; reprint, Morgan, PA: Soli Deo Gloria Publications, 1997), 69. See also Nigel Clifford, "The Westminster Directory of Public Worship (1645) in The Reformation of Worship", papers read at the 1989 Westminster Conference (Rowhedge (Colchester, Essex) Christian Design & Print, 1989), 54.

46. Owen, *The Works of John Owen*, XV:10.

prepare his prayers as to order, substance, and even the scriptural nature of the petitions. Perkins wrote,

> There are three elements in praying: (i) Carefully thinking about the appropriate content for prayer, (ii) Setting the themes in an appropriate order; (iii) Expressing the prayer so that it is made in public in a way that is edifying for the congregation.[47]

The great Matthew Henry wrote *A Method of Prayer*[48] to help ministers pray in a scriptural manner.

Next the *Directory* treats the reading and preaching of the Scriptures. The Puritans believed that the minister should read more than just the text on which he was to preach. They advocated reading through the Bible consecutively in corporate worship:

> Reading of the word in the congregation, being part of the publick worship of God, ... and one means sanctified by him for the edifying of his people, is to be performed by the pastors and teachers.
>
> All the canonical books of the Old and New Testament ... shall be publickly read in the vulgar tongue, out of the best allowed translation, distinctly, that all may hear and understand.
>
> How large a portion shall be read at once, is left to the wisdom of the minister; but it is convenient, that ordinarily one chapter of each Testament be read at every meeting; and sometimes more, where the chapters be short, or the coherence of matter requireth it.
>
> It is requisite that all the canonical books be read over in order, that the people may be better acquainted with the whole body of the scriptures; and ordinarily, where the reading in either Testament ended on one Lord's day, it is to begin the next.
>
> When the minister who readeth shall judge it necessary to expound any part of what is read, let it not be done until the whole chapter or psalm be ended; and regard is always to be had unto the time, that neither preaching, nor other ordinances be straitened, or

---

47. William Perkins, *The Art of Prophesying* (1606; reprint, Edinburgh: The Banner of Truth Trust, 1996), 78.
48. Matthew Henry. *A Method of Prayer* (reprint, Greenville, SC: Reformed Academic Press, 1994).

rendered tedious. Which rule is to be observed in all other publick performances.[49]

It is clear that preaching was to be the center piece of corporate worship. The Larger Catechism 155 expounds the importance of preaching:

How is the word made effectual to salvation?

The Spirit of God maketh the reading, but especially the preaching of the word, an effectual means of enlightening, convincing, and humbling sinners; of driving them out of themselves, and drawing them unto Christ; of conforming them to his image, and subduing them to his will; of strengthening them against temptations and corruptions; of building them up in grace, and establishing their hearts in holiness and comfort through faith unto salvation.

The *Directory* states:

Preaching of the word, being the power of God unto salvation, and one of the greatest and most excellent works belonging to the ministry of the gospel, should be so performed, that the workman need not be ashamed, but may save himself, and those that hear him.[50]

The subject matter of the sermon was to be biblical truth and they often preached consecutive, expository sermons through extended portions of Scripture: "Ordinarily, the subject of his sermon is to be some text of scripture, holding forth some principle or head of religion, or suitable to some special occasion emergent; or he may go on in some chapter, psalm, or book of the holy scripture, as he shall see fit."[51]

The singing of God's praise was another important element of Puritan worship. Davies writes,

---

49. *The Directory for the Public Worship of God*, 375, 376.
50. Ibid., 379.
51. Ibid., 379.

The Puritans, under the leadership of Calvin, re-established the importance of the praises of the congregation. As the 'elect' of God, freely chosen by him and through no merit of theirs, they had good reason to praise God. Their warrant in the Word of God came from the Psalms and the New Testament injunctions to praise God with 'psalms and hymns and spiritual songs, singing and making melody in your heart to the Lord' (Eph. v 19). It was also their invariable custom to conclude the ordinance of the Lord's supper with a psalm, on the authority of Matthew xxvi 30.[52]

The *Directory* states,

It is the duty of Christians to praise God publickly, by singing of psalms together in the congregation, and also privately in the family.

In singing of psalms, the voice is to be tunably and gravely ordered; but the chief care must be to sing with understanding, and with grace in the heart, making melody unto the Lord.[53]

Apparently the Puritans sang mostly, if not exclusively the Psalms. There is though some evidence that they did not use the term "psalms" to refer exclusively to the book of Psalms. Commenting on James 5:13, "Is anyone cheerful? Let him sing praises (Psalms), the prominent Puritan Thomas Manton wrote,

Others question whether we may sing scripture psalms, the psalms of David, which to me seemeth to look like the cavil of a profane spirit. But to clear this also. I confess we do not forbid other songs; if grave and pious, after good advice they may be received into the Church. Tertullian, in his *Apology*, showeth that in the primitive times they used this liberty, either to sing scripture psalms or such as were of a private composure.[54]

Manton goes on to recommend that the church ordinarily sings the Psalms:

52. Davies, *The Worship of the English Puritans*, 53.
53. *The Directory for the Public Worship of God*, 393.
54. Thomas Manton. *The Complete Works of Thomas Manton* (Worthington, PA: Maranatha Publications), IV: 442.

Scripture psalms not only may be sung, but are fittest to be used in the church, as being indited by an infallible and unerring Spirit, and are of a more diffusive and unlimited concernment than the private dictates of any particular person or spirit in the church. It is impossible any should be of such a large heart as the penmen of the word, to whom God vouchsafed such a public, high, and infallible conduct; and therefore their excellent composures and addresses to God being recorded and consigned to the use of the church for ever, it seemeth a wonderful arrogance and presumption in any to pretend to make better, or that their private and rash effusions will be more edifying.[55]

The Puritans, following Calvin, believed that choirs were part of the priestly service of the Old Covenant. The Roman Catholic Church had taken away singing from the congregation. The Reformation restored it. The congregation was the choir and they alone were to sing. The modern innovations of choirs, solos, praise groups, and the like, are a product of modern, non reformed evangelical Christianity.

Moreover, the Puritans contended that musical instruments should not be used in the churches. Rather the congregation should sing a capella (without accompaniment). A number of Reformed writers today suggest that musical accompaniment for congregational singing is a circumstance of worship.[56] The Puritans would not have used musical preludes, offertories, or communion music.

The Puritan service concluded with a benediction: "The prayer ended, let a psalm be sung, if with conveniency it may be done. After which (unless some other ordinance of Christ, that concerneth the congregation at that time, be to follow) let the minister dismiss the congregation with a solemn blessing."[57] They used the benedictions found in Numbers 6:24-26 and 2 Corinthians 13:14.

Provision was to be made for the offering and the collection for the poor. The *Directory* states, "The collection for the poor (after the

---

55. Ibid., 443.
56. T. David Gordon, "Presbyterian Worship: Its Distinguishing Principle"; Edmund Clowney, *The Church* (Downers Grove, IL: Intervarsity Press, 1995), 127.
57. *The Directory for the Worship of God*, 382.

observance of the Lord's Supper) is to be ordered, that no part of the publick worship be thereby hindered."[58]

The Puritans observed both sacraments within the worship service. With respect to Baptism the *Directory* states.

> Baptism, as it is not unnecessarily to be delayed, so it is not to be administered in any case by any private person, but by a minister of Christ called to be the steward of the mysteries of God.
>
> Nor is it to be administered in private places, or privately, but in the place of publick worship, and in the face of the congregation, where the people may most conveniently see and hear; and not in the place where fonts, in the time of Popery, were unfitly and superstitiously placed.[59]

The Puritans were committed in principle to the frequent observance of the Lord's Supper, in the morning worship service:

> The communion, or supper of the Lord, is frequently to be celebrated; but how often, may be considered and determined by the ministers, and other church governors of each congregation, as they shall find most convenient for the comfort and edification of the people committed to their charge. And, when it shall be administered, we judge it convenient to be done after the morning sermon.[60]

One other issue to be considered is the use of creeds. The Independent party among the Puritans opposed the use of creeds and for that reason no creeds are mentioned in the *Directory*. Nichols wrote, "But the Independents did make good their opposition to the Creed, which traditionally followed this prayer (the prayer after the sermon). They attacked it 'as an old patchery of evil stuff' and, although it was twice voted in, it was somehow lost and the *Directory* says nothing of it here. Rather, the service concludes with a second psalm and the blessing."[61] The Presbyterian party, however, used The

---

58. Ibid., 386.
59. Ibid., 382.
60. Ibid., 384.
61. James Hastings Nichols, *Corporate Worship in the Reformed Tradition*, 105. In a recent conversation Chad Van Dixhoorn, who is completing a dissertation on the Minutes of the

Apostles Creed, The *Nicene Creed*, and The *Athanasian Creed*.[62] And the
Apostles Creed was annexed to the Shorter Catechism:

> And albeit the substance of the doctrine comprised in that
> abridgment, commonly called The Apostles' Creed be fully set
> forth in each of the Catechisms, so as there is no necessity of
> inserting the Creed itself; yet it is here annexed, not as though it
> were composed by the Apostles, or ought to be esteemed canonical
> scripture, as the Ten Commandments, and the Lord's Prayer,
> (much less a prayer, as ignorant people have been apt to make both
> it and the Decalogue,) but because it is a brief sum of the Christian
> faith, agreeable to the word of God, and anciently received in the
> Churches of Christ.[63]

Having briefly surveyed the *Directory*, we note that not only does
it incorporate the general order and elements of the older forms; it
also improves on them with its clearly defined opening with a call to
worship and a prayer of adoration and invocation. Furthermore, it
makes more use of Scripture than the older forms with its inclusion
of both Old and New Testament readings. It is a great help to the
minister in its directions on prayer and the sacraments.

However, because of the tension between the Independents and
the Presbyterians, the *Directory* omits things that were included
in other Reformed liturgies. The radical independents wanted no
directory while some Anglicans desired a prescribed order. The
Preface of the *Directory* takes a middle position. All would agree
that the *Directory* is biblical in content and order, but we should
recognize that it was a compromise document. Clifford writes, that
problems developed between the English Presbyterian Puritans and
Scottish Commissioners on the one hand and the Independents on
the other: "The English Presbyterians were exAnglican Puritans,
who, in their 'nonconformity' had been used to 'reformed' editions
of the BCP (*Book of Common Prayer*). The Scottish commissioners

---

Westminster Assembly, pointed out that some Presbyterians agreed with the independents
and that he has not found a reference substantiating that the Creed was twice voted in.
62. Davies, *The Worship of the English Puritans*, 273ff.
63. *The Westminster Confession of Faith*, 319.

had used the *Book of Common Order*, the so called 'Knox's Liturgy,' which reflected the forms of Calvin's Genevan liturgy. These two groups accepted the validity of liturgical worship. And then there were the 'protocharismatic' Independents who were opposed to any kind of service book."[64] Hence the *Directory* omits the reading of the Law, the corporate confession of sin as a separate form, and the declaration of assurance. Moreover, as noted above, it omits the use of the Creeds.

Although it lacks some forms found in the older Reformational and Presbyterian orders, the *Directory* is superior to the practice of much of modern Presbyterian worship. As stated above the *Directory* has been neglected and Presbyterian worship is not easily distinguished from general practices of evangelical worship.

> But in most cases the legatees of the Westminster Assembly Puritans did not care to maintain the full prescriptions of the *Directory*. The antiliturgical current moved most of them still farther to the left. Perhaps the most faithful exponents of the *Directory* after the Restoration were the Episcopalian minority in Scotland, who were distinguished, not by the Anglican prayer book, which they did not follow, but by their use of the Lord's Prayer, the Creed, and the "Glory be to the Father" in a service modeled on the Westminster *Directory*. The Church of Scotland itself had by the end of the century come close to the position maintained by the Congregationalists against the Presbyterians at the Westminster Assembly. Presbyterians generally gave up the liturgical use of the Lord's Prayer, despite the recommendations of the *Directory*, and adopted the Congregationalist fear of the uncommented reading of Scripture.[65]

As we think about a modern application, the question remains, did the commitment to the *Directory* preclude a discretionary liturgy? The answer is "no." The Scottish Presbyterians and a good number of the English Puritans were not in principle opposed to

---

64. Clifford, "The Westminster Directory of Public Worship," 54.
65. James Hastings Nichols, *Corporate Worship in the Reformed Tradition*, 107.

a service book. The Scots used Knox's liturgy, *The Book of Common Order*. Many of the Puritans used edited forms of *The Book of Common Prayer, The Book of Common Order*, and the *Middleburgh Liturgy*. Others who criticized the *Book of Common Prayer* simply preferred another liturgy closer to the French or Dutch Reformed type. Debates of this sort had begun among the English refugees at Frankfurt in the 1550s. There the use of spoken responses had been an issue. The repetitions of the litany and the snatches of psalm verses were disliked as artificial by those who preferred what came to be the *Book of Common Order*. Thomas Cartwright, who may have been the author of the 'Waldegrave Liturgy,' urged it in Parliament in 1584 as a replacement for the *Book of Common Prayer*. A later edition was published at Middelburg in the Netherlands in 1586. The Queen disapproved of both versions, and Parliament rejected their use.[66]

When the Presbyterians, including Manton, Calamy, and Reynolds, assisted in the restoration of Charles II, they believed the king would agree to a nonimposed book of liturgy. They petitioned the King: "'We are satisfied in our judgments concerning the lawfulness of a Liturgy, or form of Public Worship, provided that it be for the matter agreeable unto the Word of God, and fitly suited to the nature of the several ordinances and necessities of the Church; neither too tedious in the whole, nor composed of too short prayers, unmeet repetitions or responsals; not to be dissonant from the Liturgies of other reformed Churches; nor too rigorously imposed; nor the minister so confined thereunto, but that he may also make use of those gifts for prayer and exhortation which Christ hath given him for the service and edification of the Church.'"[67]

The King had no intention of dealing with the Puritans and rejected their petition. Richard Baxter, hurriedly working on their behalf, put together *The Reformation Liturgy* to present to the King on their behalf. He based his liturgy on the *Directory*. It is helpful to view them side by side.[68]

---

66. Baird, *The Presbyterian Liturgies*, 92; cf. Francis Procter, *A History of the Book of Common Prayer*, with a Rationale of its Offices (London: Macmillan and Co, 1889), 84, 85.
67. Procter, *A History of the Book of Common Prayer*, with a Rationale of its Offices, 110.
68. Davies, *The Worship of the English Puritans*, 263.

A Directory for the Public Worship of God London 1644	Baxter: *The Reformation of Liturgy*, 1661
Liturgy of the Word	**Liturgy of the Word**
Call to Worship	Prayer of Approach (long or short alternative)
Prayer of Approach:	One of the three Creeds
Adoration	
Supplication	
Illumination	
	Decalogue
	Scripture Sentences (these three parts read by Minister)
	Confession and Lord's Prayer
	Scripture Sentences of Absolution and exhortation
Metrical Psalm	Psalm of Praise
	Psalms in order for the day
O.T. Lection (one chapter)	O.T. lesson (one chapter)
(Metrical Psalm)	Metrical Psalm or Te Deum (said)
N.T. Lection (one chapter)	N.T. Lesson (one chapter)
Prayer of Confession &	Prayer for King and Magistrates
Intercession	Psalm or Benedictus or Magnificat
	Prayer of Intercession
SERMON	SERMON
General Prayer and Lord's Prayer	Prayers of Intercession
Liturgy of the Upper Room	**Liturgy of the Upper Room**
Exhortation	Explication
Warning and Invitation	Exhortation
	Prayer of Confession
Words of Institution	Words of Institution
Prayer of Thanksgiving/Blessing	Prayer of Consecration and Blessing
Fraction	Fraction/Pouring
Delivery	Prayer
	Delivery
Exhortation	Prayer
Prayer of Thanksgiving	Exhortation (if there be time)
Collection of Alms	Hymn or Psalm
(Psalm)	
Blessing (Aaronic or Apostolic)	Blessing

We note that Baxter follows the order of the *Directory*, but incorporates elements from Calvin's and Knox's worship. As seen in the comparison Baxter restored the forms the *Directory* omitted (reading of the Law, Confession, declaration of pardon, and the Creed).

The *Directory* and Baxter, along with these older liturgies, offer us models for a rich, easily adaptable liturgy. In concluding this section, I have put together a liturgy that draws from the *Directory* and some of the older liturgies:

> Call to Worship (a passage that commands us to praise and worship God or is an example of the church doing so; most often from Psalms; may include votum and salutation)
> Psalm or Hymn of Adoration (focuses on the name, attribute, or work of God in praise, expression of love and adoration)
> Prayer of Adoration and Invocation (expresses love, devotion, and adoration and seeks aid of Holy Spirit in worshiping)
> Revelation of God's will (either version of the ten commandments, with Christ' summary, or another passage that reveals some part of God's moral law)
> Confession of Sin and Prayer for Sanctification (can be free or silent prayer, may use common prayer or an appropriate psalm read in unison or sung)
> Assurance of Pardon (a verse or verses read)
> When appropriate Reception of New Members and/or Baptism)
> Offering[69]
> Prayer of Thanksgiving and Supplication.
> Scripture (opposite Testament from one preached)
> Psalm or Hymn of Preparation
> Scripture with text
> Prayer for illumination
> Prayer of Application
> Psalm or Hymn of Response
> Communion service (details in Calvin's orders and the *Directory*)
> Benediction (Num. 6:24-26; 2 Cor. 13:14; 1 Thess. 5:23, 24; 2 Thess. 3:16; Heb. 13:20, 21).
> Doxology / Choral Response or Silent Prayer

Posture

The second area in which our worship is impoverished is in the use of posture. God has created us body and soul in unity, and we are to worship God with the whole person. The body affects the soul and vice versa. This unity is what makes fasting beneficial. There are a

---

69. Those who not desire to include the offering in the service, may include here a prayer of dedication.

number of biblical forms that make use of the body and can greatly enrich our worship.

The Corporate "Amen"

There is a clear biblical warrant for the corporate "Amen" (Neh. 8:6; 1 Cor. 14:16; 1 Chron. 16:36). The Puritans, following the best practices of Church history, taught the people to respond to prayer with the corporate "Amen." Davies summarizes their position: "Further, the Scriptures also taught what part the people had to play in prayer. In criticizing the responsive parts of the services in the *Book of Common Prayer*, they took their stand on Nehemiah 8:6 and 1 Corinthians 14:14-16. These references incontrovertibly declared the necessity for the pastor to pray and the people following him silently and declaring their assent in a vocal Amen."[70]

The purpose of the corporate "Amen" was to encourage the people to make the prayers their own. Perkins wrote,

> The form of prayer should be as follows: One voice, that of the minister alone, should lead in prayer, the congregation joining silently but indicating their agreement at the end by saying, 'Amen' (Neh. 8:6; Acts 4:24; 1 Cor. 14:16). This was the practice in the early church as Justin says: 'When the president has finished his prayers and thanksgivings, all the people present cry out with a favourable approbation, saying, Amen.'[71]

Later Matthew Henry wrote,

> When we join with others in prayer, who are our mouth to God, our minds must attend them, by an intelligent believing concurrence with that which is the sense and scope, and substance of what they say, and affections working in us suitable thereunto: And this the scripture directs us to signify, by saying Amen, mentally if not vocally, at their giving of Thanks, 1 Corinthians 14:16.[72]

---

70. Davies, *The Worship of the English Puritans*, 52.
71. Perkins, *The Art of Prophesying* , 77, 78.
72. Henry, *The Method of Prayer*, xi.

The corporate "Amen" enables the people to give their assent and encourages their careful listening and praying with the minister so that they will be able to give their corporate assent.

The use of a loudly spoken "Amen" at the conclusion of Psalms and Hymns is akin to the Biblical shout and further allows the people to give hearty assent to what they have sung. Revelation 5:14 and 19:4 seem to offer a biblical example of this use of the corporate "Amen."

Bodily Posture

We pay too little attention to bodily posture in prayer. Isaac Watts wrote, "But when we draw near to God in special times of worship, the work of prayer calls for a greater solemnity; and in everything that relates to it we ought to compose ourselves with greater reverence, that we may worship God with our bodies as well as with our spirits, and pay him devotion with our whole natures (1 Cor. 6:20)."[73]

The Puritans and early Reformers believed that standing or kneeling was the most appropriate posture for public prayer. Davies writes,

> If the Puritans sought the types and the matter of true prayer in the Scriptures, they also sought there for the posture for prayer. The typical Puritan posture was to stand for prayer. For this they had the authoritative examples of Abraham (Gen. xviii 22), the Levites, Priests and people (Heb. ix 25), and of our Lord (Luke xviii 10-11 and Mark xi 25). When Isaac Watts wished to persuade the Nonconformists of the eighteenth century to desist from their practice of sitting down at prayer, he assured his readers that there were three permissible attitudes for prayer warranted by the Scriptures: prostration, kneeling and standing; but that there was no divine sanction for sitting.[74]

---

73. Isaac Watts, *A Guide to Prayer* (1715; reprint, Edinburgh. The Banner of Truth Trust, 2001), 93
74. Davies, *The Worship of the English Puritans*, 51, 52.

The three primary postures for prayer in the Bible are prostration, standing, and kneeling. Sitting is not an ideal posture. The one use of the term in 2 Samuel 7:18, "Then David the king went in and sat before the Lord," is probably a reference to sitting back on his haunches in a form of kneeling. Watts wrote, "But I cannot think that sitting, or other postures of rest and laziness, ought to be indulged in solemn times of prayer, unless persons are in some respect infirm or aged, or the work of prayer is so long as to make it troublesome to maintain the one posture."[75]

Prostration, though appropriate in private prayer is not a posture made use of in corporate worship. Standing and kneeling though have been used throughout the centuries.

Standing for prayer is a posture frequently found in Scripture. Our Savior refers to it as a common posture in Mark 11:25, "And whenever you stand praying," and uses it of the posture in prayer of the Pharisee and the publican in Luke 18:13. In 2 Chronincles 20:4-5, 13 we find it used in a large public assembly. Watts wrote, "standing is a posture not unfit for this worship, especially in places where humbler gestures are not convenient. For as standing up before a person whom we respect and reverence is a token of that esteem and honor which we pay him, so standing before God, where we have not conveniences of kneeling, is an agreeable testimony to our high esteem of him whom we then address and worship." [76]

Kneeling is mentioned throughout Scripture as a fit posture in prayer (2 Chron. 6:13; Ezra 9:5; Dan. 6:10; Luke 22:41; Acts 20:36; Eph. 3:14). With respect to kneeling Watts wrote, "Kneeling is the most frequent posture used in this worship, and nature seems to dictate and lead us to it as an expression of humility, of a sense of our needs, of supplication for mercy, and of adoration of, and dependence upon him before whom we kneel. This posture has been practised in all ages and in all nations, even where the light of Scripture has never shined. And if it might be done conveniently, it would certainly be a most agreeable posture for the worship of God

---

75. Watts, *A Guide to Prayer*, 95.
76. Ibid., 94.

in public assemblies, as well as in private families or in our secret chambers."[77]

Calvin also used kneeling as an appropriate posture in corporate prayer. In commenting on the need to introduce the promise of pardon and reconciliation in the liturgy, he wrote, "And I would have introduced this custom from the beginning, but some fearing that the novelty of it would give offence, I was over easy in yielding to them, so the thing was omitted, and now it would not be seasonable to make any change; because the greatest part of our people begin to rise up before we come to the end of the confession."[78] The French churches in 1559 stated the same conviction that the people should kneel to pray:

> That great irreverence which is found in divers person, who at public and private prayers do neither uncover their heads or bow their knees, shall be reformed; which is a mater repugnant unto piety, and giveth suspicion of pride, and scandalizes them that fear God. Wherefore all pastors shall be advised, as also elders and heads of families, carefully to oversee, that in time of prayer all persons, without exception or acceptation, do evidence by these exterior signs the inward humility of their hearts, and homage which they yield to God; unless any one be hindered from so doing by sickness or otherwise.[79]

The practice of looking up in prayer is also Biblical. "To lift up the eyes to heaven," wrote Watts, "is a very natural posture of prayer, and therefore the psalmist so often mentions it (Ps. 121:1; 123:1; 141:8). Though sometimes under great dejection of spirit and concern for it is very decent with the publican to look down as it were upon the ground, as being unworthy to lift up our eyes to heaven where God dwells (Luke 18:13).[80]

Standing is the most appropriate posture for the reading of God's Word. It was the posture used by Ezra in Nehemiah 8:5 and

---

77. Ibid., 94.
78. Quoted in Baird, *The Presbyterian Liturgies*, 22.
79. Ibid., 27
80. Watts, *A Guide to Prayer*, 97. See also John 17:1; Matt. 14:19

seemed to be the universal practice of the synagogue.[81] We stand in reverence for God and His Word.

One other posture to mention is the corporate lifting of hands (Neh. 8:6; 1 Tim. 2:8). Of course when I mention raising hands, one immediately thinks about the current trend of individuals raising hands as they are singing. This is not the practice I am recommending. In the first place, hand-raising is a posture primarily used in prayer, not for singing. Second, all our acts in corporate worship are to be corporate acts and not individual ones. Johnson teaches a proper use of this posture:

> Moses' famous prayer during Israel's battle with Amalek provides a good example, but there are any others as well (Exod. 17:9ff; Pss 28:1,2, 63:4,141:2, 119:47, 134:2, 141:2, 143:6, etc.). So then, if hands are to be raised in worship it should be done either symbolically on behalf of the congregation by the minister, or by the whole congregation itself throughout the prayer as a posture for intercession.[82]

I think it is also appropriate for prayer of praise and would recommend it for the opening prayer of adoration and invocation and perhaps the sung *Doxology* or *Gloria*.

Needless to say, since these are forms they are not required, but the use of some or all of them will free our worship from abstract intellectualism. One ought to institute them, however, in a way that will not confuse or disrupt the congregation. The introduction of each form of liturgy or posture should be preceded by careful instruction. Remember Bannerman's caution:

> This third mark is necessary, in order that the canon of Church order under consideration may not be interpreted so widely as to

---

81. Some note that in Luke 4:17-20 Christ stood to read and sat to teach. In the synagogue, sitting seemed to be the posture for teaching, but standing is also a posture in the Bible for preaching (Acts 2:14). The posture of standing is more fitting for the proclamatory nature of preaching.

82. Terry Johnson. *Reformed Worship*: Worship That is According to Scripture (Greenville, SC: Reformed Academic Press, 2000), 57.

admit of the indefinite multiplication of rules and rubrics, even in matters that stand the two other tests already mentioned, – that is to say, in matters merely circumstantial, and not determinable from Scripture. Even in the instance of such, there must be a sufficient reason, either in the necessity of the act, or in the manifest Christian expediency of it, to justify the Church in adding to her canons of order, and limiting by these the Christian liberty of her members. There must be sufficient reason, in the way of securing decency or preventing disorder, to warrant the Church in enacting regulations even in the circumstances of worship as contradistinguished from its ceremonies. Without some necessity laid upon it, and a sufficient reason to state for its procedure, the Church has no warrant to encroach upon the liberty of its members.... Even in matters lawful and indifferent, not belonging to Divine worship itself, but to the circumstance of it, the Church is bound to show a necessity or a sufficient reason for its enactments.[83]

I have put forth these suggestions on liturgy and posture to stimulate the Church's thinking about these matters. It is my hope to provoke our Presbyterian congregations at least to move to a thoughtful adaptation of the Westminster *Directory*, if not to an even more biblically warranted, historically rich Reformational liturgy.

With respect to forms of voice and posture I would ask: "Is not the bodiless approach to worship practiced by many Presbyterian and Reformed congregations a species (though not as dangerous) of the soulless worship often attributed to prescribed forms? Does not God intend us to worship Him with body and soul as whole people?" May our worship abound to the Glory of God.

---

83. Bannerman, *Church of Christ*, I:356, 357.

Chapter 7

Worship from the Heart[1]

Terry L. Johnson

Jesus says because "God is spirit," worship must be not only "in truth," but also "in spirit." Remember, He is responding to the question raised by the Samaritan woman. Her question is, where ought man to worship, "in this mountain" or "in Jerusalem" (John 4:20),[2] "in our building or yours," and by extension, "according to this ritual of that?" She is concerned with the externals of worship. Jesus sides with the Jews (and Biblical revelation) regarding the truth content and form of worship. But as for the place, the location, the building, that now is irrelevant. "Neither place," He says (v. 21). The place and other externals of worship are not the issue any longer. If the building and location are insignificant, then what is significant? Internal matters are. In addition to being Biblical in structure and content, worship must also be conducted in the right "spirit." It is offered in the name of Jesus, who is the "truth" (John 14:6) and in the power of the Holy Spirit, apart from whom no one can say Jesus is Lord (1 Cor. 12:3). The internal matters of worship – the intent, the motive, the intensity, the sincerity, the reverence – are critical.

Are we now adding something to the regulative principle? Not

1. This chapter is a companion to chapter [1], "The Regulative Principle" and has been adapted from *Reformed Worship: Worship That is According to Scripture* (Greenville, SC: Reformed Academic Press, 2000) for presentation and publication.
2. Scripture quotations are taken from the New American Standard Version unless noted otherwise.

at all. Rather, the regulative principle is concerned with more than truth. We who care a great deal about formal, objective correctness ought to be careful about this. The very fact that few people today care about form means that those who do – who have zealously reacted to the banalities surrounding them – are vulnerable to the problem of making an idol out of correctness *per sē*. Jesus, citing Isaiah before him, condemned the religious leaders of his day, saying, "this people honors Me with their lips, but their heart is far away from Me," (Matt. 15:8).

What they were saying about the Lord was true; nevertheless, their hearts were "far away," and consequently they worshiped "in vain." Both the form and heart of worship must be correct. New Testament worship, prompted and inspired by the Holy Spirit, will be predominately spiritual and internal in ways that Old Testament worship was not. Here are the differences.

Internal or of the Heart
First, worship that is "in spirit" is from the heart. Because God is spirit, He must be worshiped spiritually, internally, from the heart. When we sing we "make melody with our hearts to the Lord" (Eph. 5:19; see also Col. 3:16). What is true of singing is true of all the elements. True worship is not a matter of sacred places, but the spiritual condition of the heart. God's presence is in heaven. There are no holy buildings, holy places, or holy things through which God's blessing is uniquely mediated. Palestine is not a "Holy Land," where God is more present than in other places. Our place of worship is not "God's house," or a "sanctuary," as though God were more present in it than in other buildings. God has made no promises to convey His blessing in connection with the place or location of worship. At the time of the dedication of Independent Presbyterian Church of Savannah's new church building in 1891, it was never called a "sanctuary." It was called the "church building" or "church house." God dwells in His people. They are the "living stones" which become "a spiritual house" for God (1 Pet. 2:5; see also Eph 2:19-22). The building only becomes a house for God when God's people are present within it. This seemed to be better

understood a hundred years ago than it is today. But the point is that worship can never be merely a matter of getting my body in the right building at the right time for the right ritual.

"What about the Old Testament?" we are repeatedly asked. "Did they not have holy buildings, a holy land, and holy symbols?" Yes, indeed they did, and Jesus is abolishing them. This is why it is crucial that the symbolic, typological, and temporary nature of Old Testament worship be understood. Visual pictures were given to Israel of the spiritual realities that would be fulfilled in Christ. Lambs were sacrificed; incense was burned; blood was sprinkled; priestly garments were worn. Old Testament worship was prominently symbolic because it was pre-incarnational. Jerusalem, the temple, the priests, the altars, the incense, and the sacrifices were necessary then because through them God provided pictures of the Christ who would come. These sense stimulating types, however, were surpassed by the anti-type, Christ. He, having come, is apprehended not by continuing types, but by faith through His portrayal in the gospel. The types, in other words, were by design temporary and of necessity inferior to the revelation of the anti-type in the gospel.

Again, we must be careful not to overstate the case. The difference is one of emphasis. The New Testament sacraments are symbolic presentations of the gospel as well. They are "sensible signs" whereby "Christ and the benefits of the new covenant are represented," (Shorter Catechism 92). There is nothing inherently wrong with symbols. Likewise the Old Testament worship was not devoid of "spirit" and "truth." To maintain otherwise would be absurd. Of course there was great concern for spirit and truth in Old Testament worship; indeed, the symbols of the Old Testament were never ends in themselves, but were always meant to point to the internal and spiritual. The physical temple pointed to Christ's body and to His spiritual temple, the church (John 2:21; 2 Cor. 6:16). The sacrificial lambs pointed to the Lamb of God (John 1:29). The blood of bulls and goats (which could never put away sin) pointed ahead to the "precious blood, as of a lamb unblemished and spotless, the blood of Christ" (Heb. 10:4; 1 Pet. 1:19). The priests and their garments pointed to Christ, our great High Priest

(Heb. 2:17,18). The "sacrifices of God" that worshipers present have always represented a "broken and contrite heart" (Ps. 51:17).[3] The Old Testament worshiper aspires that "all that is within (him)" might "bless His holy name" (Ps. 103:1,2). There was truth and spirit in the Old Testament, but not in the magnitude or with the clarity found in the New.

So what is the difference? It is a difference of emphasis and proportion. The Old Testament was filled with symbols in anticipation of Christ. These symbols are by nature temporary. The New Testament has only two, Baptism and the Lord's Supper. Thus the New Testament worship is "in spirit" in that it does not have the numerous symbols and types that Old Testament worship did. Calvin's comments on John 4 are to the point: "By these words (i.e., "in spirit") he meant not to declare that God was not worshiped by the fathers in this spiritual manner, but only to point out a distinction in the external form, viz., that while they had the Spirit shadowed forth by many figures, we have it in simplicity."[4] Jesus, then, is emphasizing the spirituality of New Testament worship over against the symbolic and typological nature of the Old.

The church has at times succumbed to the temptation to return to typological worship and thought again of its ministers as priests, its buildings as temples, the Lord's Table as an altar, and the Lord's Supper as a sacrifice. It has reverted to incense, processions, and clerical garb. Through ritual, ceremonies, art, pageantry, drama, dance, and sometimes music, it has sought to stimulate and inspire faith. This was exactly the thinking and practice of the Medieval church, for which pictures were "the books of the unlearned." According to Philip Schaff, "sacred drama ... was fostered by the

---

3. Perhaps a parallel example may help. We read in John's gospel that "the law was given through Moses; grace and truth were realized through Jesus Christ," not because the Old Testament was all law and utterly devoid of grace and truth, nor because the New Testament is all grace and utterly devoid of law, but as a matter of emphasis (John 1:17). Again, of course there was grace and truth then. But there was more emphasis on law in the Old Testament and on grace in the New Testament. There is more truth now in the sense that it is fuller and clearer in Christ.
4. John Calvin, "On The Necessity of Reforming the Church" in Selected Works of John Calvin (reprint, Grand Rapids: Baker Book House, 1983), 1:128.

clergy and first performed in churches, or the church precincts" and became "in some measure a medieval substitute for the sermon and the Sunday School."[5] This supplanting of the central role that the sermon played in the early church was a disastrous development in church history, as is every attempt to externalize Christian worship.

Let us summarize our conviction. Why would any movement in the direction of symbol over spirit be seen negatively by the proponents of Biblical or Reformed worship? We so respond for the following reasons:

1. The Old Testament symbols were temporary by nature. The temple and everything in connection with it were only meant to fill a need for a time. They were a dim picture of the Messiah until His glory was "beheld" in Jesus Christ (John 1:14).

2. Symbols by nature are inferior to verbal revelation. This is why the church has no "dumb sacraments," as J. A. Motyer has put it. The sacraments are always accompanied by an explanatory word. They are not self interpreting. They depend on the word in ways that the word does not depend on them. Thus the law, unlike God's revelation in Christ, is only a "shadow" and "not the very form of things" (Heb. 10:1). Christ is the "very form of things." The point of the Book of Hebrews is that the church must not go back to the Aaronic symbols and types (3:12 4:13; 6:18; 7:10, esp. 10:26-31; 11-13). You have the substance; you do not need the shadow. Do not waste time looking at the shadow of your loved One when He Himself is standing there before you.

3. Symbols other than the two instituted by Christ are a distraction from the ordained means of grace. What Hughes Old said of the Reformers' attitude toward Baptism is true of all worship generally: "It was because the Reformers prized so highly the divinely given signs that they had such disdain for those signs of merely human intervention which obscured them."[6]

---

5. Philip Schaff, *History of the Christian Church* (1907; reprint, Grand Rapids: William B. Eerdmans Publishing Co., 1947), 5:869.
6. Hughes O. Old, *The Shaping of the Reformed Baptismal Rite in the Sixteenth Century* (Grand Rapids: William B. Eerdmans Publishing Co., 1992), 286.

4. Services dominated by symbols and accompanying rituals will tend toward formalism. The emphasis on the external in worship draws attention away from, and has more often than not become a substitute for, the internal, the heart and its motives, opening the door to soulless, heartless, rote worship.

Extraneous symbols, rituals and movements, harmless in isolation, perhaps even symbolically significant in the eyes of many, are to be avoided if they are not required by Scripture or immediately germane to the service itself. "A visually elaborate" setting, says Godfrey, "would interfere with our spiritual ascent, binding our minds too much to earth."[7] Paul speaks of Jesus Christ being "publicly portrayed as crucified" before the "eyes" of the Galatians (Gal. 3:1). This can only be a metaphorical reference to preaching. The gospel read and preached is a better portrayal of Christ than any material symbol. Unauthorized symbols divert attention and time away from those means (including the ordained symbols) which God has promised to bless. Remember, faith is the conviction of things not seen (Heb. 12:1)! True faith comes through the word (Rom. 10:17). True worship then must be primarily (though not exclusively) nonmaterial, nonsensual, and nonsymbolic. In true worship we ascend to God in heaven by faith. By faith we apprehend God on His throne of grace and worship Him there. By faith we see Christ in His gospel.

Thus, worship that is "in spirit" is from the heart. As we have noted, those of us who are most concerned about correctness in worship must not ever lose sight of the goal of worship: fellowship with God. What are we doing in worship? We are "drawing near" to God (Heb. 4:15,16; 10:16-22). We are coming into His presence (Jas. 4:8-10). We are seeking and calling upon Him (Isa. 55:6). Our great passion is to meet with our God. Our outlook must be that of the Psalmist: "One thing I have asked from the Lord, that I shall seek: that I may dwell in the house of the Lord all the days of my life, to behold the beauty of the Lord, and to meditate in His temple," (Ps. 27:4). What is the one thing that he seeks above all else? That

---

7. See chapter 2, Robert W. Godfrey, "Calvin and the Worship of God," p. 31..

he may "dwell in the house of the Lord" and "behold the beauty of the Lord." He continues, "When Thou didst say, 'Seek My face,' my heart said to Thee, "Thy face, O Lord, I shall seek,'" (Ps. 27:8).

It is God Himself that the psalmist seeks through the forms of Old Testament worship. The Old Testament saints longed fervently to experience God's personal presence in and through their typological system.

As the deer pants for the water brooks, so my soul pants for Thee, O God. My soul thirsts for God, for the living God (Ps. 42:1, 2).

O God, Thou art my God; I shall seek Thee earnestly; my soul thirsts for Thee, my flesh yearns for Thee, in a dry and weary land where there is no water. Thus I have beheld Thee in the sanctuary, to see Thy power and Thy glory. Because Thy loving kindness is better than life, my lips will praise Thee. So I will bless Thee as long as I live; I will lift up my hands in Thy name. My soul is satisfied as with marrow and fatness, and my mouth offers praises with joyful lips. When I remember Thee on my bed, I meditate on Thee in the night watches, for Thou hast been my help, and in the shadow of Thy wings I sing for joy. My soul clings to Thee; Thy right hand upholds me (Ps. 63:1-8).

Whom have I in heaven but Thee? And besides Thee, I desire nothing on earth. My flesh and my heart may fail, but God is the strength of my heart and my portion forever. For, behold, those who are far from Thee will perish; Thou hast destroyed all those who are unfaithful to Thee. But as for me, the nearness of God is my good; I have made the Lord God my refuge, that I may tell of all Thy works (Ps. 73:25-28).

How lovely are Thy dwelling places, O Lord of hosts! My soul longed and even yearned for the courts of the Lord; My heart and my flesh sing for joy to the living God.... How blessed are those who dwell in Thy house! They are ever praising Thee.... For a day in Thy courts is better than a thousand outside. I would rather stand at the threshold of the house of my God, than dwell in the tents of wickedness. For the Lord God is a sun and shield; the Lord gives grace and glory; no good thing does He withhold from those who walk uprightly. O Lord of hosts, how blessed is the man who trusts in Thee! (Ps. 84:1, 2, 4, 10-12).

Here we see the passion with which the Psalmist seeks for God, particularly in and through public worship. He "thirsts," "seeks earnestly," "yearns," and "clings." God's "loving kindness" for him is "better than life." Besides God he desires "nothing on earth." God's "nearness" is his "good." God's "dwelling places" are "lovely," and he longs and yearns for them. Relish and meditate on this deeply experiential language and do not settle for less. Come to God in Christ and feed upon the Bread of Life, and quench the thirst of your soul with Living Water (John 6:35; 7:37).

This is our aim week by week in our worship services. We are worshiping God in heaven whom we see there in all His glory through the eye of faith. This is why we emphasize preparation for worship. Our hearts must be right. Faith is critically important. Do not come to worship with only one minute to spare. Do not think that all one need do is place one's body in the right building at the right time, where the right ritual is being performed. Arrive early. Pray your heart into a receptive, attentive condition. Ready yourself to see God by faith. God must be worshiped "in spirit," in the right spirit, with the right attitude.

Simple

Second, worship "in spirit" is simple. New Testament worship is devoid of procedural and ceremonial complexity. This follows closely on all that we have seen thus far of Biblical and spiritual worship. It is simple. It has no Jerusalem, no Temple, and no Levitical instructions. Having said this, we wish to clarify what we do not mean. Sometimes it is argued that because there is no Book of Leviticus, that is, no elaborate set of procedural instructions for worship, in the New Testament, it must be that God has granted to the church complete freedom to worship as it sees fit. "Calvin's response," to this argument, says Godfrey, "would be that the absence of a Levitical book in the New Testament reflects more the simplicity of the church's worship in Christ than creative freedom … the New Testament is full and complete as a guide and warrant for the simple worship of the children of God in the Spirit. No more freedom is given in the New Testament to invent forms of worship than was given in the Old."[8]

Detailed instructions in the New Testament would be appropriate if New Testament worship were meant to be elaborate in ritual, rich in symbolism, and complex in procedure. This was true of the Old Testament Levitical instructions which foreshadowed Christ. The Levitical priests were required to carry out their ministrations through detailed ritual, symbolism, and procedure. Let us remind ourselves of what was involved. The Old Testament required precise conformity to extensive and particular details regarding the externals of worship. These included the following:

- the *dimensions* of the tabernacle/temple (Exod. 26-27; 1 Kings 6–7; 2 Chron. 3)

- The *furniture* of the tabernacle/temple, including the curtains (Exod. 26:1-14), boards and sockets (Exod. 26:15-30), the ark of the covenant (Exod. 25:10-22), the table of showbread (Exod. 25:23-30), the golden lampstand (Exod. 25:31-40; Num. 8:1-4), the veil and screen (Exod. 26:31-37), the bronze altar (Exod. 27:1-8; see also 1 Kings 6; 2 Chron. 4).

- *priestly garments* worn, including the breastpiece, ephod, robe, turban, sash and tunic (Exod. 28, 30).

- *ritual details* including the consecration of priests (Exod. 29:1-9, Lev. 8; Num. 8:1-22), the sacrifices (Exod. 29:10-30; Lev. 16:1–17:16; Num. 28, 29), the incense (Exod. 30:1-21, 34-38), the priestly food (Exod. 29:31-37), the anointing oil (Exod. 30:22-23), the sacrificial animals (Lev. 22:17-33), and other priestly regulations (Lev. 21:1–22:16).

---

8. Ibid., 10,11.

- a schedule of regular offerings including daily morning and evening (Exod. 29:38-46; Num. 28:18), weekly Sabbath (Num. 28:9-10), and monthly (Num. 28:11-15).

- calendar of Holy days, including Passover (Lev. 16:29-34, 23:5; Num. 28:16), Unleavened Bread (Lev. 23:6-8; Num. 28:17ff), Pentecost (Lev. 23:9-25; Num. 28:16ff), the Day of Atonement (Lev. 23:26-32; Num. 29), and the Feast of Booths (Lev. 23:38-44).

Nothing anywhere in the New Testament parallels any of this. The closest New Testament ordinances to which we might point would be the sacraments of the Lord's Supper and Baptism. But still we find nothing like the procedural details found in the Old Testament. Consider just a small part of what was required of Aaron and the priests in offering atoning sacrifices.

> Aaron shall enter the holy place with this: with a bull for a sin offering and a ram for a burnt offering. He shall put on the holy linen tunic, and the linen undergarments shall be next to his body, and he shall be girded with the linen sash, and attired with the linen turban (these are holy garments). Then he shall bathe his body in water and put them on. And he shall take from the congregation of the sons of Israel two male goats for a sin offering and one ram for a burnt offering.... And he shall take a firepan full of coals of fire from upon the altar before the Lord, and two handfuls of finely ground sweet incense, and bring it inside the veil. And he shall put the incense on the fire before the Lord, that the cloud of incense may cover the mercy seat that is on the ark of the testimony, lest he die. Moreover, he shall take some of the blood of the bull and sprinkle it with his finger on the mercy seat on the east side; also in front of the mercy seat he shall sprinkle some of the blood with his finger seven times, (Lev. 16:3-5, 12-14, etc.).

"Then he shall ... and he shall ... and he shall ... and he shall," etc. Similarly detailed New Testament instruction would have been given to ministers leading worship if they had been meant to have such. Ministers might have been commanded to begin services by sprinkling holy water, lighting incense, bowing to the east three times while crossing themselves and saying the "Our Father." A whole calendar of seasons and Holy days paralleling those of the Old Testament might have been given. In other words, a ritual of approach to God, with defined procedure, rich in symbolism, anchored to the calendar, might have been given. But there is none of this. This does not mean that the church is free to make of worship what it wishes. It does mean that our worship is to be simple, straightforward, without elaborate ritual, devoid of complex procedure, liberated from the calendar and nature's cycles, and limited in its use of symbols to those instituted by Christ – the Lord's Supper and Baptism. For the church to devise worship that is encumbered by ritual, symbolism, and procedure is to undermine the intent of God that our worship be simple and is to return to the shadows of the Old Testament. Do not go there. Do not revive the pomp and circumstance of medieval liturgies.

Neither should we embrace the high-voltage extravaganzas of contemporary worship. Do not create a new priesthood of technicians, artists, and actors. Because our worship is simple, it is also catholic: it can be conducted and enjoyed at any place, at any time, whatever the income, education, or technological prowess of those involved. It can be conducted in an igloo in Alaska, a grass hut in the Congo, or in a grand cathedral in Paris. God may now be worshiped in Samaria or Jerusalem. This is to say that simplicity serves the goal of catholicity. We repeat the implication of Hebrews 8–10: the Levitical ordinances were "a copy and shadow of the heavenly things," but Christ "has obtained a more excellent ministry," (8:5, 6). The entrance of Christ into heaven itself, and not the earthly temple, "a mere copy of the true one," of necessity means the abolition of the old "copy" (9:23ff). The Law, he says, was "only a shadow of the good things to come," which have come in Christ (10:1). He writes,

> Since therefore, brethren, we have confidence to enter the holy place by the blood of Jesus, by a new and living way which He inaugurated for us through the veil, that is, His flesh, and since we

have a great priest over the house of God, let us draw near with a sincere heart in full assurance of faith, having our hearts sprinkled clean from an evil conscience and our bodies washed with pure water, (Heb. 10:19-22).

His point is that we should not return to the complex symbols, rituals, and procedures by which the people of God approached God in the Old Testament. This way of worship has been abolished in Christ, who performed all the priestly and sacrificial tasks on our behalf, once for all. Our way is a "new and living way" of approach. Our sacrifice is "a sacrifice of praise to God, that is, the fruit of lips that give thanks to His name," not a material sacrifice upon an altar following a prescribed procedure (Heb. 13:15). The glimpses of the Church's worship provided in the New Testament bear out this point. The early Christians devoted themselves to "the apostle's teaching, and to fellowship, and to the breaking of bread, and to prayer," (Acts 2:42). They followed not the richly elaborate services of the temple, but the simple and unadorned worship of the synagogue. "They did not take over the rich and sumptuous ceremonial of the Temple," notes Hughes Old, "but rather the simpler synagogue service with its Scripture reading, its sermon, its prayers, and its psalmody."[9] Their services were simple services of the word, sacraments, and prayer. Ours should be as well.

The "style" of New Testament preaching provides a case study of how the early church understood the principle of simplicity. Addressing first century Greeks given to excessive and manipulative rhetorical flourishes, the Apostle Paul argues that the simplicity of the gospel requires simple packaging, lest the means of presentation obviate the message: "For Christ did not send me to baptize, but to preach the gospel, not in cleverness of speech, that the cross of Christ should not be made void," (1 Cor. 1:17).

"Cleverness" in speech, that is, a message dressed up in the sophisticated techniques of the Greek orators, would "void" the cross. Think of Bible verses pasted to the midsections of belly-dancers (not too far fetched; remember Larry Flint's experiment

---

9. Old, *Worship*, 43

combining centerfolds with Bible verses). Marshall McLuhan was right: the medium is the message. The medium can shout so loudly that the message is buried. The Apostle Paul employed a simple style appropriate to a simple message: "And when I came to you, brethren, I did not come with superiority of speech or of wisdom, proclaiming to you the testimony of God … and I was with you in weakness and in fear and in much trembling," (1 Cor. 2:1, 3).

His simple style of proclamation was suited to the simple message of "Christ crucified": "For I determined to know nothing among you except Jesus Christ, and Him crucified, (1 Cor. 2:2). He was careful to preach simply because only a simple style of speech would highlight the simplicity of the message, whereas a sophisticated style would undermine it: "And my message and my preaching were not in persuasive words of wisdom, but in demonstration of the Spirit and of power," (1 Cor. 2:4).

When unbelievers came to repent and believe, it would be not because the preacher was clever, not because He preached with "superiority of speech or of wisdom," or "in persuasive words of wisdom." Rather, his simple style left the "demonstration of the Spirit and of power" in plain view, "that your faith should not rest on the wisdom of men, but on the power of God," (1 Cor. 2:5). The positive response of faith to a gospel message would not be response to a man and his gifts, his charm, his worldly persuasiveness, but to the Spirit.

Give heed as the Apostle Paul once again contrasts "craftiness" and the clear "manifestation of the truth into every man's conscience."

> Therefore, since we have this ministry, as we received mercy, we do not lose heart, but we have renounced the things hidden because of shame, not walking in craftiness or adulterating the word of God, but by the manifestation of truth commending ourselves to every man's conscience in the sight of God, (2 Cor. 4:1, 2).

Gospel preaching does not require tricks or contrived manipulation of hearers' emotions. It is simply the "manifestation of the truth" to the "conscience" of the listeners. If we are right in citing Paul's preaching as a case study in simplicity, then the implications for each element of worship and for the whole service are clear: everything about our worship is to be simple. Nothing is to be clever. Nothing is to draw attention to the learning, the wisdom, the sophistication, the beauty, the complexity of the medium. Simple readings (as in the Bible, not the philosophers), plain style preaching, unadorned praying, and hearty singing ought to characterize our worship. Frankly, this makes everything about leading worship and participation more difficult. The leaders cannot fall back on processionals, incense, liturgy, ceremony, and ritual; nor may they rely on lightshow, drama, dance, band, and multimedia presentations. The participants cannot sit back and enjoy the "show" as an audience for whom these liturgists or technicians perform. Men with depth of character and godliness are the only vessels through which spiritual and simple worship will flow. Open minds and hearts are the only kind in which it will be received.

Reverent

Third, worship that is "in spirit" is reverent. The spirit or intrinsic attitude of acceptable worship is that of reverence. The saints are to "offer to God an acceptable service with reverence and awe," (Heb. 12:28). Worship is never to be conducted with a light or frivolous touch. When we pray, we pray not merely "Our Father," but "Our Father who art in heaven, hallowed be Thy name." Our concern in prayer and all our worship is that God's name be honored and revered, or hallowed, because He is the Father in heaven. True worship must always be serious, substantial, solid, sober, reverent.

What is reverence? The Bible does not leave us to pour into that word whatever content we wish. Reverence is righteous fear. Missing from the whole discussion of worship today is an appreciation of the Biblical concept of the "fear of God," which was unmistakably central to Old Testament spirituality. "It is the decisive religious factor in Old Testament piety," says one theological dictionary.[10] In the Old Testament "true religion is often regarded as synonymous

---

10. Colin Brown (ed.), *The New International Dictionary of New Testament Theology* (Grand Rapids: Zondervan Publishing House, 1975), 1:622.

with the fear of God," says another.[11] The fear of the Lord is the first sign of true belief (Exod. 14:31), and it is the beginning of wisdom (Heb. *yirah*; Prov. 1:7; Ps 111:10). The Lord's eye is upon those that fear Him (Ps. 33:18); He encamps about them and they suffer no want (Ps. 34:7, 9); His mercy is great toward them (Ps. 103:11); He pities them (Ps. 103:13); He blesses them (Ps. 128:1); He fulfills their desire (Ps. 145:19); and He takes pleasure in them (Ps. 147:11). While this fear is not terror, neither is it bland appreciation, nor simple disquiet nor diffidence. There is a fear that is "due" or owed to God (Ps. 90:11). Consequently, those who fear God with righteous fear also are said to "tremble." Those who are approved of God are those who are "humble and contrite of spirit, and who tremble at (His) word," (Isa. 66:2). "Hear the word of the Lord, you who tremble at His word," (Isa. 66:5). In Psalm 96:9, "Worship the Lord in holy attire" parallels "Tremble before Him, all the earth." Worshiping and trembling go hand-in-hand. All the earth is called to tremble before our God (Ps. 77:18; 99:1; 104:32; Isa. 64:2; Jer. 33:9). Even our rejoicing is with trembling: "Worship the Lord with reverence, and rejoice with trembling," (Ps. 2:11).

Other physical expressions of reverence are described as well. These manifestations also help us to understand its meaning. The Psalmist says, "At Thy holy temple I will bow in reverence for Thee," (Ps. 5:7b). Because the Psalmist reverences God, he bows. Again, the Psalmist says, "Come, let us worship and bow down; let us kneel before the Lord our Maker," (Ps. 95:6).

Bowing and kneeling are appropriate responses for one who is in the presence of God (Ps. 138:2). Moses "made haste to bow low to the earth and worship," when God passed before him (Exod. 34:8). Solomon knelt as he prayed (2 Chron. 6:3), and the whole people "bowed down" as they "worshiped and gave praise to the Lord," (2 Chron. 7:3). Similarly, Ezra fell on his knees in confession, lay prostrate, and later the whole people "bowed low and worshiped the Lord with their faces to the ground," (Ezra 9:5, 6; 10:1; Neh. 8:6).

---

11. J. D. Douglas, ed., *The New Bible Dictionary* (Leicester, England: Inter-Varsity Press, 1962), 365.

When we move into the New Testament is there any significant change? No, the reverent piety of the Old Testament, the piety of the Psalms, of the Prophets, and of Proverbs, is the piety of the New Testament, only more so. Jesus assumed this continuity in saying, "And do not fear those who kill the body, but are unable to kill the soul; but rather fear Him who is able to destroy both soul and body in hell," (Matt. 10:28).

While this is not terror, it is a strong fear (Grk., *phobos*) that Jesus commanded. He assumed this continuity in His parable of the persistent widow, who approached a judge who "did not fear God and did not respect man," (Luke 18:1, 2, 4). The New Testament defines the ungodly as those who do not fear God (Rom. 3:18), whereas Christians are those who are "walking in the fear of the Lord," (Acts 9:31). The fear of God is regularly appealed to as a motivation for Christian living; Christians are "perfecting holiness in the fear of God" (2 Cor. 7:1), "subject to one another in the fear of God" (Eph. 5:21), and they "conduct (them)selves with fear during the time of (their) stay upon earth," (1 Pet. 1:17). This last reference bears examination: "And if you address as Father the One who impartially judges according to each man's work, conduct yourselves in fear during the time of your stay upon earth," (1 Pet. 1:17). Here the themes of sonship and fear are brought together. If the judge is our Father, we are to conduct ourselves with fear. (cf. Rom. 11:20; Col. 3:22; Heb. 4:1; 1 Pet. 2:17). According to the final book of the Bible, heaven is populated by those who fear God (Rev. 11:18). Both the calls of the gospel and the calls to worship found in the Revelation are calls to fear God (Rev. 14:7; 15:4; 19:5).

Neither is fear in the New Testament without trembling, prostration, and bowing. The Apostle Paul says, "So then, my beloved, just as you have always obeyed, not as in my presence only, but now much more in my absence, work out your salvation with fear and trembling," (Phil. 2:12). "Fear and trembling" are joined here and elsewhere in the New Testament as they are in the Old Testament. The Corinthians are commended because their obedience was accompanied by "fear and trembling" (2 Cor. 7:15; see also, 1 Cor. 2:3; Eph. 6:5). Similarly, the Apostle John, when given a vision of

Christ upon His throne, "fell at His feet as a dead man," (Rev. 1:17). Paul concludes the extended prayer that began his epistle to the Ephesians by saying, "For this reason, I bow my knees before the Father," (Eph. 3:14). In Philippians, he promises that one day, "that at the name of Jesus every knee should bow, of those who are in heaven, and on earth, and under the earth, and that every tongue should confess that Jesus Christ is Lord, to the glory of God the Father." (Phil. 2:10,11).

Finally, we read of the twenty-four elders of Revelation that they "fell down before Him who sits on the Throne," that they "fell down and worshipped," (Rev. 4:10; 5:14; see also, 5:8). Old Testament and New Testament reverence is a godly fear that the saints have expressed through trembling, kneeling, bowing, and prostration.

Even if God were not concerned about posture, He certainly is explicit about the deepest attitudes which produce such bodily manifestations. Some authors want to avoid concepts like "serious" and "solemn," and advocate instead a friendly, light, informal atmosphere for worship, but one wonders how such an ambiance could possibly be created while still remaining true to the Biblical concept of reverence.[12] How else does one describe the mood of an assembly where the worshipers may be trembling, kneeling, bowing, or lying prostrate before the Almighty?

What about joy? That depends on what one means by joy. Christian joy is not the joy of the bar room or the ball field, but of those who fear the God whom they love. Again it may be helpful to make some distinctions. Even in the athletic world there is a difference between the joy expressed when the winning touchdown is scored and that expressed at the awards banquet two months later. In both cases the emotion is joy, yet the manner of expressing it differs as one moves from one setting to another. Similarly the joy of worship is not like that of the arena. Such joy is not an emotional

---

12. Frame finds "no scriptural reason" to believe that worship services should be conducted in a "solemn atmosphere." He reduces "dignity" to "a code word for formality," and claims that "the New Testament nowhere commands formality in worship." "All in all" he says, "it seems to me that the relevant considerations favor an informal service with a friendly, welcoming atmosphere and contemporary styles in language and music" (*Worship*, 82, 84).

high expressed by highfives, by jumping up and down, by screams and shouts. I once heard a preacher ask why we do not get as excited in church as we do at the football stadium. The answer is, that kind of excitement is unsuitable for public worship; gospel joy is a different kind of pleasure. "Delight" and "fear" stand side by side in Psalm 112:1. As we have just noted, Christian joy is compatible with "trembling" (Psalm 2:11). Presumably the twenty-four elders were filled with joy even as they fell prostrate before God. Indeed prostration and joy were conjoined in the experience of the wise men, who "rejoiced exceedingly with great joy ... and fell down and worshiped Him," (Matt. 2:10, 11). Our joy is a deep emotion, similar to peace, experienced at a level unrecognized by the world. It is not the noisy exuberance and excitement of the arena, but is "inexpressible and full of glory," (1 Pet. 1:8). John Newton phrased it this way:

> Savior, if of Zion's city
> I, through grace, a member am,
> Let the world deride or pity,
> I will glory in thy name:
> Fading is the worldling's pleasure,
> All his boasted pomp and show;
> Solid joys and lasting treasure
> None but Zion's children know.

"Pomp and show" is the "wordling's pleasure." It fades quickly. The world knows only the fleeting pleasure of temporary excitement. It is experienced in a moment and then vanishes. Our joys are the "solid joys" that only "Zion's children" experience. Bard Thompson, in *Liturgies of the Western Church*, explains that Calvin's liturgy "was directed *Soli Deo Gloria*, though in the same subdued and austere fashion that shaped all of Calvinist piety."[13] Our joy is a reverential joy, in public displayed with restraint. Ostentatious displays of zeal, whether by shouting, by raising hands, by leaping about, or by other

---

13. Brad Thompson, *Liturgies of the Western Church* (Philadelphia: Fortress Press, 1961), 193.

such physical manifestations, have been restrained in Reformed circles by a sense of what is appropriate in public worship service, as well as the desire not to draw attention to oneself or to claim too much for oneself. We do not pray so as to be seen by man, whether on the street corner or in the public assembly. God alone is to be glorified (Matt. 6:1-18).

Wisely Conducted

Fourth, worship that is "in spirit" is wisely conducted. In the Presbyterian Church in America (my denomination), we regrettably are split between pragmatists, who are ready to jettison all the distinctives of Reformed worship for the sake of "success" in ministry, and some purists, who are attempting to lift Reformed worship out of the seventeenth century, undiluted and unaltered, and introduce it into the twenty-first century. What is needed is a new breed of "pragmatic purists," wise and sensible leaders who will champion Reformed worship but who will go about reforming today's worship wisely. We need "wise master builder(s)" who will repudiate the quickbuilding expedients of "wood, hay, stubble," and build only out of the wordrich elements of "gold, silver, precious stones," (1 Cor. 3:10-15). But as "wise masterbuilders" they will proceed with caution, sensitivity, and discernment.

Foolishness is manifest on both sides of the worship issue, both by those who follow the contemporary trends reducing the Biblical content of public services (with less Bible read, preached, sung, and prayed), and by those who in the name of Reformed worship have reinstituted its distinctives too quickly, with insufficient explanation, and in indigestible quantities. The congregations of the former are starving on a milkonly diet while those of the latter are choking on indigestible red meat. Reform your worship. But do so wisely.

When you elders lead worship, you must set the right tone and pace. You must not rush. You must not crawl. You must be reverent, not frivolous; joyous, not woeful.

When you preach, expounding a text, do not just give a lecture – illustrate it, but do not let the whole sermon become storytelling. Aim initially at thirty minutes, not fifteen ("sermonettes breed

Christianettes," says John Stott), rather than fifty to sixty minutes, unless your congregation is already accustomed to longer, substantive expositions. Why not? Because it is unwise to preach sermons that are either too short or too long for the capacity of the congregants.

When you pray (referring here to the traditional pastoral prayer), do not cheapen the value of prayer by reducing it to two minutes, but do not try the patience of your people by praying for 7-10 minutes, either.

When you sing, avoid silly camp-fire or revival-meeting songs, but do not overwhelm your people with weighty psalms and hymns all at once, either. Proceed with discernment and wisdom.

Hopefully, over time, we may be able to reform today's worship. There are indications that give one hope. Many of our young people are looking for something more rooted in history and substantial in content than the worship of the babyboomers. Colleen Carroll's recent book *The New Faithful*, argues this very point. The simple, spiritual, reverent worship of the Reformed church may prove to be just the food upon which the hungry souls of our day are longing to feast.

Chapter 8

The Biblical Case for Exclusive Psalmody[1]

Brian Schwertley

Introduction

In this chapter, we shall argue that the inspired Psalms of Holy Scriptures are the only songs authorized by the Scriptures for use in the religious worship of God. While this is the minority view among Reformed and Presbyterian churches today, from the sixteenth century until the late eighteenth century virtually all Reformed churches held to exclusive psalmody. It most certainly is the position set forth by the Westminster Standards.[2]

---

1. I would like to thank Greenville Presbyterian Theological Seminary for inviting me to present this paper. Discussions such as this are very important because: (1) the topic of worship has generally been neglected during the last century and, (2) in matters of worship, most modern Presbyterian churches have more in common with Wesleyan, Baptist, Lutheran and Charismatic churches than with the Westminster Standards. It is my hope and prayer that conferences such as this will be used of God to reform His Church.

2. That the Westminster Standards endorse exclusive psalmody is proven by the following points: (1) *The Westminster Confession of Faith's* enumeration of the parts of ordinary religious worship lists "the singing of psalms with grace in the heart" (21.5) not the singing of psalms and hymns. (2) *The Directory for the Publick Worship of God* says, "It is the duty of Christians to praise God publickly, by singing psalms together in the congregation, and also privately in the family." In the immediate context the *Directory* mentions the use of "a psalm book" and the lining out of the psalms for those who cannot read. This observation proves that the word "psalms" refers explicitly to the canonical psalms of Scripture. Therefore, "psalms" in the *Directory* is not a general term referring to any sacred song used in religious worship as many uninspired-hymn advocates assert. (3) The minutes of the Westminster Assembly show beyond a shadow of doubt that the assembly of divines only permitted the 150 canonical psalms of the Bible to be used in public worship (see Brian Schwertley, *Exclusive*

The case for exclusive psalmody is very simple. It flows from two basic principles. The first argument is rooted in a strict and consistent application of the regulative principle of worship to the element of singing in public worship.[3] The canonical Psalms are authorized for use in New Covenant public worship while uninspired hymns are not. The second primary argument is based on the sufficiency of the Psalter as a New Covenant manual of praise. The book of Psalms is inspired, organized by God Himself and meets all the needs of believers for the element of singing praise in public worship. Therefore, the idea that God's inspired hymn book is inadequate, defective, and out of date, and therefore ought to be superseded or improved upon by the uninspired compositions of sinful men, must be emphatically rejected. God requires and deserves only the very best when it comes to singing praise – the inspired, infallible, divine songs of Scripture. As for the fallible, uninspired hymns of men, the biblical evidence will show that there is no warrant and no need.

The argument from the regulative principle is both positive and negative. First, it must be demonstrated from Scripture that

---

Psalmody: A Biblical Defense [Covenanted Reformation Press: Haslett, MI, 2002], Appendix. Available free at www.reformedonline.com). (4) Presbyterians did not allow uninspired hymns for about 250 years, until 1788 when the P.C.U.S.A. *Directory* changed the original Westminster *Directory's* "singing of psalms" to "singing Psalms and hymns." The first official Presbyterian hymn book did not come into existence until 1831. For an excellent account of how and why Presbyterians abandoned exclusive psalmody see Michael Bushell, *The Songs of Zion: A Contemporary Case for Exclusive Psalmody* [Pittsburgh: Crown & Covenant, 1993 (1980)], 197-217.) The reason for considering Presbyterian church history is: if the early Presbyterians actually believed that the term "psalms" was general and included uninspired religious songs, then why did they purposely exclude them for centuries? To ignore the Presbyterian practice of exclusive psalmody – both before, during, and after the Westminster Assembly – and then to import a meaning to the word "psalm" that explicitly contradicts the early Presbyterian belief and practice with regard to public worship is exegesis of the worst sort. Furthermore, if the Westminster divines intended the term "psalm" to include uninspired hymns, then they were negligent, hypocritical, and sinful for forbidding what they believed God required.

3. When defining the regulative principle it is important to note that divine warrant can refer to an explicit command of God (e.g., "Do this in remembrance of Me," Luke 22:19), or logical inference from Scripture (i.e., there may not be an explicit command, but when several passages are compared they teach or infer a scriptural practice); or biblical historical example (e.g., the change from the seventh day to the first day of the week for corporate public worship).

Jehovah requires the singing of Psalms when He is worshipped. This point may seem obvious and unnecessary; but, given the fact that one of the central arguments against exclusive psalmody is that God does not command the singing of Psalms, but only the singing of praise (which is taken as a very general term),[4] positive warrant for canonical psalmody must be demonstrated. Second, the absence of positive warrant in the Bible for the use of uninspired hymns in the public worship of God must be demonstrated.

The singing of the Spirit inspired Psalms is supported by approved historical examples, specific commands, and deduction.

The Biblical Case For Exclusive Psalmody

The fact that God has placed within the canon of inspired Scripture a collection of 150 worship songs itself proves that God requires these songs to be used in public worship.[5] The Holy Spirit authored the Psalms, providentially organized them into a book, placed them in the middle of the Bible, and on several occasions commanded God's people to sing them. Unless a professing Christian is a radical dispensationalist, Manichean or modernist, he has absolutely no reason to exclude any of the 150 Psalms from public worship. Even those Reformed churches that believe that uninspired hymns are authorized have a moral obligation to sing or chant all 150 Psalms

---

4. The argument that the singing of Psalms is not commanded is found in R. A. Morey, "Exclusive Psalmody," Baptist Reformation Review 4, no. 4 (Winter 1976): 43 ff. Stephen Pribble, *The Regulative Principle and Singing in Worship* (Greenville Presbyterian Theological Seminary, 1995), originally published in *The Harbinger*, January-February, 1994). Joe Morecraft III, *How God Wants Us to Worship Him*: An Exposition and Defense of the Regulative Principle of Worship (Cumming; Georgia: Triumphant Publications, 2001), 153-154. Pribble's article popularized this argument in theologically conservative Presbyterian circles. For a more extensive refutation of Pribble's article than space allows in this small article, see Brian Schwertley, *Exclusive Psalmody*, 8-32, 51-56. Michael Bushell, *The Songs of Zion* (Pittsburgh: Crown and Covenant Publications, 1977),12-15, 56-106.

5. That the book of Psalms is clearly designed by God to be sung is indicated by the musical terminology found in the Psalm titles and throughout the Psalms themselves. There is the mention of chief musicians and various types of musical instruments as well as the names of melodies by which certain Psalms were to be sung. The Psalms are constantly referred to as songs, psalms (melodious songs), and hymns. While it is true that the Psalms can be read, chanted, prayed, and so on, they were and are clearly intended to be sung by God's people.

from a faithful translation.[6] In order to be faithful to God's holy word, every Reformed and Presbyterian church should have a complete Psalter for singing for every member of the church. The very common practice of using a hymnal that is almost exclusively uninspired materials mixed with some gross paraphrases of some Psalms, a few entire Psalms and some Psalm fragments is a clear violation of Scripture, disrespectful of the Holy Spirit who authored the Psalms, a sign of humanism in the church[7] and is an indication of declension.

Historical Examples from Scripture
Several historical examples are recorded in the Bible of Psalms or their counterparts being used in public worship (see 1 Chron. 6:31-48; 16:7-36; 2 Chron. 29:25-30). Inspired songs of praise were sung not only by the Levitical choirs but also by the whole assembly of the people of God (e.g., Exod. 15:1; 2 Sam. 1:17-18; 1 Chron. 16:36; 2 Chron. 23:13; 29:27-30; Psalm 30:4; 137:1-16). The use of Psalms for singing praise was also the practice of Jesus and the apostles (e.g., Matt. 26:30; Eph. 5:19; Col. 3:16; Jas. 5:13).

Only Inspired Songs Used
A careful examination of the Scripture passages that mention the songs used in worship and how these songs were composed reveals that God alone authorizes and accepts divinely inspired songs for His praise. The clearly discernable pattern throughout God's word regarding the text of worship songs is that only people who had the prophetic gift composed such songs. Therefore, divine inspiration is

---

6. Those who argue that the placing of an inspired hymn book in the middle of the canon is not significant and is not a clear indication of what God intends to be used in the church's worship "might as well argue that the composition of the canon provides no specific indication that the sixty-six books in the canon are those to be used when the word of God is read in the church's worship" (Sherman Isbell, *The Singing of Psalms*, part XII, online at http://members.aol.com/RSISBELL/psalms12.html.).

7. Hymnals in evangelical and Reformed churches contain songs by Unitarians, Socinians, Arminians and feminists. Tragically, once a church becomes used to singing a hymn that contains doctrinal error, it is almost impossible to eliminate such a hymn due to the emotional attachment of people to that hymn. Perhaps that is one reason that God requires only inspired, infallible songs in the worship in the church.

the biblical norm and requirement for the content of praise songs used in public worship. There are so many examples in the Bible that show the connection between writing songs of praise and prophetic inspiration that it is astounding that this fact is largely ignored in Reformed churches today. There are the examples of Miriam (Exod. 15:20-21), Deborah (Judg. 5), Isaiah (e.g., 5:1; 21:1 ff.) and Mary (Luke 1:46 ff.). The Psalms of 1 Corinthians 14:26, whether an Old Testament Psalm or a new Psalm, were written under the inspiration of the Holy Spirit.

Most of the worship songs in the Bible were written by King David (seventy-three bear his name).

David was a prophet (2 Chron. 29:25-30) who wrote his songs by means of a special gift of the Holy Spirit (2 Sam. 23:12; Acts 1:16). The New Testament repeatedly refers to David as a prophet when quoting his songs (cf. Matt. 22:43-44; Mark 12:36; Acts 1:16-17; 2:29-31; 4:24-25). Psalm 90 was written by Moses, a prophet. Two Psalms were written by Solomon (72, 127) who was also a prophet.

What is particularly noteworthy is that God even inspired the Levitical musical guilds to write songs for public worship. In 2 Kings 23:2 and 2 Chronicles 34:30 the term "Levite" and "prophet" are used interchangeably. The worship of the temple musicians and singers is referred to as prophecy in Scripture (1 Chron. 25:1-7). What they wrote and sang was the product of divine inspiration. The Bible refers to the first worship leader appointed by David (Heman) as a "seer" (1 Chron. 25:5), a term synonymous with the word "prophet." Twelve Psalms (50, 73-83) are attributed to Asaph, who was appointed by David as a chief temple musician (1 Chron. 6:39; 15:17; 16:5 ff.; 2 Chron. 5:12). Centuries after the death of David, Scripture declared that the Levites sang praises to the LORD with the words of David and Asaph the seer (2 Chron. 29:30). Jeduthun, a chief temple singer during the reign of Josiah, is called "the king's seer" in 2 Chronicles 35:15. If God's people held to the position of most modern Presbyterians that worship songs may be either inspired or uninspired, then why did the production of new worship songs cease in the Jewish church when the Old Testament canon of Scriptures was closed? Where is the old covenant version of the Trinity Hymnal where a few inspired songs are intermingled with a mass of fallible, uninspired, human compositions?

There have been many attempts by opponents of exclusive psalmody to refute the assertion that divine inspiration was a requirement for the composition of worship songs to be used in the church. One author asserts that exclusive psalmody reverses the order of importance of preaching and singing praise because it teaches that the element of singing praise is more closely regulated than preaching.[8] There are a number of problems with this argument. It assumes that preaching is more important than singing praise. Preaching is more important in the sense that, through applicatory preaching, believers are sanctified and become acquainted with the meaning of worship and the sacraments. However, as both an element of worship and an activity that continues through eternity, praise should not be regarded as less important than preaching. Further, the argument assumes that God is making a statement regarding the relative importance of a particular element of worship by means of the different regulations regarding each part of worship. A more logical explanation is that the different purposes of each element of worship required different regulations. Believers are not to question God as to why He sets the rules the way He has. They are simply to trust and obey. The Bible does not specify why Jehovah has so strictly regulated the singing of praise. The simple answer is that God's nature and character demanded it. James A. Kennedy writes:

What is praise? The word is derived from the word 'price.' But who knows God's price or value? To prepare a complete and sufficient manual of praise one must know, on the one hand, all the divine excellences, for they are to be set forth in sufficient measure and due proportion; and, on the other hand, the whole range of human devotional feeling called forth by contemplating the divine perfections. But such vast knowledge is only possible to one to whom a divine revelation has been made. And to give

---

8. Leonard Coppes, "Exclusive Psalmody and Doing God's Will as it is Fulfilled in Christ," *The Harbinger* (Nov.-Dec. 1993).

adequate expression to this knowledge, divine inspiration is an absolute prerequisite....God evidently deemed it necessary to have His praises prepared thus, for as a matter of fact He inspired David, Asaph, and others to compose them. And He never puts forth divine power unless it is necessary. God kept the manual of praise strictly under His control. Why should He be indifferent to this matter now? And why should we be put off without a divine book for this dispensation? Are we not as worthy of such a perfect book as the Old Testament Church?[9]

Another author argues that the Bible requires only theological accuracy in the composition of worship songs. The problem with his argument is that he does not offer any scriptural texts or examples to back up his claims – not one. Further, the hymn book used by the denomination in which this person serves as a pastor not only has errors in it, but has hymns written by Unitarians and Arminians.[10] Even the small, theologically conservative Presbyterian denominations that permit uninspired, manmade hymnals have not been able to produce a totally theologically accurate hymnal.

A Reformed Baptist writer quotes several examples of worship songs that are not found in the book of Psalms as proof that divine inspiration was not necessary. The problem with this argument is that every song he refers to was given by divine inspiration (e.g., Exod. 15:20-21; Judg. 5; Isa. 5:1; 26:1 ff.; Luke 1:46 ff. 1 Cor. 14:26). His argument is self-refuting. Another author quotes from Isaiah

---

9. "The Psalms: The Divinely Authorized and Exclusive Manual of Praise" in *The Psalms in Worship*, ed. John McNaugher (1907; reprint, Edmonton: Still Water Revival Books, 1992), 60-61.

10. Many popular hymns now sung by Presbyterians were written by men and women who espoused various heretical views. "Nearer My God to Thee," by Sarah Flower Adams (1805–1848); "In the Cross of Christ I Glory," by Sir John Bowring (1792–1872); and "It Came upon the Midnight Clear," by Edmund Sears (1810–1910), were all written by Unitarians. Several popular hymn writers, such as Frances Havergal, Fanny Crosby, and Harriet Beecher Stowe, were advocates of, or quite sympathetic to, the rising tide of feminism and it could be argued with some force that the feminization of the church's worship in the nineteenth century greatly contributed to the acceptance of Arminianism and modernism in the P.C.U.S.A. For a discussion of the heretical views of various hymn writers and theologically inaccurate and heretical popular hymns, see: Louise F. DeBoer, *Hymns, Heretics, and History: A Study in Hymnody*, forthcoming by the American Presbyterian Press.

38:20 – "The Lord was ready to save me; therefore we will sing my songs with stringed instruments all the days of our life, in the house of the Lord" – as proof that uninspired songs were used in public worship in the Old Testament era.[11] This author assumes that since these songs, written by King Hezekiah, were never inscripturated, therefore they must be uninspired. This argument fails when we consider that many prophecies and inspired writings did not make it into our Bibles. (There are Old Testament prophets named of whom we have no surviving oracles. There is the missing letter of Paul to the Corinthians, as well as the volumes of sayings, proverbs, and teachings that Christ spoke to His disciples). The fact that Hezekiah's songs (except the one recorded in Isa. 38) did not make it into our Bible does not tell us at all whether or not they were inspired. In fact, the passage under discussion, if anything, indicates that his songs were inspired. Note the transition from the singular ("me") to the plural ("we"). The king identifies himself with the Levitical choir of the Temple, which functioned as a musical prophetic guild. In any case, there certainly is not a shred of evidence that Hezekiah composed uninspired songs. That assertion is assumed, not proven.

There are "Reformed" pastors who argue that the fact that every instance of worship song in the Bible is divinely inspired has no significance for today's church. They reason that since worship songs are in the Bible, which in itself is divinely inspired, they of necessity must also be inspired. This reasoning is fallacious for two reasons. First, the Bible contains many infallibly recorded statements of uninspired words. The Bible records individuals' lying, examples of bad theology, and even Satan's lying to Jesus. No one would argue that Satan's lies were divinely inspired. Second, and even more significant, is that the Holy Spirit emphasizes that songs of worship came not simply from anyone who decided to write a song, but only from seers and prophets. Further, if the old covenant people of God held to the same position as modern advocates of uninspired hymns, then why is there absolutely no archeological evidence for the use of uninspired hymnals in the Old Covenant church?

---

11. Stephen Pribble, *The Regulative Principle and Singing in Worship*, 11-12.

Commanded by God

The book of Psalms contains several commands to praise Jehovah: "Oh come, let us sing to the Lord! Let us shout joyfully to the Rock of our salvation. Let us come before His presence with thanksgiving; let us shout joyfully to Him with psalms" (Ps. 95:1-2; see also 81:2; 98:4-6; 100:2). This point gives us the opportunity to consider two objections commonly raised by opponents of exclusive psalmody regarding the claim that believers are commanded to sing Psalms. First, they point out that not one divine imperative is connected to the singing of *mizmor*, which is the specific Hebrew word meaning Psalm. Believers are only commanded to "sing praise" (*zammero*), or "sing songs" (*zemirot, zimrah*). In other words, the Bible does not command the singing of Psalms, but merely the singing of praise. The singing of praise, we are told by some, is a general term that is inclusive of the uninspired hymns so common today. Second, they point out that there are historical examples in Scripture of God's people singing worship songs that are not included in the book of Psalms.

These objections raise three questions: (1) Does one need to find a divine imperative connected to the word *mizmor* to conclude that the singing of Psalms is commanded by God? (2) Does the command to "sing praises" authorize the use of uninspired hymns in public worship? (3) Does the fact that there are examples in the Bible of people singing worship songs not included in the canonical Psalter disprove exclusive psalmody?

The first two of these questions will be answered by considering the biblical meaning of "sing praise." The meaning of "sing praise" is a matter of biblical interpretation (or hermeneutics). What is the proper method for determining the meaning of this expression? Should one take the meaning of "sing praise" from ancient Greek paganism, from modern American evangelical church practice, or from the Bible? The answer to this question is obvious. Only the sacred Scriptures can legitimately tell us what God had in mind when He commanded the covenant people to "sing praise." The essential question is, What does God's word teach regarding this subject? The following points demonstrate that the command to "sing praise" refers solely to inspired worship songs and definitely includes the canonical Psalter. First, it has already been demonstrated that the prophetic gift of divine inspiration was a prerequisite for writing worship songs to be used by the church (e.g., 2 Sam. 23:1, 2; Acts 1:16, 17; 1 Chron. 25:17; 2 Chron. 29:30; 34:30). Second, every example of worship songs in the Bible is divinely inspired (e.g., Exod. 15:20-21; Judg. 5; Isa. 5:1; 26:1 ff.; Luke 1:46 ff; 1 Cor. 14:26). There are no examples of uninspired worship songs in the sacred Scriptures. Not one. Third, God has placed a psalm book right in the middle of our Bibles, which in Hebrew Scriptures is called Book of Praises (*Sepher Tehillim*).[12] If a Jew heard the phrase "sing praise" he would immediately think of the collection of inspired praise songs currently in liturgical use. He would never have applied the expression "sing praise" to *uninspired* human poetry, for such songs were not introduced into public worship until the fourth century after Christ.[13] Fourth, the praise of Jehovah is the main characteristic of the book of Psalms. Indeed, the term "hallelujah" which means "praise Yahweh" *only* occurs in the Psalter. "Of the 206 occurrences

12. A. F. Kirkpatrick writes: "In the Hebrew Bible the title of the collection is "Book of Praise," or simply, "Praises": *Sepher Tehillim* abbreviated into *Tillim* or *Tillin*. This title was known to Hippolytus and Origen in the first half of the third century AD, and to Jerome. Though the word praise occurs frequently in the Psalter, only one Psalm (cxlv) bears the title A Praise, and the name "Book of Praises" probably originated in the use of the collection as the hymn-book of the Second Temple" (*The Book of Psalms*, [Grand Rapids, MI: Baker Book House, 1982], xiv-xv). W. S. Plumer writes: "The name of this collection of songs in the Hebrew is Book of Praises, or Praise-Songs.... From the Greek Testament we get the titles, PSALMS, and BOOK OF PSALMS. These names are chosen by inspiration." (*Psalms: A Critical and Expository Commentary with Doctrinal and Practical Remarks*, [1867; reprint, Carlisle, PA: The Banner of Truth Trust, 1975)], 18). When one considers that the titles Book of Praises (Hebrew) and Book of Psalms (Greek) are used as synonyms in Scripture, one can see the absurdity of advocating uninspired hymns with the mizmor argument.
13. After a careful study of the worship of the early church, Philip Schaff, ed., "Nicene and Post-Nicene Fathers: Eusebius" Church History, Life of Constantine the Great, and Oration in the Praise of Constantine (reprint, Peabody, MA: Hendrickson Publishers, 1994), 1:247, footnote 14: "So far as we are able to gather from our sources, nothing, except the Psalms and New Testament hymns (such as the "Gloria in Excelsis," the "Magnificat," the "Nunc Dimittis," etc.), was as a rule sung in public worship before the fourth century (the practice which had sprung up in the church of Antioch seems to have been exceptional; see Kraus, p. 673). Before the end of that century, however, the practice of singing other hymns in the service of the church had become common, both in the East and West."

of *hll*, "praise" in the Old Testament (146 verbal, 60 nominal), about two-thirds are in the Psalms or in phrases taken from the Psalms."[14] When a divinely inspired prophet writes a worship song and the worship song contains the command "sing praise," simple logic dictates that the command applies directly to the inspired song or songs – not to a composition by an uninspired writer. Fifth, if the expression "sing praise" is a general term that included uninspired hymns, then why is a collection of uninspired hymns completely absent from the post-exilic Jewish church, the apostolic church, and the post-apostolic church? If uninspired hymnody existed, it is truly remarkable that not one collection of uninspired worship songs survived. It is even more amazing considering how easily copies of such materials would have been spread throughout the Roman Empire. "The paucity of extant hymns from the early centuries of the church," writes Bushell, "is rather striking and can only be explained as a result of the firm adherence of the church as a whole to the inspired Psalms."[15]

The attempt to interpret the expression "sing praise" as inclusive of uninspired hymns must be rejected. It is exegetical malpractice to impose modern meanings upon biblical concepts. In the opinion

14. James Linburg, editor-in-chief, David N. Freedman, "Book of Psalms" in The Anchor Bible Dictionary (New York: Doubleday, 1992), 5:523. See Michael Bushell, The Songs of Zion, 154-167. While one can find uninspired Christian songs written for private use quite early, the use of uninspired songs in public worship became widespread in the fourth century as a response to the first hymn writers: the Gnostics.

15. Michael Bushell, *The Songs of Zion*, 156. After this comment Bushell (pp. 146-147) quotes Phillip Schaff: "We have no complete religious song remaining from the period of persecution (i.e., from the first three centuries) except the song of Clement of Alexandria to the divine Logos – which, however, cannot be called a hymn and was probably never intended for public use; the Morning Song and the Evening Song in the Apostolic Constitutions, especially the former; and the so-called Gloria in Excelsis, which, as an expansion of the hymn of the heavenly hosts, still rings in all parts of the Christian world. Next in order comes Te Deum, in its original eastern form. The "Ter Sanctus" and several ancient liturgical prayers may also be regarded as poems. Excepting these hymns in rhythmic prose, the Greek church of the first six centuries produced nothing in this field which has had permanent value or general use. It long adhered almost exclusively to the Psalms of David, who, as Chrysostom, says, was first, middle and last in the assemblies of the Christians, and it had, in opposition to heretical predilections, even a decided aversion to the public use of uninspired songs. "The Greek and Latin Hymnology," British and Foreign Evangelical Review (1866), 680.

of this author it is a vain attempt to justify current practice instead of deriving our practice from Scripture alone.

But what about the fact that there are examples of God's people corporately singing inspired songs outside the Psalter? Does not this alone disprove the doctrine of exclusive psalmody? This point is the best objection to exclusive psalmody, for it is based upon very clear historical examples instead of speculation and exegesis. The following observations apply to this objection: (1) It cannot be used as warrant for the use of uninspired hymns in public worship. At the very most it would authorize use of the handful of inspired worship songs that were not included in the Psalter (e.g., Exod. 15:119; Deut. 32:1-43; Judg. 5; Isa. 5:1-30; 26:1-21; Luke 1:46 ff.). Reformed churches today that use uninspired hymn books with some Psalms and Psalm fragments thrown in would be vastly better off if they used only inspired songs in public worship. Such a revival of Reformed worship would stop the rapid spread of so-called "celebrative worship" (i.e., Arminian, Charismatic, man-centered, hedonistic worship) among the conservative Presbyterian denominations; (2) God Himself organized the final, inscripturated hymn book for the church – the 150 Psalms. The fact that Jehovah did not include every inspired song in the Psalter indicates that not all inspired songs were intended by God for perpetual use in the church. Some inspired songs were given by God for specific, unique occasions. A number of these "songs" or poetic prophecies were spoken on only one occasion by one person.[16] Without any indication that God intended the few inspired songs outside the divine hymn book for perpetual use, the early Presbyterians decided to exercise caution. These songs outside the book of Psalms were not approved for public worship. One may disagree with this argument or consider it a weak deduction. But since there is not one shred of biblical evidence that uninspired songs were ever used for the praise of Jehovah, if there is going to be a debate among Reformed believers

---

16. For example, Luke 1:46-55 was spoken by Mary; Luke 1:68-79 was spoken by Zechariah. There is no indication in the immediate context that either prophecy was even sung (e.g., vs. 46, "And Mary said;" vs. 67, "Zechariah prophesied … saying"); Isaiah 5 was sung by Isaiah the Prophet (v. 1, "I will sing indeed") to the rebellious people of Judah.

it ought to be between exclusive Psalm singers and those Christians who want to include the handful of other inspired worship songs which are found outside of the Psalter.

The Psalms and Apostolic Worship

The singing of divinely inspired songs in worship is not only an Old Testament worship ordinance, but it is also a new covenant era ordinance. Further, like the Old Testament, the New Testament does not authorize the use of uninspired compositions for public worship.[17]

In the Gospel accounts of the Lord's Supper, the Holy Spirit gives information that indicates that Christ and the apostles sang Psalms at the institution of the Lord's supper. Both Matthew and Mark say that immediately after the institution of the holy supper Jesus and the apostles sang a hymn. "And when they sang a hymn [lit., "when they had hymned"], they went out to the Mount of Olives" (Matt. 26:30; cf. Mark 14:26). Virtually all commentators believe that the word "hymn" in these passages refers to a Psalm or Psalms from the Hallel (i.e., Ps. 113–118). James Morison writes: "Or Psalm, as it is in the margin and the Geneva: or very literally, And when they had hymned (*humnesantes*). The word does not imply that it was but one hymn or Psalm that was sung or chanted. And if the tradition, preserved among the Jews, is of any weight in such a matter, the hymning at the conclusion of the supper would embrace Ps. cxv., cxvi., cxviii., which constitute the second part of the Jewish Hallelujah, or Hallel, as they call it. The other part of the Hallel

---

17. Because this study must be kept reasonably short we will not discuss Acts 16:25 and James 5:13. Regarding these verses, only the broad context of Scripture can define "sing praise" (Jas. 5:13) or "singing hymns" (Acts 16:25). The broad context of Scripture always applies the phrase "sing praise" to inspired worship songs (see the discussion above). Note also, that humneo (Acts 16:25) is the same word used to describe the psalm-singing at the last supper (Matt. 26:30; Mark 14:26). Given the fact that: a) Pious Jews and Jewish proselytes often committed many of the psalms to memory for devotional use; and, b) uninspired hymns would not become normative in the church for another three centuries, it is extremely unlikely that these terms refer to uninspired worship songs. If in the new covenant church there were a change from the Old Testament practice of the exclusive use of inspired materials in praise to the use of uninspired materials, there would be some solid evidence for so radical a change. Such evidence is lacking.

consisted of Ps. cxiii., cxiv., which was customarily chanted at the commencement of the feast."[18]

Matthew Henry points out that if Jesus and the disciples had departed from the normal Jewish practice of singing the Psalms after the Paschal meal, it probably would have been recorded in the Gospel accounts, for it would have been a new practice. He notes, "Singing of Psalms is a gospel ordinance. Christ's removing the hymn from the close of the Passover to the close of the Lord's Supper, plainly intimates that he intended that ordinance should continue in his church, that, as it had not its birth with the ceremonial law, so it should not die with it."[19] If the head of the church directly connected the singing of Psalms to the new covenant ordinance of the Lord's Supper and used inspired songs for praise, comfort and edification, should not His bride do likewise?

Two passages which are crucial to the exclusive psalmody debate are Ephesians 5:19 and Colossians 3:16. These passages are important because they are used as proof texts by both exclusive psalm singers and those who use uninspired hymns in worship. Paul writes, "And do not be drunk with wine, in which is dissipation; but be filled with the Spirit, speaking to one another in Psalms and hymns and spiritual songs, singing and making melody in your heart to the Lord" (Eph. 5:18-19). Again, the Apostle writes, "Let the word of Christ dwell in you richly in all wisdom, teaching and admonishing one another in psalms and hymns and spiritual songs, singing with grace in your hearts to the Lord" (Col. 3:16).

Before we consider the question of how these passages relate to public worship, we first will consider the question "what does Paul

---

18. James Morison, *A Practical Commentary on the Gospel According to St. Matthew* (1884; reprint, Minneapolis: Klock and Klock, 1981), 537. The following commentators and theologians concur with Morison: A. A. Hodge, Alfred Plummer, R. C. H. Lenski, David Hill, Art Gundry, B. Harvie Branscomb, John Peter Lange, William Hendriksen, G. Campbell Morgan, R. V. G. Tasker, C.H. Spurgeon, Matthew Henry, William Lane, David Dickson, Henry Barcley Swete, Alfred Edersheim, John Gill, Ezra P. Gould, and A. T. Robertson. It is providential that when Jesus was about to enter the humiliation, torture, agony, abandonment, and darkness of Golgotha He had the words of victory upon His lips (read Psalm 118:22-29).

19. Matthew Henry, *Commentary on the Whole Bible* (reprint, McLean, VA: MacDonald Pub., n. d.), 5:392.

mean by psalms, hymns, and spiritual songs?" This question is very important, for many advocates of uninspired hymnody point to this passage as proof that uninspired hymns are permitted in public worship by God. When examining passages such as Ephesians 5:19 and Colossians 3:16, one should not make the common mistake of importing our modern meaning or usage of a word, such as hymn, into what Paul wrote over nineteen hundred years ago. When a person hears the word "hymn" today, he immediately thinks of the extra biblical non inspired hymns found in the pews of most churches. The only way to really determine what Paul meant by "psalms, hymns, and spiritual songs" is to determine how these terms were used by Greek speaking Christians in the first century.

When interpreting religious terminology used by Paul in his epistles, there are certain rules of interpretation that should be followed. First, the religious thinking and worldview of the apostles was essentially derived from the Old Testament and Jesus Christ, not Greek heathenism. Therefore, when Paul discusses doctrine or worship, the first place to look for help in understanding religious terms is the Old Testament. We often find Hebrew expressions or terms expressed in *koine* Greek. Second, we must keep in mind that the churches that Paul founded in Asia consisted of converted Jews, Gentile proselytes to Old Testament Judaism (God-fearers), and Gentile pagans. These churches had the Septuagint, a Greek version of the Old Testament. When Paul expressed Old Testament ideas to a Greek-speaking audience, he used the religious terminology of the Septuagint. If the terms hymns (*humnois*) and spiritual songs (*odais pheumatikais*) were defined within the New Testament, then looking to the Septuagint for the meaning of these words would be unnecessary. Given the fact, however, that these terms are rarely used in the New Testament and cannot be defined within their immediate context apart from knowledge of the Old Testament, it would be exegetically irresponsible to ignore how these words are used in the Septuagint.

When we examine the Septuagint, we find that the terms psalm (*psalmos*), hymn (*humnos*), and song (*odee*) used by Paul clearly refers to the Old Testament book of Psalms and not ancient or modern uninspired hymns or songs. Bushell writes:

> *Psalmos* ... occurs some 87 times in the Septuagint, some 78 of which are in the Psalms themselves, and 67 times in the psalm titles. It also forms the title to the Greek version of the psalter....
> *Humnos* ... occurs some 17 times in the Septuagint, 13 of which are in the Psalms, six times in the titles. In 2 Samuel, 1 & 2 Chronicles and Nehemiah there are some 16 examples in which the Psalms are called 'hymns' (*humnoi*) or 'songs' (*odai*) and the singing of them is called 'hymning' (*humneo, humnodeo, humnesis*)....
> *Odee* ... occurs some 80 times in the Septuagint, 45 of which are in the Psalms, 36 in the Psalm titles.[20]

In twelve Psalm titles we find both "psalm" and "song"; and in two others we find "psalm" and "hymn." G. I. Williamson explains, "Psalm seventy-six is designated 'psalm, hymn and song.' And at the end of the first seventy-two Psalms we read 'the hymns of David the son of Jesse are ended' (Ps. 72:20). In other words, there is no more reason to think that the Apostle referred to Psalms when he said 'psalms,' than when he said 'hymns' and 'songs,' for all three were biblical terms for Psalms in the book of Psalms itself."[21] To ignore how Paul's audience would have understood these terms and how these terms are defined by the Bible, and then instead to import non biblical modern meanings into these terms is exegetical malpractice.

One of the most common objections to the idea that in Ephesians 5:19 and Colossians 3:16 Paul is speaking of the book of Psalms is that it would be absurd for the apostle to say, "sing psalms, psalms, and psalms." This objection fails to consider the fact that a common literary method among the ancient Jews was to use a triadic form of expression to express an idea, act, or object. The Bible contains many examples of triadic expression. For example: Exodus 34:7 – "iniquity and transgression and sin"; Deuteronomy 5:31 and 6:1 – "commandments and statutes and judgments"; Matthew 22:37

20. Michael Bushell, *The Songs of Zion*, 85-86.
21. G. I. Williamson, *The Singing of Praise in the Worship of God*, 6.

– "with all your heart, with all your soul, and with all your mind" (cf. Mark 12:30; Luke 10:27); Acts 2:22 – "miracles and wonders and signs"; Ephesians 5:19 and Colossians 3:16 – "psalms and hymns and spiritual songs." "The triadic distinction used by Paul, Kiddie argues, "would be readily understood by those familiar with their Hebrew O.T. Psalter or the Greek Septuagint, where the Psalm titles are designated psalms, hymns, and songs. This interpretation does justice to the *analogy* of Scripture, i.e., Scripture is its own best interpreter."[22]

The interpretation that says that "psalms, hymns, and spiritual songs" refers to the inspired book of Psalms also receives biblical support from the immediate context and grammar of these passages. In Colossians 3:16 we are exhorted: "Let the word of Christ dwell in you richly...." In this passage the word of Christ is very likely synonymous with the word of God.

> In 1 Peter 1:11 it is stated that 'the spirit of Christ' was in the Old Testament prophets and through them testified beforehand the sufferings of Christ and the glory which should follow. If, as is definitely stated, the Spirit of Christ testified these things through the prophets, then Christ was the real Author of those Scriptures. Prominent among those prophecies, which so testified concerning Christ, is the Book of Psalms, and therefore Christ is the Author of the Psalms.[23]

After Paul exhorts the Colossian church to let the word of Christ dwell in them richly, he immediately points them to the book of Psalms, a book which comprehends "most beautifully and briefly everything that is in the entire Bible;"[24] a book far superior to any human devotional book, which Calvin called "an anatomy of all parts of the soul;"[25] a book which is "a compendium of all divinity."[26] Do we let the Scriptures, the word of Christ dwell within us when we

---

22. J. W. Keddie, *Why Psalms Only?*, 7.
23. M.C. Ramsey, *Purity of Worship* (Presbyterian Church of Eastern Australia, 1968), 20.
24. Martin Luther, "Preface to the Psalter, [1528] 1545" Luther's Works, tr. C.M. Jacobs (Philadelphia: Muhlenberg Press, 1960), XXXV:254.
25. John Calvin, *Commentary on the Book of Psalms*, tr. James Anderson (Edinburgh: Calvin Translation Society, 1845), I:xxxvi-xxxix.
26. Basil, quoted in Michael Bushell, *The Songs of Zion*, 18.

sing uninspired human compositions in worship? No, we do not! If we are to sing and meditate upon the word of Christ, we must sing the songs that Christ has written by His Spirit – the book of Psalms.

The grammar also supports the contention that Paul was speaking of the book of Psalms. In our English Bibles the adjective "spiritual" modifies only the word songs ("spiritual songs"). In the Greek language, however, when an adjective immediately follows two or more nouns, it modifies all the preceding nouns. John Murray writes,

> Why does the word *pneumatikos* [spiritual][27] qualify *odais* and not *psalmois* and *hymnois*? A reasonable answer to this question is that pneumatikais qualifies all three datives and that its gender (fem.) is due to attraction to the gender of the noun that is closest to it. Another distinct possibility, made particularly plausible by the omission of the copulative in Colossians 3:16, is that 'Spiritual songs' are the genus of which 'psalms' and 'hymns' are the species. This is the view of Meyer, for example. On either of these assumptions the psalms, hymns, and songs are all 'Spiritual' and therefore all inspired by the Holy Spirit. The bearing of this upon the question at issue is perfectly apparent. Uninspired hymns are immediately excluded.[28]

If one wants to argue that "spiritual" does not apply to psalms and hymns, then one must answer two pertinent questions. First, why would Paul insist on divine inspiration for songs, yet permit uninspired hymns? We can safely assume that Paul was not irrational.

27. We should be very careful not to define the word "spiritual" in these passages in the modern sense of "religious." The word "spiritual" here refers to something that comes from the Spirit of God, and thus is "inspired" or "God-breathed." B. B. Warfield, "The Presbyterian Review" 1 (July 1880):561, quoted in Michael Bushell, *The Songs of Zion*, 90-91), writes of *pneumatikos*: "Of the twenty-five instances in which the word occurs in the New Testament, in no single case does it sink even as low in its reference as the human spirit; and in twenty-four of them is derived from *pneuma*, the Holy Spirit. In this sense of belonging to, or determined by, the Holy Spirit, the New Testament usage is uniform with the one single exception of Ephesians 6:12, where it seems to refer to the higher though superhuman intelligence. The appropriate translation for it in each case is spirit-given, or spirit-led, or spirit-determined."
28. John Murray, "Song in Public Worship" in *Worship in the Presence of God*, eds. Frank J. Smith and David C. Lachman (Taylors, SC: Greenville Seminary Press, 1992), 188.

Second, given the fact that "psalms" refers to divinely inspired songs, it would be unscriptural not to apply spiritual to that term. Furthermore, since we have already established that psalms, hymns, and spiritual songs refer to the divinely inspired book of Psalms, it is only natural to apply spiritual to all three terms. Since the book of Psalms is composed of divinely inspired or spiritual psalms, hymns, and songs, we obey God only when we praise Him using the biblical Psalter; uninspired hymns do not meet the scriptural criteria for authorized praise.[29]

Another question that should be considered regarding these passages is: "Do these passages refer to formal public worship services or to informal Christian gatherings?" Since Paul is discussing the mutual edification of believers by singing inspired songs in private worship, it would be inconsistent on his part to allow uninspired songs in the more formal public worship settings.

The Book of Revelation contains a number of examples of worship song (e.g., 4:8, 11; 5:9-13; 7:10-12; 11:17-18; 14:2-3; 15:3-4; 19:1, 2, 5, 6). Regarding these songs we may well inquire, "Do these allusions to worship in heaven teach us anything regarding what we are to sing in public worship and how we are to conduct public worship at the present time?" Clearly, they do not, for the following two reasons: (1) The Book of Revelation is apocalyptic literature, and therefore was not meant to be a literal guide or pattern for public worship. If it were, we would all be Romanists, for Revelation describes an "altar" (6:9; 8:3, 5; 9:13; 11:1; 14:18; 16:7); "incense" (8:4); "trumpets" (1:10; 4:1; 8:13; 9:14); "harps" (5:8; 14:2; 15:2) and even the "ark of the covenant" (11:19). We also

---

29. Some scholars argue for the use of uninspired hymns on the basis of alleged hymn fragments within the New Testament. This argument will not stand for the following reasons. (1) Church practice must be based on sound biblical exegesis, not the speculations or theories of modernist theologians and commentators. (2) The so-called hymn fragments do not resemble Greek or Hebrew-style metrical songs; neither do they follow any discernable musical laws. (3) Scholars are not in agreement as to what is a hymn fragment and what is not. (4) There is not a shred of evidence that the apostolic or post apostolic church used these so-called hymn fragments. If we are going to depart from the worship of our covenanted Reformation we need real evidence (i.e., divine warrant) not speculations.

would have to be mystics, for Revelation has every creature, including birds, insects, jellyfish, and worms, praising God (5:13). Apocalyptic literature uses figurative language and dramatic imagery to teach spiritual lessons. "The important thing in watching a drama is not the props," according to William Cox, "but the message they help to portray."[30] Similarly Bushell argues, "The Book of Revelation is filled to overflowing with obscure rites, with thrones and temples, and with a whole host of liturgical acts that cannot possibly relate to our own circumstances of worship. The attempt to derive elements of worship from such apocalyptic literature can only lead to liturgical chaos."[31]

Furthermore, even if one wanted to take the apocalyptic scenes of worship in heaven as normative for the church today, they still would not authorize the use of uninspired hymns, for the songs sung by the angels, four living creatures, and sinless heavenly saints "are in the nature of the case inspired compositions, proceeding as they do from heaven itself and the very throne and presence of God."[32] But (as noted) the apocalyptic worship scenes, with their altar, incense, harps, and other ceremonial images clearly cannot be applied to the new covenant church without Scripture's contradicting itself, which is impossible.[33]

An examination of the relevant biblical passages relating to singing praise has shown that the singing of Psalms is commanded, is supported by numerous historical examples, and meets the

---

30. William E. Cox, *Studies in Final Things* (Philipsburg, NJ: Presbyterian and Reformed, 1966), 159.

31. Michael Bushell, *The Songs of Zion*, 94-95.

32. Ibid., 94.

33. Some writers appeal to the "new song" mentioned in Revelation 14:3 as scriptural authorization for the composing of "new songs" today. A study of this phrase in Scripture, however, will prove that the biblical phrase "new song" has nothing to do with composing new uninspired songs after the close of the canon. The phrase "new song" in the Old Testament can refer to a song that has as its theme new mercies or new marvels of God's power (e.g., 40:3; 98:1). But keep in mind that this phrase is used only to describe songs written under divine inspiration. This fact limits "new songs" to the inspired songs of the Bible. Since the phrase "new song" is only used to describe songs written by people who had the prophetic gift, and did not apply to other Israelites, it therefore certainly does not apply to Isaac Watts, Charles Wesley, or any other uninspired hymn writer.

Another meaning of "new song" refers not to a song describing new mercies, but rather to singing a song anew; that is, with a thankful, rejoicing heart; with a new impulse of gratitude. The song may in fact be very old, but as we apply the inspired song experimentally to our own situation, we sing it anew. This is probably the meaning of

scriptural requirement that all worship songs be produced by divine inspiration. Since there is no scriptural authorization for the use of uninspired songs in public worship, Reformed churches should abandon their use and return to the biblical attainments of our covenanted Reformation.

The Sufficiency of the Psalter

Although we have established that singing inspired Psalms is biblical, it is also necessary to establish that the book of Psalms is a sufficient manual of praise for the new covenant church. This point is important for two reasons. First, if the biblical Psalter is sufficient for praise in the new covenant dispensation, the use of new uninspired materials is unnecessary. Indeed, it would be sacrilegious to place fallible uninspired songs along side infallible inspired songs when they are neither commanded nor needed. Second, one of the most common arguments against exclusive psalmody is that the Psalter is an inadequate manual for praise at this time in redemptive history. In other words, the church needs worship songs written after Christ's redemptive work was completed to look back and reflect upon what Jesus has accomplished. However, once we understand that the Psalter more than adequately meets all the needs of the new covenant church as a manual of praise, such objections are overthrown. When approaching a thrice-holy God, infinite in perfections, should we not use only the very best worship songs available?[34]

The Psalter reveals such a clear portrait of Christ and His work that any suggestion that they are inadequate in their exposition of Christ's work betrays a deficient understanding of their content.

"sing a new song" in the Psalms, which use the phrase, yet do not discuss new mercies. For example, Psalm 33 uses the phrase "sing a new song," and then discusses general well-known doctrines: creation, providence, and hope and trust in God. Also, there is a sense in which all the Old Testament songs are "new songs" for the new covenant Christian, in that we sing the Psalms with an understanding and perspective unknown to Old Testament believers. Because of God's expression of love in and by Christ, Jesus and the Apostle John can even refer to a well-known Old Testament commandment (Lev. 19:18) as a "new commandment" (John 13:34; 1 John 2:7; 2 John 5).

34. Bushell writes: "That man who prefers a humanly composed song to one written by the Spirit of God, when the latter fully suits his purposes, is, to say the least, lacking in spiritual discernment. And that man who would mix together in one book the inspired

The Psalms teach Christ's divinity (Ps. 45:6; 110:1), His eternal sonship (Ps. 2:7), His incarnation (Ps. 8:5; 40:7-9), and His mediatorial offices as Prophet (Ps. 40:9-10), Priest (Ps. 110:4), and King (Ps. 2:7-12; 22:28; 45:6; 72; 110:1). The Psalms give us Spirit inspired details regarding Christ's betrayal (Ps. 41:9), His agony in the garden (Ps. 22:2); His trial (Ps. 35:11), His rejection (Ps. 22:6; 118:22), His crucifixion (Ps. 22; 69), His burial and resurrection (Ps. 16:9-11), His ascension (Ps. 24:7-10; 47:5; 68:18), and His second coming and judgment (Ps. 50:3-4; 98:6-9). They also tell us of the victory of Christ's kingdom (Ps. 2:6-12; 45:6 ff.). Some Psalms reveal so much vital information regarding Christ's person and work that they are called messianic Psalms (Ps. 2, 8, 16, 22, 40, 45, 69, 72, 110).[35]

The Psalms are a treasure house of biblical doctrine. One can learn more about God from the Psalter than a hundred hymnals. The Psalms tell us about: God's self existence (Rev. 33:11; Ps. 115:3), His absolute perfection (Ps. 145:3), His immutability (Ps. 102:26-28), His eternality (Ps. 90:2; 102:12), His omnipresence (Ps. 139:7-10), His omniscience (Ps. 94:9; cf. 1:6; 37:18; 119:168; 139:14), His omnipotence (Ps. 115:3), His veracity (Ps. 25:10; 31:6), His sovereignty (Ps. 22:28; 47:2, 3, 7, 8; 50:10-12; 95:3-5; 115:3; 135:5-6; 145:11-13), His wisdom (Ps. 19:1-7; 33:10, 11; 104:1-34), His goodness (Ps. 36:6, 9; 104:21; 145:9, 15, 16), His mercy (Ps. 136; 86:5; 145:9), His longsuffering nature (Ps. 86:15), His holiness (Ps. 22:3; 33:21; 51:11; 71:22; 78:41; 89:18-19; 98:1; 99:3, 5, 9; 103:1; 105:3; 106:47; 111:9), His righteousness (Ps. 119:137), and His retributive justice (Ps. 58:11). The Psalms teach that God is the creator (Ps. 89:47; 90:2; 96:5; 102:25; 104) and the Savior (Ps. 19:14; 28:9; 106:21). They teach His providence (Ps. 22:28; 104:14), His hatred of sin (Ps. 5:4; 11:5), His punishment of

---

songs of God with the uninspired songs of sinful men (as if the latter were in any way comparable with the former in majesty, holiness, and authority) is, whether he knows it or not, guilty of sacrilege, of bringing the things of God down to the level of sinful men. The only way to avoid this charge is to claim that the Psalms are in a very real sense outdated, so much so that even frail and sinful men may presume to improve upon them" (*The Songs of Zion*, 11).

35. Ibid., 23-24.

the wicked (Ps. 7:12, 13; 11:6), and His chastening of His people (Ps. 6:1; 94:12; 118:18).

The Psalms contain a theological balance and fullness that is astounding. From the Psalter we learn of general and special revelation (Ps. 19:1-2; 103:7), original sin (Ps. 51:5), total depravity and the universality of sin (Ps. 14:1-3; 53:1-3), justification by faith and the free remission of sins (Ps. 32:1 ff.; 51:1-5; 103:1-13; 106; 130:4; 143:2), repentance (Ps. 51:1-4; 3-9), kingdom victory (Ps. 2, 45, 46:7-11, 47, 72), and the judgment of the wicked and the blessing of the righteous (Ps. 9:16; 37:28; 59:13; 73:26-27). The Psalter informs us that the gospel will go to all nations (Ps. 67:1-7; 72:6-17; 87:4-6; 98:1-9; 106:5; 148:11). Bushell writes,

> The Psalter recognizes the reality of sanctification, on the one hand, but never loses sight, on the other, of man's inherent depravity. Side by side with emphatic assertions of personal integrity (e.g., 7:3 ff, 17:1 ff, 18:20 ff; 26:1 ff; cf. Acts 20:26 ff; 23:1; etc.) one finds "the fullest recognition of personal sinfulness (51:5; 69:5), of man's inability to justify himself before God (130:3ff; 143:2), of his need of pardon and cleansing and renewal (32:1; 65:3), of his dependence on God for preservation from sin (19:12 ff.), of the barrier which sin erects between him and God (66:18; 50:16); as well as the strongest expressions of absolute self-surrender and dependence on God and entire trust in Him."[36]

A common objection to the sufficiency of the Psalter is that the new covenant church should not rely solely upon a book of praise that uses types, symbols, and prophecies to describe the work of Christ. When we consider that we now have a completed canon in which the types, symbols, and prophecies are interpreted and fully understood, this objection has no merit. It is absurd to suggest that at the precise time when the Psalter can be fully understood and be even more edifying for the people of God, it is no longer sufficient. The Psalms are much more comprehensible and useful with the New Testament than without it. "Our belief," writes Bushell, "in the sufficiency of the Psalter for New Testament worship is in large part

---

36. Ibid., 21-22.

a consequence of our understanding of the organic connection that exists between the two Testaments. They proclaim the same Gospel, exalt the same Christ, and confirm the same covenant (Gal. 3:6-18; Rom. 4:9-25), and it is in no wise inconceivable that they should enjoin the use of the same Psalter in worship."[37]

Conclusion

Many of the conservative Presbyterian denominations are drifting toward a dark and uncertain future in matters relating to worship. At the present time modern, Arminian, Charismatic, man centered will worship is replacing the old fashioned hymnody that was popular throughout the nineteenth and most of the twentieth centuries. Many older, more conservative believers are attempting to stem the tide against the so called "celebrative" worship. They argue that worship must be reverential, majestic, and must be done decently and in order. The "conservative" uninspired hymn singers, however, are losing and will continue to lose the battle against the trend toward charismatic style worship. The reason for this failure is simple. One cannot effectively argue against human autonomy in worship while holding to a position of autonomy oneself. The uninspired hymn singers opened the door, and the advocates of "celebrative worship" are all too happy to walk through it. The progression from the uninspired hymn book to the overhead projector is logically and spiritually quite natural. If Reformed and Presbyterian churches are to avoid being steam rolled by new gimmicks in worship that appeal to the flesh, they must adhere to a strict interpretation and application of the regulative principle. They must return to the perfect, sufficient, inspired hymn book of the Bible – the Psalter.[38]

---

37. Ibid., 26-27.

38. If crucial sections of the Westminster Standards are ignored or completely redefined in a manner that contradicts the plain historical meaning of the Standards (e.g., accepting the idea that the terms "psalms" and "psalm book" are inclusive of uninspired hymnals), will this not eventually lead to a shift in authority from the original intent of the Standards to an unwritten, historically relative, arbitrary standard? It surely will. (For a refutation of common objections to exclusive psalmody, see my *Exclusive Psalmody, A Biblical Defense*, chap. 3.)

Chapter 9

A Defense of Biblical Hymnody

Benjamin Shaw

For much of the history of the Reformed Church, some would say for much of the history of the church, the content of worship song has been drawn exclusively from the Book of Psalms. For much of the past two centuries, however, the use of songs other than those of the Psalter has been the more common practice. A study of that transition, and the historical, theological, and Biblical motives and rationale that produced it would be useful. That is not, however, our purpose here.

Rather, our purpose is to determine, as far as we are able in the space allotted to us, what Scripture requires concerning the content of worship song.[1] This investigation will proceed in a twofold fashion. We will first examine the arguments for exclusive psalmody as they are set out by our opponent – Mr. Brian Schwertley. In this portion of the study, we hope to show that these arguments are insufficient to prove their conclusion. The second part of the study will then set out, as far as we are able, what we believe to be the true Biblical requirements for a worship song.

---

1. This argument presumes the legitimacy of the regulative principle of worship as set forth in the *Westminster Confession of Faith* 21.1, which says, "But the acceptable way of worshipping the true God is instituted by Himself, and so limited by His own revealed will, that He may not be worshipped according to the imaginations and devices of men, or the suggestions of Satan, under any visible representation, or any other way not prescribed in the holy Scripture."

The Arguments for Exclusive Psalmody

The arguments presented here are those set out by our opponent in his own work, which he (and we) believe to be a fair and faithful presentation of those arguments as they have been made throughout the history of this discussion.[2] In his work, Brian Schwertley presents six general arguments in favor of the exclusive use of the Book of Psalms for the content of worship song. At the conclusion of each of these arguments we will evaluate the argument for its strength and applicability for accomplishing its purpose. At the end of this portion of the argument, we will then give an evaluation of the entirety of Schwertley's argument.

Specific Commands

This argument observes that the Book of Psalms contains several specific commands to the end that God should be praised by the singing of Psalms. Schwertley then cites such passages as Psalm 81:2; 95: 1-2; 98:4-6; 100:2; and 105:2.[3] While these are certainly commands to praise the Lord, they are all *general* commands. There is nothing implied in them which would limit the praise to the content of these particular psalms, or even to the Book of Psalms as a whole.

Designed by God for Singing

Schwertley argues that the very design of the Book of Psalms indicates that God intended it to be used as a song book. This is shown in a number of ways. There is musical terminology found in the psalm titles and in the psalms themselves. The "chief musician" is mentioned in a number of psalm titles. Various musical instruments are mentioned in both the titles and the bodies of the psalms. Names of melodies are given in the titles of some of the psalms. Finally, the language of these compositions refers to them frequently as

---

2. Brian M. Schwertley, *Exclusive Psalmody: A Biblical Defense* (Saunderstown, RI: American Presbyterian Press, 2002). The arguments are all presented in Chapter 2 "The Testimony of Scripture," pp. 8-32.
3. The verse citations given throughout are for English versions of the Bible. The Hebrew versification may differ in some instances.

songs, psalms (which Schwertley defines as "melodious songs"), and hymns. This collection of observations says to Schwertley that the Psalms were thus "clearly intended to be sung by God's people."

However, this data is not as forceful as Schwertley apparently believes. There is a variety of terminology found in the titles of the psalms. Some of these terms designate the author, such as David or Asaph. Other terms probably designate certain types of compositions; such as psalm (55 psalms), song (14 psalms), prayer (5 psalms), *maskil* (13 psalms), *miktam* (6 psalms). Other terms may be musical terms, such as *shiggaion* (Ps. 7) or *gittith* (Ps. 8, 81, and 84). Other terms may be the names of tunes, such as "according to *alamoth*" (Ps. 46).[4] The term "to the chief musician" (found in 55 psalm titles) may refer to the leader of the temple singers (cf. 1 Chron. 15:21).[5] None of these terms occurs in all of the psalms, and 45 of the psalms have none of these terms, though an author may be designated.[6] There is no general title to the Book of Psalms, except the conventional Hebrew title "praises." Thus it seems that the evidence of the Book of Psalms cannot lead to the conclusion that all of these compositions were intended for use in the public worship of God, though some of them may well have been used so in the temple services of the Old Testament period.

Historical Examples

Schwertley states that there are numerous historical examples (that is, recorded in Bible history) of Psalms used in public worship. He cites the following passages: 1 Chronicles 16; 2 Chronicles 5:13; 20:21; 29:30; and Ezra 3:11.

1 Chronicles 16 records a psalm (though the word "psalm" is not used here) that is duplicated in part in Psalm 105 (1 Chron. 16:8-11 is found with almost identical wording in Ps. 105:1-15) and in Psalm 96 (1 Chron. 16:23-33 is repeated almost verbatim in Ps.

---

4. The reader should note that if these terms do designate tune titles, God did not see fit to preserve the tune for the general use of His people.
5. This term also occurs in Habakkuk 3:19 at the end of his prayer.
6. Those interested in a fuller discussion of these issues are referred to Derek Kidner, "Psalms 1-72", Tyndale *Old Testament Commentaries* (Downers Grove: Intervarsity Press, 1973), 32-43.

96:1-13). 2 Chronicles 5:13 refers to the temple musicians praising God. The verse only mentions one line of what is sung, and it does not correspond precisely to any Psalm verse, though part of the wording is identical to the refrain of Psalm 136. 2 Chronicles 20:21 reports that Israel was led in battle by the singers. Again, only one line of what they sang is given, and the last part of it corresponds to the refrain of Psalm 136. 2 Chronicles 29:30 record the commend of Hezekiah "to sing praises to the Lord with the words of David and Asaph the seer." No song content is specified. In Ezra 3:11, the priests and Levites are described as praising God at the laying of the foundation of the new temple. One line is given, which partly corresponds to the refrain of Psalm 136.

Schwertley goes on to say that "the Psalms or their (inspired) counterparts" were used by the Levitical choirs, and taught to the common people, citing as examples Exodus 15:1; 2 Samuel 1:18; 2 Chronicles 23:13; Psalm 30:4; 137:1ff; Matthew 26:30; James 5:13.

With regard to Exodus 15, it is clear that this song was sung at the defeat of the Egyptians, but no instruction is given for the people to learn it, nor is there any evidence that the song was sung again on other occasions. In 2 Samuel 1:18, David orders that his lament over the deaths of Saul and Jonathan be taught to the sons of Judah. Again, however, there is no indication that this song was sung on other occasions. In 2 Chronicles 23:13, when Athaliah is deposed, the temple singers and the people sing praise, but nothing is recorded to indicate what they sang. Psalm 30:4 simply instructs the people to sing praise. Psalm 137 records that, while in captivity, the people were ordered by their captors to "sing us one of the songs of Zion." What these songs might have been is not defined. Matthew 26:30 states that Jesus and the disciples sang a hymn after the Last Supper. Again, the content of the hymn is not given.[7] In a similar way, James instructs those who are joyful to sing psalms, but unless one assumes Schwertley's conclusion, those "psalms" are not defined.

---

7. It is commonly asserted that this hymn was "the Great Hallel," including Psalm 118 and some others. That this became the practice in later Judaism is clear, but it is doubtful that this practice went back to the first century.

In short, it is clear that the people of Israel were instructed to sing praise to God, and on some occasions were instructed to learn particular compositions. However, there is no indication in any of these passages that the entirety of the Book of Psalms was used. In fact, some of the compositions the people were instructed to learn (the Song of Moses in Deut. 32 and David's lament in 2 Sam. 1) do not appear in the Book of Psalms. This evidence, whatever its worth, gives no support to the idea that the people of God were limited to the Book of Psalms to provide the content for their public praise.

Placed in the Canon
The canonical argument is a bit like Anselm's ontological argument for the existence of God – either the reader sees it or he does not. The premise is that the fact that the Book of Psalms is in the canon of Scripture is proof positive that these compositions, and only these, were given by God for His people's use in their public worship. In this, it seems to ignore several facts. First, not all of the compositions in the Book of Psalms are songs. Some are prayers, as is indicated in their titles. Some are meditations on particular subjects, such as Psalm 119's meditation on the Word of God. Some are individual in nature (indicated by the presence of the first person pronoun throughout) while others are communal. Some are historical recitations, such as Psalm 78. Others are essentially brief theological treatises, such as Psalm 139. This great diversity of both type and subject matter would seem to argue against these all being intended for the public, corporate praise of God's people.

A second consideration is the fact that many of the psalms are include in the title "to the chief musician." This may indicate that these compositions were intended for public worship, or that they originated in that context. But even if they originated in that context, it does not necessarily follow that that is their sole, or even primary, purpose. In addition, many of the psalms have no title, let alone one that specifies "to the chief musician." It seems to be a logical leap to conclude that these also were necessarily intended for use in public worship. In short, this author does not see the logical defensibility of the argument.

Only Inspired Songs Used
Next, Schwertley states that in the Scriptural examples, only inspired songs are used in the public worship of God. Hence, for example, there is the song of praise in Exodus 15 and the Song of Deborah in Judges 5. Schwertley also refers to the songs of Isaiah: the Song of the Vineyard in chapter 5 and the song of chapter 26. It is apparent that these songs are divinely inspired. However, it is not apparent that any of these songs were ever in use in the stated public worship of the Old Testament Church.

However, with regard to the Psalms, Schwertley rightly points out that the authors of many of the Psalms were also denoted prophets. David, while not specifically called a prophet, is included with others called prophets in 2 Chronicles 29:25-30, and in 2 Samuel 23:2, David says, "The Spirit of the LORD spoke by me." Other writers of psalms such as Heman (1 Chron. 25:5), Asaph (2 Chron. 29:30), and Jeduthun (2 Chron. 35:15) are all called "seer," which is an equivalent term for prophet (1 Sam. 9:9). Schwertley is mistaken, however, when he claims that "Levite" and "prophet" were used interchangeably, due to the close connection of worship song with inspiration.[8] 2 Kings 23:2 says, regarding Josiah, "The king went up to the house of the LORD and all the men of Judah and all the inhabitants of Jerusalem with him, and the priests and the prophets and all the people." The parallel passage in 2 Chronicles 34:30 says, "The king went up to the house of the LORD and all the men of Judah, the inhabitants of Jerusalem, the priests, the Levites and all the people." Because of the similarity in the listing, Schwertley has assumed that "prophets" in 2 Kings 23 is equivalent to "Levites" in 2 Chronicles 34. The problem with that assumption is first, that it is an equivalence drawn nowhere else in Scripture and second, fails to take into account the books where these statements are made. The Books of Chronicles regularly distinguish between the priests and the Levites, recognizing them as belonging to separate classes. The Books of Kings never use the term "Levite," but always subsume the Levites under the priests as two classes of temple functionaries. On

8. Schwertley, *Exclusive Psalmody: A Biblical Defense*, 13.

the other hand, the Books of Chronicles rarely mention prophets, while the Books of Kings make frequent reference to prophets. Thus, the Levite is not to be regarded as a prophet.

In sum, it is clear that many songs were given to the Old Testament church by inspiration. Many of these were recorded in the Scriptures. Some, perhaps, were not. What is not clear, however, is that only inspired songs were used in the temple worship of the Old Testament church. Despite Schwertley's assertions to the contrary, there is simply no evidence as to what particular songs were sung in the temple. We have reference to a few, and allusion to others, but it is simply more that the evidence will bear to say that only inspired songs were used in the temple. In addition, it seems to be the case that songs other than those included in the Book of Psalms were used in Old Testament worship. There are, for example, the songs of Hezekiah (Isa. 38:20). As far as we can tell, these were not inscripturated, in the Book of Psalms or elsewhere, though Schwertley insists that they were used in Old Testament worship.

The Psalms and Apostolic Worship

Schwertley also argues that all examples of worship song in the New Testament point to the apostolic use of inspired songs only. This he attempts by looking at several passages or collection of passages, which we, in turn, shall consider.

First, Matthew 26:30 – "*After singing a hymn, they went out to the Mount of Olives.*" The issue here is what Christ and the disciples sang. The usual view is that they sang part of the "Great Hallel" (Ps. 113–118). Schwertley cites approximately a dozen commentators who hold to that view. While it may well be the case, it may also not be the case. The common view is based on the Mishna, a work of the Jewish rabbis that originated late in the second century. While it may accurately represent earlier practices, this is not at all certain, due to the fact of the great upheaval in Judaism in the first and second centuries. In AD 70, the temple was destroyed. About AD 130, the Jews were driven out of Palestine. These two events introduced radical changes into the understanding and practice of Judaism, to the extent that it is uncertain how accurately the rabbinic material, such as the Mishna, reflects the actual practice of Judaism in the period prior o the destruction of the temple.

The next passage utilized by Schwertley is Acts 16:25 – "*But about midnight Paul and Silas were praying and singing hymns to God.*" With regard to this passage, Schwertley simply begs the question, saying, "Although there is no way for us to know conclusively what Paul and Silas sang, given the fact that there is not a shred of evidence for uninspired hymnody within the New Testament, it is very likely that they were singing Psalms."[9] This is simply assertion, based on the assumption that what he intends to prove is indeed the case.

The third passage summoned by Schwertley is Ephesians 5:19, Colossians 3:16, James 5:13. The view of Schwertley is that these passages all refer to the use of the Book of Psalms in both public and private worship. It is our contention instead that these verses clearly extend the use of praise in the Christian church beyond the bounds of the Book of Psalms. As a result, the exegesis of these passages will be developed more fully in the argument for Biblical hymnody as it is set out below.

The hymns of the Apocalypse constitute the fourth collection of passages from which Schwertley attempts to defend his presupposition. There are a number of hymns, or hymn fragments in the Book of Revelation: 4:8, 11; 5:9-13; 7:10-12; 11:17-18; 14:23; 15:34; 19: 1, 2, 5. A number of observations may be noted about these passages. In the first place, in several of these passages the words are said, not sung, so they do not qualify as worship song. This is the case with 4:8, 11; 5:12-13; 7:10-12; 11:17-18; 19:1-6. The only explicit references to singing and song in Revelation are in 5:9; 14:3; and 15:3. In each case the singing involves the singing either of a new song (5:9; 14:3) or the song of the Lamb (15:3). The songs of 5:9 and 14:3 are also songs of the Lamb as is clear from the context. In none of these three cases, nor in the other passages cited by Schwertley, is the wording even remotely connected with the content of one of the compositions from the Book of Psalms. Schwertley argues that "new song" means either a new, inspired song

9. Schwertley, *Exclusive Psalmody: A Biblical Defense*, 19.

referring to new mercies or marvels of God, or it refers to singing an old, inspired song "with a new impulse of gratitude."[10] Now it should be noted that while the content of the song is specified in 5:9 and 15:3, it is not specified in 14:3. It is simply identified as "a new song."

Schwertley rightly makes the point that the Book of Revelation is apocalyptic literature and must be interpreted carefully. It is also true that many passages in Revelation probably refer to the church, rather than to heaven. In addition, the new songs that are sung are specifically called songs of the Lamb – a theme absent from the Book of Psalms. That is not to say that the sacrificial work of Christ is absent from the Book of Psalms. It is not. But the identification of Christ's role as the Lamb of God is an identification that is not found *per se* in the Book of Psalms. At the very least it is safe to conclude from the Book of Revelation that the worship of the church is to include the song of the Lamb, and the content of that song is not specified, nor can it be found in the Book of Psalms.

Arguments for Biblical Hymnody: Exegetical Considerations
A careful examination of the arguments in favor of exclusive psalmody has found those arguments to be weak and inconclusive. A different solution must then be sought to the question as to what Christians are commanded to sing in their public worship.

First, we shall consider Ephesians 5:19 and Colossians 3:16. These two passages are almost identical. Ephesians 5:19 says (my translation), "speaking to one another with (or, by means of) psalms and hymns and spiritual songs, singing and psalming in your hearts to the Lord." Colossians 3:16 says (my translation), "the word of Christ let dwell in you richly, with all wisdom teaching and admonishing one another, with psalms, hymns, spiritual songs singing with grace in your hearts to God." In these verses, the primary command is to sing, with the content of that song being defined as psalms, hymns, and spiritual songs. Schwertley notes, we must interpret this statement not so much in the context of the secular Greek usage of the first century, but in the context of the Septuagint, the Greek

---

10. Schwertley, *Exclusive Psalmody: A Biblical Defense*, 28-29.

translation of the Old Testament.[11] However, Schwertley fails to note that Paul and the other New Testament writers were under an obligation to their readers not to use confusing or ambiguous language, an obligation we can be sure that they, as inspired writers, fulfilled. In addition, it is not simply the context of the Septuagint that is involved, but that of the Hebrew Old Testament behind the Septuagint.

The terms Paul uses in Ephesians 5:19 and Colossians 3:16 are the Greek words *psalmos* (psalm), *humnos* (hymn), and *hode* (song). As Schwertley properly notes, these terms are used frequently in the Septuagint. One must be very careful in the evaluation of this data, however. It is certainly the case that these words are used primarily in the Book of Psalms, because that is the sole book in the Old Testament devoted to songs of any kind. Thus, it is more important to note where the terms are used outside of the Book of Psalms, and to what these terms refer in those other contexts. In addition, it is necessary to look at these terms in relation to the Hebrew text.

The word *psalmos* is used to translate seven different Hebrew words, ranging from the very general word "praises" (the title of the Book of Psalms in Hebrew) to the word "psalm" (Hebrew *mizmor*, usually translated "psalm" in English). This indicates that the translators of the Septuagint did not recognize the word *psalmos* as a technical term referring to a portion of the Book of Psalms, but rather a more general word, referring to a song of almost any sort.

The word *humnos* is used to translate five different Hebrew words, ranging from "praises" to "prayer" and "song." Again, the evidence suggests that *humnos* did not function as a technical term for the Septuagint translators, but as a general term for any religious song.

The word *hode* is used by the Septuagint to translate six different Hebrew words, ranging from "burden" (a technical term used in

11. "First, the religious thinking and world view of the apostles was essentially from the Old Testament and Jesus Christ, not Greek heathenism. Therefore, when Paul discusses doctrine or worship, the first place to look for help in understanding religious terms is in the Old Testament" (Schwertley, *Exclusive Psalmody: A Biblical Defense*, 20).

the prophets to indicate a word of judgment) to "song" and "psalm." As with the other terms, this does not reflect any idea that this is a technical term referring to an inspired composition, but a word that refers to many different types of sung compositions.

In short, the use of these three terms in the Septuagint is such that the three terms individually, and the three terms together, simply refer to songs of many kinds, but particularly songs of praise to God. It is not at all likely that Paul's readers would have understood here a reference to the Book of Psalms, for the following reasons. First, unless Ephesians 5:19 and Colossians 3:16 are references to the Book of Psalms, the threefold phrase occurs nowhere else. This hardly makes the case that this was some kind of common shorthand reference to the Book of Psalms. Second, when the Book of Psalms is explicitly referred to in the New Testament, it is done in one of the following ways: 1) "the Book of Psalms" (Luke 20:42; Acts 1:20); 2) "the Psalms" (Luke 24:44); or 3) by reference to the specific psalm: Acts 13:33, "written in the second psalm," Acts 13:35, "also in another psalm." Hence, it seems extremely unlikely, if Paul had intended to direct the Ephesian and Colossian churches to the Book of Psalms as the manual for praise that he would have used an obscure and uncertain phrase used nowhere else in Scripture instead of a clear and explicit statement.

Therefore, the phrase, "psalms, hymns, and spiritual songs" does not refer to the Book of Psalms. Instead it refers to any type of song, defined by the context, which would praise God and edify His people. The modifier "spiritual" applies to "song" and not to "psalms" and "hymns" for one simple reason. A song (hode), as the word is used in Scripture, may be either a sacred or a secular composition, whereas "psalms" and "hymns" are, by their nature, directed to God.[12]

---

12. Schwertley, *Exclusive Psalmody: A Biblical Defense*, 23-4, argues (depending heavily on Professor John Murray) that "spiritual" applies to all three terms, and thus indicates "Spirit-inspired." Unfortunately, the data from the actual use of the term in the New Testament does not support this conclusion. The primary use of "spiritual" is in contrast with "carnal" or "fleshly." In Ephesians 6:12, it is used to refer to "spiritual" wickedness. Thus, the meaning in Ephesians 5:19 is to distinguish songs concerning spiritual matters from non-spiritual songs.

Finally, with regard to these two passages, the context is that of the public worship of God. The admonition is with regard "to one another," not to oneself. Thus, the purpose of singing in the context of public worship is the mutual edification of the saints by means of psalms and hymns directed to God, and songs concerning spiritual matters. This instruction does not omit singing from the Book of Psalms, in fact it encourages the use of the Book of Psalms. But it does not limit the content of worship song to the Book of Psalms. Rather, any song (or hymn or psalm) that expresses God's revealed truth adequately and accurately fulfills this admonition.

Next we consider James 5:13. This passage does not deal with public worship. Nor does it deal exclusively with the Book of Psalms. Instead, it is the direction that if anyone is cheerful, he is to psalm. Unfortunately, English does not have a verb that means "to sing psalms." As a result, the English "sing psalms" has a natural tendency to create in the mind of the reader that the phrase means "he is to sing from the Book of Psalms." But that is not what the word means. Rather, it means to sing praises, of whatever type, with the possible implication that it is to be done to musical accompaniment. Thus, the man who is cheerful is to praise God for providing the things that have made him cheerful. There is nothing in the language of James 5:13, either implicitly or explicitly, that requires that the cheerful man use one of the chapters of the Book of Psalms.

Arguments for Biblical Hymnody: Theological Considerations
Schwertley, citing Bushell, states that "one of the most common arguments used against exclusive Psalmody is 'that the psalter is doctrinally and spiritually insufficient to meet the worship needs of the New Testament church.'"[13] The sensitive Christian reader almost naturally rebels against the idea that some portion of Scripture is not adequate for Christian use, and Schwertley's argument seems compelling on the face of it. However, in showing the doctrinal and spiritual riches of the Book of Psalms, Schwertley misses a very important point.

---

13. Schwertley, *Exclusive Psalmody: A Biblical Defense*, 33.

The Lord Jesus Christ used the entire Old Testament to instruct His disciples regarding His person and work (Luke 24:27, 44-45). While some of those passages were from the Psalms, many were not. Thus, the Lord Jesus Himself demonstrated, in His instruction of the disciples, that the Book of Psalms was inadequate to fully treat His person and work; that is, it was doctrinally inadequate. The whole of the Old Testament was needed. In addition, many of the New Testament passages that deal with spiritual instruction for the believer draw on Old Testament material from outside the Psalms. This seems to indicate that the Book of Psalms is also spiritually inadequate for the New Testament believer. We have no wish to deny the great doctrinal and spiritual profundity of the Book of Psalms. There are rich treasures in that Book with which too many Christians are unfortunately unaware. However, the fact that the Book of Psalms contains depths ignored by many modern Christians does not prove the adequacy of the Psalter as the hymnal for the church. As noted above in the critique of Schwertley's position, it is in fact not proven that the Psalter was the exclusive hymnal of the Old Testament church. The Lord Jesus Himself proved its inadequacy for the New Testament church. Thus to limit the praises of the New Testament church to the Book of Psalms is to deny the principle that Jesus Himself set before us.

Another consideration is this. The Old Testament, in a certain sense, was adequate for the preaching of the gospel. Jesus preached the gospel to the disciples from the Old Testament. The disciples, until the gospels and epistles of the New Testament began to appear, preached the gospel from the Old Testament. However, Jesus designated the twelve as apostles, His official spokesmen, led by the Spirit into all truth, to add to the Old Testament. Thus, Jesus' own actions, and those of the apostles, indicates that however adequate the Old Testament might have seemed in its own right, the Lord Jesus Christ deemed it inadequate for the church. He saw to it that the New Testament was added, in order that those things that appeared in the Old Testament in types, symbols, shadows, and prophecies might be completed by the antitypes, the things symbolized, the things foreshadowed, and the fulfilled prophecies. Thus, while it would not be wrong to sing the truths of Christ and His gospel under the shadows and types found in the Book of Psalms, it would certainly be wrong to limit the church to the Book of Psalms for its praise, since those shadows and types are explained for us in the pages of the New Testament, and we, if we would be faithful to Christ, must also sing those truths in the full and glorious manner in which they are set forth in the New Testament.

Conclusion

It is certainly the case that many hymns currently sung by the church of Christ are doctrinally weak and spiritually shallow. However, that is not an argument against the singing of hymns. It is an argument only against singing weak and shallow hymns. Schwertley failed to demonstrate exegetically that Scriptural teaching requires the singing of the Book of Psalms and only the Book of Psalms by the Christian Church. He also failed to deal adequately with the theological conundrum faced by the exclusive psalmodist that Jesus did not leave His church with the shadows and types of the Old Testament, but provided for them the full and clear disclosure of the meanings of those shadows and types in the pages of the New Testament. Further, Christ's apostles, when they had the opportunity to state clearly that we, as the church, were to edify one another by the use of the Book of Psalms, did not say that. Instead, Paul instructed us to sing psalms, hymns, and spiritual songs. This list no doubt includes the Book of Psalms, but it certainly also extends beyond the limits of that Book to compositions using the full and clear revealed truths of the New Testament, that we might praise our God in spirit and in truth with a sound understanding of what we sing.

Chapter 10

The Few on behalf of the Many: An Examination of Choirs in the Light of Scripture, Church History, and Practical Theology

Cliff Blair

John Calvin, whose name is so often joined in the popular mind with the doctrines of predestination and reprobation, did not consider either of those tenets to be of the first importance in true religion. Neither did Calvin give a preeminent place to justification, the great battleground doctrine of the Reformation. Rather, he wrote: "If it be inquired, then, by what things chiefly the Christian religion has a standing existence amongst us, and maintains its truth, it will be found that the following two not only occupy the principal place, but comprehend under them all the other parts, and consequently the whole substance of Christianity: that is, a knowledge, first, of the mode in which God is duly worshipped; and, second, of the source from which salvation is to be obtained."[1]

This serious regard for worship found expression a century later in the Westminster Confession of Faith which declares: "But the acceptable way of worshiping the true God is instituted by himself, and so limited by his own revealed will, that he may not

---

1. John Calvin, *The Necessity of Reforming the Church* (1544; reprint, Dallas: Protes-tant Heritage Press, 1995), 15.

be worshiped according to the imaginations and devices of men, or the suggestions of Satan, under any visible representation, or any other way not prescribed in the Holy Scripture, (21.1)." The divines understood this doctrine of regulated worship to arise from numerous points in Scripture, chief among them being the second commandment as indicated by their catechisms.[2] With this high conception of the place and content of worship in view, the followers of Calvin and the later Assembly have sought to include in their worship nothing that lacked biblical warrant. While good men may differ over the biblical warrant for any given element of corporate worship (i.e., the Lord's prayer, the use of hymns, etc.) all honest men who make a claim to stand in the theological stream of Calvin and the Assembly ought to seek to justify their inclusion or exclusion of specific elements in their worship.

This paper will seek to give such a justification for the rejection of the use of choirs that are distinct from the congregation as a whole in corporate worship.[3] Positively stated, we will advocate that the congregation is the choir in the worship of God's people. To establish this position we will examine the pertinent biblical data from both testaments (section 1). This position will also be shown to be consonant with the practice of the Church in the stronger phases of her history (section 2). Lastly, we will answer some popular objections and offer some practical considerations in light of our thesis (section 3).

The Biblical Data

Old Testament: When a person sets out to examine the role and justification for choirs in modern corporate worship, he soon discovers something interesting: the almost total absence of anything in the way of a sustained argument on their behalf. Despite the near ubiquity of choirs in twenty-first century churches, the

---

2. Larger Catechism questions 107-110 and Shorter Catechism Questions 49-52.
3. Particularly in view are choirs that sing in worship while the congregation is silent. Some consideration will be given in section 3 to choirs distinct from the congregation, but singing in unison with them. Specifically not in view in this paper are choral concerts or other musical performances outside of the worship services of the Church.

overwhelming impression one is left with is that they have been assumed proper, not demonstrated to be so. In contrast with the battles over the inclusion of hymnody and the use of musical instruments that raged in the nineteenth century, and to a lesser degree still do, there is near silence on the matter of choirs. Forty years ago James White rightly observed: "In light of such widespread developments [of choirs] it seems strange that there have been few inquiries into the theological presuppositions of the choir in common worship. Rarely, even in the schools of sacred music, is the purpose of the choir in Protestant worship discussed."[4] On the rare occasions that a biblical argument for the inclusion of choirs in worship is ventured, they are invariably justified by recourse to the Levitical choirs of the Old Testament.[5]

The data concerning the choirs is somewhat scattered, but comes primarily in passages from the time of the monarchy (in Kings and Chronicles) and then briefly in passages from the period of the restoration (in Ezra and Nehemiah). Gathering these disparate passages together we will provide an overview of the choirs and follow that material with pertinent observations.

The choirs were originally appointed from among the three Levitical clans (Kohath, Gershon, and Merari) by David and served first in the services of the tabernacle and later the temple (1 Chron. 6:31-47; 16:37-42; 25:2-6, etc.). In addition to their clan leadership, the choirs were also presided over by those appointed on the basis of musical skill (1 Chron. 15:22, 27; 25:7-8; and the more than fifty Psalm titles directed to the choir director).[6] The choirs were composed of both singers and musicians[7] (1 Chron. 15:16-21)

---

4. James F. White, "The Church Choir: Friend or Foe?" *The Christian Century*, 23 March, 1960, 355.

5. John Frame, *Worship in Spirit and Truth* (Phillipsburg, NJ: P&R, 1996), 127-9; Joe Morecraft III, *How God Wants Us to Worship Him* (San Antonio: Vision Forum, 2001) 193-5; and with less precision Robert Webber, *Worship Old and New* (Grand Rapids: Zondervan Publishing House, 1982), 178, who alludes to finding "the roots of sound in the early church are found in the Old Testament heritage."

6. The New Brown, Driver and Briggs Hebrew–English Lexicon says of the ambiguous phrase *lamenatseach*: "in titles of Psalms has probable simple meaning, of musical director or choirmaster," (664). NASB: choir director; KGV: chief Musician; NIV: director of music.

using a variety of instruments (cymbals, harps, lyres, etc.; see also 1 Chron. 16:42).

In David's declining years, and with a view to the coming temple, he made changes regarding these musicians. He decreed their total number to be 4,000 (1 Chron. 23:5); lowered the starting age from 30 to 20 (1 Chron. 23:3, 24, 27); and clarified their functions: "They are to stand every morning to thank and to praise the LORD, and likewise at evening, and to offer all burnt offerings to the LORD, on the sabbaths, the new moons and the fixed festivals in the number set by the ordinance concerning them, continually before the LORD (1 Chron. 23:30-31)." So integral was the work of the choir with duties of the temple that they were exempted from other requirements "for they were engaged in their work day and night" (1 Chron. 9:33).

In addition to detailing their regular duties, Scripture records the presence of the musicians on a number of key occasions. Indeed, it was in the midst of the service of the Levitical musicians that the new temple was originally filled with the cloud (2 Chron. 5:11-14). They were present when treacherous Athaliah was overthrown (2 Chron. 23:12-13); when Hezekiah purified the temple (2 Chron. 29:27-28); and they are also noted as being "at their stations according to the command of David" during Josiah's great Passover celebration (2 Chron. 35:15).

After the above passages, choirs are largely undocumented in Scripture until the return from the exile. Mention of the returning musicians is made in both the first (Ezra 2:41; Neh. 7:44) and second waves of exiles (Ezra 7:7).[8] No great detail is given of their activities in Jerusalem until the dedication of the reconstructed wall around

---

7. Henceforth references to the Levitical choirs or musicians should be understood as encompassing both.

8. It is important to distinguish the Levitical singers mentioned in Ezra 2:41, 70; 7:7; Nehemiah 7:1, 44, 73, etc. from the "singing men and women" in Ezra 2:65 and Nehemiah 7:67. In commenting on Ezra 2, Derek Kidner observes: "The singers were distinct from the temple choirs of verse 41 and were simply a pleasant addition to a wealthy establishment: cf. 2 Samuel 19:35" "Ezra and Nehemiah," Tyndale *Old Testament Commentaries*, vol. 11 (Downers Grove, Ill.: Inter-Varsity Press, 1979) 44. Similarly, C. F. Keil states: "The Israelites had from of old employed singing men and singing women...

the city. In Nehemiah 12 a stirring ceremony is described where two great Levitical choirs proceed along the walls and converge at "the house of God ... they offered great sacrifices and rejoiced because God had given them great joy" (Neh. 12:40, 43).[9]

When the above passages are considered as a whole some simple and pertinent conclusions can be drawn regarding the relation of the Levitical choirs and contemporary ones. As their name implies they were wholly constituted by Levites. That is, they were priestly in constitution and function. Their service was tied to the temple service, specifically to the sacrifices. As Hughes Old comments, "It was during the actual immolation of the sacrifice that the singing of the psalms played its primary role. While the sacrifice was being burned on the altar a psalm of praise and thanksgiving was sung by the Levites as the one who offered the sacrifice circumambulated the altar (Pss. 25, 26)."[10] As such, those who would base modern choirs on this precedent have to ask themselves some questions: what office are modern choir members fulfilling? What are the requirements of that office? The Old Testament priests served in a mediating role between God and His people – do modern advocates of choirs claim that for themselves? If not, then how do Levitical choirs justify the modern practice? These musicians were office bearers who met specific qualifications: male[11] Levites from the

these, because they sang and played for hire, are named along with the servants and maids, and distinguished from the Levitical singers and players." *Ezra, Nehemiah, and Esther,* trans. Sophia Taylor (reprint; Grand Rapids: William B. Eerdmans Publishing Co., n.d.), 47. Such observa-tions should be obvious from the separate mention of both groups in the same passage, but we underscore them here as this will be important for our later discussion of the Levitical choirs.

9. The pageantry of the event is heightened in the original by a change of vocabulary. The expression rendered "companies of them that gave thanks" (KJV) or "choirs" (NASB) (vv. 31, 38, 40) is the noun *hattodoth* (meaning thanksgivings or confessions) rather than the usual word for singers or choir *hammeshorrim* (*piel* plural participle form of *shir*). "Almost as though these choirs were the embodiment of what they sang." Kidner, 126.

10. Hughes Oliphant Old, *Worship That is Reformed According to Scripture* (Atlanta: John Knox Press, 1984), 41.

11. It is important to underscore that these were not mixed choirs as is sometimes implied. For example, the NIV Dictionary under its discussion of "Heman," one of the leaders of the Levitical choirs, cites 1 Chron. 25 and declares "His ... three daughters were in the choir." Similarly, *The New Nave's Topical Bible* under its discussion of "women" says they served in these choirs, citing the same verse and the verses from Ezra and Nehemiah which mention

families of Asaph, Heman, and Jeduthun (1 Chron. 25:1-7; 2 Chron. 35:15, etc.), between the ages of 20 and 50, who, as Levites, were set apart for their work by God's appointment and the most sober of ceremonies (cf. Num. 8:5-15). Is there really any connection between that and modern choirs that are based on little more than an aptitude (or even mere willingness) to sing publicly?

New Testament: When we turn to the New Testament the case for singing is easily made – but the case for *choirs distinct from the congregation* becomes far more difficult. This is particularly true if that case is made from the Levitical Choirs. Temple worship is no longer the norm, nor is there a distinct earthly priesthood, nor is there anything that approximates an example of the practice. Rather, what we find is a broad assumption of singing by all true worshipers.

There are only two narrative examples of singing in the New Testament.[12] The Lord's Supper is said to conclude with all the participants "singing a hymn" (Matt. 26:30 and Mark 14:26). The other is in Acts 16 where "Paul and Silas were praying and singing hymns of praise to God, and the prisoners were listening to them." It is interesting to note that this is the only place in the N.T. where others are said to be listening and not outwardly participating in singing hymns – and they are unbelieving prisoners.

There is one passage that touches on singing that might be categorized as didactic: 1 Corinthians 14:15: "What is the outcome

---

female singers in contradistinction to the Levitical choirs (see footnote 8 above.) Both sources have misread the passage, which happens if verses 5 and 6 are taken out of context. 1 Chron. 25:5-6 says in part: "God gave fourteen sons and three daughters to Heman. All these were under the direction of their father to sing in the house of the LORD...." The larger context makes clear that only his sons were in the choir. The "all these" of verse 6 is the "subscription to the enumeration of vers. 2-5." C. F. Keil, *Chronicles*, trans. Andrew Harper (reprint; Grand Rapids: William B. Eerdmans Publishing Co., n.d.), 272. That the daughters are named as an indication of God's blessing on Heman and not as participants in the choir is clear from v. 1 which states: "David ... set apart for the service some of the sons of Asaph and of Heman and of Jeduthun." and also from, the balance of the chapter which lists the service of all twenty four sons named in verses 2-4 – but says nothing of the daughters.

12. In addition to the two passages here, Old suggests that Acts 4:23-31 may be congregational singing of a psalm (v. 24 "they lifted their voices to God with one accord"). The point is debatable; if it is granted it only underscores the thesis of this paper. See Old's discussion, 43-44.

then? I shall pray with the spirit and I shall pray with the mind also; I shall sing with the spirit and I shall sing with the mind also." This verse says little about singing *per se*, and more about the right use of our faculties and our deportment in corporate worship. It is a call for "a balance between rationalism and emotion. And ... that singing be done for edification."[13]

There are three passages in the New testament that are exhortations to singing: Ephesians 5:19, Colossians 3:16, and James 5:13.[14] James is manifestly private in character and does not touch on matters of corporate worship except in one regard: it assumes a familiarity with worship songs. Where would such familiarity likely develop? Most naturally, it would develop from singing in worship (not being sung to, or for, in worship). Paul's parallel passages in Ephesians and Colossians rely on the same assumption as James. Whether they envision a private or corporate setting (or both) is debatable and immaterial. If they assume a private setting the verses do not speak to the issue before us. More, to the point, if a corporate setting is assumed they provide an argument against choirs distinct from the congregation. This is made clear by an examination of the underlying grammar. The phrases "speaking to one another"

---

13. Mary Hopper, "Music and Musical Instruments" in *Baker Encyclopedia* of the Bible, (1997). A further note on 1 Corinthians. 14:26 "... When you assemble, each one has a psalm, has a teaching,...." This verse gives no indication if the psalm brought was to be sung or spoken, whether it was of charismatic origin or not, or what further use of the psalm would be made at later gatherings. What is certain is that no sound argument for solos can rest on so vague a foundation (and one so tangential to Paul's concerns in this passage). Even less credible is the notion that a psalm brought "When you assemble" would then be given only to a portion of the congregation to sing. Hughes Old, *Worship That is Reformed According to Scripture*, 43, speculates that this verse "probably means that the whole congregation is to sing a psalm, but it may indicate that the first Christians had cantors like the synagogue. The cantor would sing the text while the congregation answered by singing 'Hallelujah' after each verse. It did not mean that everyone was supposed to get up and sing a solo." Even if Old's tentative speculation of a cantor is correct, this still requires the participation of the entire congregation.

14. Ephesians 5:19 "speaking to one another in psalms and hymns and spiritual songs, singing and making melody with your heart to the Lord;" Colossians 3:16 "Let the word of Christ richly dwell within you, with all wisdom teaching and admonishing one another with psalms and hymns and spiritual songs, singing with thankfulness in your hearts to God." James 5:13 "Is anyone among you suffering? Let him pray. Is anyone cheerful? Let him sing praises."

(Ephesians) and "admonishing one another" (Colossians) both employ the same pronoun: *heautou*. This is a reflexive pronoun. Wallace reminds us that the force of the reflexive pronoun is "to indicate that the subject is also the object of the action of the verb. The pronoun thus "reflects back" on the subject ... the reflexive pronoun is used to highlight the participation of the subject in the verbal action, as direct object, indirect object, intensifier, etc."[15] Thus, in both verses, the speaking to "one another" is such that identifies the speaker and hearer as inclusive of one another (as is the case in congregational singing) not exclusive (as with a choir distinct from the congregation).

In addition to the passages considered thus far, there are those from the book of Revelation which can be called eschatological (Rev. 5:9-10; 14:3; 15:3).[16] What is chiefly notable in these passages is that all of God's people are envisioned as worshiping and singing. There is no distinct choir, the people are the choir. Such an observation comports perfectly with the overall theology of the priesthood in the New Testament. While the singing in the temple of the Old Testament was performed by priestly choirs (who served under the ministration of a high priest), so too in the New. But now the singing is done by all of God's people who have become a kingdom of priests (1 Pet. 2:5, 9; Rev. 1:6, 5:10, 20:6) and who serve under the ministration of the high priest (see Hebrews, especially chapters 7-9). This connection between the priesthood of all believers and their corporate singing of praise is made clear in Rev. 5:9-10 (see footnote 16 below). It comes through also in Hebrews where Christ is pictured (by the quotation of Ps. 22) leading the praise of God's people from "the midst of the congregation" (Heb. 2:12); and also, the people of God (not a portion of them) are exhorted to

---

15. Daniel B. Wallace, *Greek Grammar Beyond the Basics* (Grand Rapids: Zondervan Publishing House, 1996), 350.

16. Revelation 5:9-10 "And they sang a new song, saying, 'Worthy art Thou to take the book, and to break its seals; for Thou wast slain, and didst purchase for God with Thy blood men from every tribe and tongue and people and nation. And Thou hast made them to be a kingdom and priests to our God; and they will reign upon the earth.'" Revelation 14:3 "And they sang a new song...." Revelation 15:3 "And they sang the song of Moses the bond-servant of God and the song of the Lamb...."

"continually offer up a sacrifice of praise to God, that is, the fruit of lips that give thanks to His name" (Heb. 13:15).

Thus we see that the biblical data from both testaments argues strongly for the congregational choir. That line of reasoning that seems at first glance to offer the strongest support for modern choirs – an appeal to the Levitical choirs – actually argues against them. Further, the New Testament's great emphasis on corporateness[17] is underscored by congregational singing and implicitly denied by the segregation of a portion of the congregation to sing separately. The textual, grammatical, and theological evidence all points toward one practice in corporate worship: congregational singing. Let us next consider to what degree that direction has been followed by the Church throughout her history.

Church History

One of our earliest windows into the ancient church comes from the famous letter of the Governor of Bithynia, Pliny the Younger, to the Emperor Trajan (c. 112). Therein he describes the worship of the early Christians as they described it to him: "On an appointed day they had been accustomed to meet before daybreak, and to recite a hymn antiphonally to Christ, as to a god, and to bind themselves by an oath, not for the commission of any crime but to abstain from theft, robbery, adultery and breach of faith, and not to deny a deposit when it was claimed."[18] Thus, from the earliest days of postbiblical Church history we see congregational singing as the norm for the worship of God's people.[19] In fact, it would be some

17. Romans 12:5 "we are one body in Christ"; Ephesians 4:16 "being fitted and held together by that which every joint supplies"; Colossians 2:19 "holding fast to the head, from whom the entire body, being supplied and held together by the joints and ligaments, grows with a growth which is from God."

18. Henry Bettenson, ed., *Documents of the Christian Church* (London: Oxford University Press, 1943), 4-5.

19. Pliny's letter is by no means a singular witness from the early Church. Eusebius makes numerous references to such in his *Ecclesiastical History* (e.g., V, xxviii, 5; VII, xxx, 10; X, iii, 3) as do Socrates Scholasticus (VII, viii) and Sozomen (in reference to the hymnody of St Ephraim, III, xvi) in their works of the same title. Terry Johnson (likely in reliance on Old) states that "numerous references [to congregational Psalm singing] from the sermons of Augustine, Basil the Great, and Chrysostom" abound. Terry L. Johnson, ed., *Leading in Worship* (Oak Ridge, TN: Covenant Foundation, 1996), 11, n. 16.

centuries before choirs developed. Most agree that it was in the early medieval period that the complexity of the music grew and "singing became the privilege of the monks and clerics, and the congregation was put in the position of watching and listening."[20] Old writes of this period: "More and more it was the monks who were charged with the praise of the church."[21] Fortunately, this did not last: "With the Reformation the praises of the church took a very different direction. The Reformers wanted the whole congregation to sing the praises of the church. They wanted the people to sing in their own language and in music simple enough for the people to learn."[22] Focusing on John Calvin, James Hasting Nichols observes that the Reformers did not see their efforts as an innovation but a restoration to the practice of the ancient Church as it was based on Scripture: "Calvin knew, as did the ancient church, that 'each Christian bears the exalted title of sacrificer' and has his rightful place in the corporate offering of praise and intercession. The people should understand and, insofar as possible, unite themselves to voice the sung and spoken prayer of the service. So they had done in the third and fourth centuries."[23]

Thus it was that under the leadership of the great Reformers such as Calvin, Luther, and Bucer, that singing was rightfully restored to the congregation as a whole. The Reformation era and the centuries that followed saw a steady production of Psalters and hymnals designed with the great aim of equipping God's people to fulfill their calling to sing praises unto Him.

It was not till the nineteenth century that this state of affairs in Protestantism began to alter. The source of this regression can be traced to a person and a movement. The person was John Jebb, and the movement was the Anglo-Catholic movement within the Church of England. James White describes Jebb's role thus:

---

20. Webber, *Worship Old and New*, 179.
21. Old, *Worship That is Reformed According to Scripture*, 47.
22. Ibid.
23. James Hastings Nichols, Corporate Worship in the Reformed Tradition (Philadelphia: Westminster Press, 1968), 15. The quotation is from *Operi Calvini*, ed. by G. Baum, E. Cunitz, E. Ruess (Brunsvigae, 1884), XXVII. 407. Indeed, so clear was Calvin's intent to reform the practices of his day according to the pattern of the early Church that he titled his service book *The Form of Prayers According to the Custom of the Early Church*.

In 1841 at Jebb's suggestion [Walter Farquhar] Hook introduced a full choral service modeled after the cathedral service into the new parish church which he was building in Leeds. Before this time the only form of choir common in English parish churches was a small band of musicians in the west gallery. Beyond the occasional anthem its participation in the service was negligible. Jebb convinced Hook that the choral services, maintained since ancient times in the cathedrals, might profitably be used in parish churches. It should be noted that in the cathedral service the choristers and clergy were generally the only worshipers and that the cathedral service was not designed for the participation of a congregation. Nevertheless, Jebb felt that the cathedral service could be used in some parish churches and advocated this use in his book *The Choral Service of the United Church of England and Ireland* (1843). Hook made a major innovation in giving the choir an important place in the worship of the parish church. His practice of dressing the choir in surplices and placing them in the chancel was soon widely adopted largely for an architectural reason. During the 1840's the Cambridge Camden Society was actively promoting the building of "correct" fourteenth century Gothic churches with their characteristic deep chancels. The vested choir very neatly solved the problem of what to do with the chancels…. Within a few decades nearly every Anglican parish had adopted the novel practice of filling the chancel with a choir of laymen.[24]

Nichols recounts many of the same details, and states that, "Jebb explicitly opposed congregational singing as a 'mistaken and modern notion.' Congregations should sit and hear the professionals do it correctly."[25] Nichols opines: "Perhaps the most unfortunate legacy of the AngloCatholic movement to the Reformed churches generally has been this epidemic of chancels and theatrical choirs."[26]

Oddly, this "epidemic" went largely unchallenged and undocumented. Within American Presbyterianism, there is little evidence of a great debate on this point – which is all the more striking

24. White, "The Church Choir: Friend or Foe?", 355.
25. Nichols, *Corporate Worship*, 161. The quotation is cited from G. W. O. Addleshaw and F. Etchells, *The Architectural Setting of Anglican Worship* (London: Faber & Faber, Ltd., 1948), 219.
26. Ibid., 161-62.

when one considers the sacerdotal implications of the enterprise. Julius Melton says of this period simply: "The nineteenth century was witnessing changes even in Old School Presbyterian piety and worship. But few persons seemed to be very much disturbed by this."[27] The minutes of the General Assembly of the Presbyterian Church (Old School) of 1867 record at least one comment on the matter:

> The introduction of choirs or musical instruments can be justified only as they serve this end (to inspire and express devotion) and aid or accompany sacred song; and no display of artistic skill, no delicacy of vocal training, no measure of musical ability, compensates for the violation, or even neglect, of the proprieties of divine worship. The Assembly, therefore, cannot observe, without serious concern, the great and growing evil, that the music of the sanctuary, instead of ministering to the praise of God, should so often be perverted to carnal ends, being secular in character and associations, unsuited to congregational use … the Scriptures nowhere recognize the service of song as to be performed by the few in behalf of the many; but teach us that the Lord delights in the praise of all the people.[28]

The decades that followed the great changes brought by the revivalist fever of the Second Great Awakening were not auspicious for following such restrained reasoning. As Melton describes the middle third of the nineteenth century: "History had challenged American Presbyterian churches by suddenly creating 'audiences' at their Sunday services which included large numbers of nonchurch people. To meet this challenge the services began to be changed from periods of adoring God and edifying Christians into opportunities for convincing and convicting the 'unsaved.'"[29] Those changes included (among other things) the widespread inclusion of choirs in worship. Those choirs, admitted in the days of revivalism for reasons

---

27. Julius Melton, *Presbyterian Worship in America* (Richmond, VA: John Knox Press, 1967), 42.
28. Quotation from William E. Moore, *Presbyterian Digest*, (1873), 781, cited in Joseph A. Pipa, Jr., "Unpublished lecture notes of Covenantal Worship."
29. Melton, *Presbyterian Worship*, 57.

of aesthetics and the unexamined theological motives rooted in the AngloCatholic movement, are still with the vast majority of the Protestant Church today. Few would argue that the Church's worship has been significantly prospered in those years.

Objections Answered with some Practical Observations
The argument against choirs is not without objections. In this section we will answer some of the common objections, and make some practical observations touching on the matter in general.

Objection: John Frame states that choirs are justified by biblical examples of antiphonally arranged psalms: "Scripture does not require that all singing be done by the whole congregation. In fact, some psalms seem to be arranged for antiphonal or callresponse performance: see Psalm 136, for example, and the alternation of curses and blessings in Deuteronomy 27:12-13 and Joshua 8:30-35. Choirs and soloists simply represent divisions in the labor of worship. It is good to sing; it is also good to meditate while others are singing."[30]

Answer: This objection rests on some dubious assumptions. First, this assumes that congregational singing ceases to be such unless every member of the congregation sings every word. Secondly, this objection assumes that any pause within a song by any portion of those singing for any reason (including aesthetic) is the direct equivalent of a group of people who are not participating at all. Both assumptions are patently ridiculous. This is like suggesting the driver of a car becomes a passenger whenever he lifts his foot from the accelerator. When one hears a choral work with an antiphonal portion, one does not conclude that the portion of the group that sang intermittently alternated back and forth from being a part of the group and a part of the audience. Further, Frame's assertion that choirs or soloists are but means of dividing the labor of worship implies what? That while the choir sings, the listener can rest from worshiping? His final assertion that it is "good to meditate while others are singing" is merely that, an assertion, without any evidence that God would call such a meditation worship. If such things as

---

30. Frame, *Worship in Spirit and Truth*, 129.

resting while others worship, and meditating while others sing, are needful in worship, then when will the laboring choir members enjoy them? Furthermore, where is the biblical warrant for such a philosophy of music in worship?

Objection: Joe Morecraft, in his recent book on worship, marshals the arguments of Professor Benjamin Shaw who questions the presuppositions of a rejection of choirs.[31] Shaw argues that the rejection of choirs rests on the assumption that the Old Testament "choirs and instruments are inherently ceremonial in character and cannot be anything else. The reason that the ceremonial law has been abrogated is that it has been fulfilled in Christ. But what is there about choirs that point to Christ?"[32]

Answer: We refer the reader back to section 1 to see that the Old Testament choirs were indeed inherently ceremonial – not inherently as objects, but in function. The singers and musicians were appointed from the priestly class to priestly functions. All such functions have been fulfilled in Christ, the true high priest. Further, Psalm 22:22, which is quoted in Hebrews 2:12, pictures Christ leading the praise of God's people from "the *midst* of the congregation." In such a description we see the office of Levitical singer (indeed the choirmaster) fulfilled in Christ.

Objection: Frequently, choirs in worship are justified on aesthetic grounds. "Many people," states White, "would state that the real purpose of choral music is to add beauty to the service."[33]

Answer: The simple answer to such an appeal is to request the biblical warrant for such a standard for determining what should and should not be done in worship. "The relationship of beauty and common worship is highly ambiguous. The Bible does not praise beauty as an abstraction.... Beauty is certainly not the end of Christian worship."[34] The second answer is to question the standard

---

31. Interestingly, while Morecraft adheres to Shaw's arguments, Shaw does not. In a recent private conversation, he said to this author that he has significantly changed his position and no longer believes there is biblical warrant for choirs in worship.
32. Benjamin Shaw, *Studies in Church Music* (Taylors, SC: GPTS Press, 1993) cited in Morecraft, *How God Wants Us to Worship Him*, 194.
33. White, "The Church Choir: Friend or Foe?", 355.
34. Ibid.

for beauty: is there not something powerfully beautiful in the singing of all of God's people together: men and women; young and old? Thirdly, one needs to ask this question: beautiful to whom? God has called for His people to sing His praises to Him (Pss. 9, 27, 47), to make a joyful noise to Him (Pss. 66, 81, 95, etc.), to enter His gates with thanksgiving (Ps. 100) –if He is pleased by such things, who are we to reject them.

Objection: Some who wish to have choirs argue that it is an important opportunity for people to exercise their gifts in the service of the Lord. Or similarly, some argue for the choir on the grounds of aiding the whole congregation in their singing.

Answer: These are excellent motives and should be encouraged. However, the question the person blessed with musical gifts needs to ask is not can or *should* I serve the Lord with them in corporate worship–but what is the best way to do so? A case can be made that a choir *singing in unison with the rest of the congregation* may serve to guide the voices of the less gifted. If such a choir were restricted from singing apart from the congregation then they would not be in direct conflict with the biblical principle of congregational singing argued for in this paper. Additionally, we would observe, if the aid of congregational singing were the aim of such a choir, it seems manifestly clear that they would assemble in the rear of the assembly, and not in the front as is the common practice. Better still, why assemble at all? Could not such a choir of gifted singers, meet regularly to improve their own natural endowments, and then serve the assembly by dispersing among them? G. Vandooren envisions just such a scenario in his work *The Beauty of Reformed Liturgy*: "The only use for a choir I would see is in supporting congregational singing. From my youth I remember that choirs trained themselves mostly in good Psalm singing , and you could notice that in church! Now, with several new tunes, a choir could perform some *diakonia* or service here. It would not even be necessary to sit together as a choir in church. Spread throughout the congregation, their support will be noticeable."[35]

---

35. G. Vandooren, *The Beauty of Reformed Liturgy*, (Winnipeg: Premier Publishing, 1980), 51-52. White, "The Church Choir: Friend or Foe?" *The Christian Century*, 23 (March 1960),

Additionally on this point, we need to examine the very premise that choirs will necessarily improve congregational singing. Melton, commenting on the church music arising in the nineteenth century, says, "The advanced tastes of organists and choirs often turned the more pedestrian laymen into bewildered observers during musical portions of the service rather than into participants."[36] Arguments for (or against) the notion that choirs distinct from the congregation will enhance that congregation's singing are inherently problematic. Such arguments are necessarily anecdotal, subjective, and subject to a host of variables. Still, to suggest that a passive audience (whose best singers have been segregated from them) will have their singing measurably improved by observing others sing seems, at best, unlikely.

Conclusion

We have seen that the case for choirs in public worship is no case, but a mere assumption. It cannot rest on the precedent of the Levitical choirs without partaking of a sacerdotal theology that is completely at odds with the priesthood of all believers taught in the New Testament. Church history has shown that choirs have been advanced at just those times when sacerdotal theology was waxing (in the medieval period and in connection with the Anglo Catholic movement of the nineteenth century). Further, those seasons of Church history that have been the most vigorous and fruitful (i.e., the early centuries and the Reformation) have been those most distinctly marked by congregational singing in the worship of God's people. Lastly, we have seen that many of the objections to the biblical principles advocated here have either already been met; fall from the failure of their own assumptions; or can be answered in a manner that comports with our thesis.

When all of these things are considered, no place remains for choirs in worship independent of God's people united in Christ.

356, makes similar comments: "There is no reason why the choir cannot be used to encourage congregational singing... Some notable experiments have been tried in which trained choir members where scattered throughout the congregation with the intention of encouraging singing on the part of all worshipers."
36. Melton, *Presbyterian Worship*, 101.

Rather, what remains is for those people to unite their voices in praise as we answer His call "from the throne, saying, Give praise to our God, all ye his servants, ye that fear him, the small and the great" (Rev. 19:5).

List of Contributors

Rev. Cliff Blair is the pastor of Redeemer Orthodox Presbyterian Church in Charlotte, North Carolina. He is a graduate of Greenville Presbyterian Theological Seminary.

Dr. Robert S. Godfrey is Professor of Church History and President of Westminster Theological Seminary in California. He received his Ph.D. from Stanford University.

Rev. Terry L. Johnson is the senior pastor of the Independent Presbyterian Church in Savannah, Georgia.

Dr. Joseph A. Pipa, Jr. is the President of Greenville Presbyterian Theological Seminary and also serves as Professor of Systematic and Historical Theology. He received his Ph.D. from Westminster Theological Seminary, Philadelphia.

Dr. Morton H. Smith has served as a dean and Professor of Systematic and Biblical Theology at Greenville Presbyterian Theological Seminary since its founding in 1987. He received his Th.D. from the Free University of Amsterdam.

Rev. Brian Schwertley is the pastor of Covenanted Reformed Presbyterian Church in Bear Creek, Wisconsin.

Rev. Benjamin Shaw is Assistant Professor of Hebrew and Old Testament at Greenville Presbyterian Theological Seminary and also serves as Academic Dean. He received his Th.M. from Princeton Theological Seminary, and is currently a Ph.D. candidate at Bob Jones University.

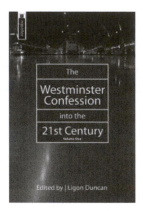
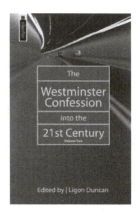

The Westminster Confession into the 21st Century

Volume One & Volume Two

Edited By Ligon Duncan

Contributors include:
Michael Horton, Mark Dever, Philip Ryken, Doug Kelly,
Timothy George, Richard Gaffin, David Wright, Paul Helm

In the first two of four volumes, Ligon Duncan has assembled an impressive array of contributors from a variety of ecclesiastical backgrounds. The aim is simple - to enable the 21st Century to understand the Westminster Confession more fully, and so bring about the same kind of rugged, vigorous, intelligent and self-sacrificing Christianity that was the result of its initial publication over 350 years ago.

'...a most worthy undertaking and, to my mind, one that is quite timely not only because of the anniversary of the Assembly but also because of the clear need in Presbyterian and Reformed circles for scholarly work on the Reformed tradition and its confessions.'

Richard A. Muller,
P.J. Zondervan Professor of Historical Theology
Calvin Theological Seminary, Michigan

'If the historic confessions are to be preserved for the future, it will take the kind of sympathetic historic description and effective doctrinal argumentation displayed in this book. It is a volume that Christians who adhere to other confessions, or those who feel that Westminster did not say the last word, should value as much as those who believe in the entire adequacy of Westminster for today.'

Mark A. Noll
McManis Professor of Christian Thought
Wheaton College, Illinois

ISBN 1-85792-862-8 (Volume 1)
ISBN 1-85792-878-4 (Volume 2)

Christian Focus Publications

publishes books for all ages

Our mission statement –

STAYING FAITHFUL

In dependence upon God we seek to help make His infallible Word, the Bible, relevant. Our aim is to ensure that the Lord Jesus Christ is presented as the only hope to obtain forgiveness of sin, live a useful life and look forward to heaven with Him.

REACHING OUT

Christ's last command requires us to reach out to our world with His gospel. We seek to help fulfill that by publishing books that point people towards Jesus and help them develop a Christ-like maturity. We aim to equip all levels of readers for life, work, ministry and mission.

Books in our adult range are published in three imprints.

Christian Focus contains popular works including biographies, commentaries, basic doctrine and Christian living. Our children's books are also published in this imprint.

Mentor focuses on books written at a level suitable for Bible College and seminary students, pastors, and other serious readers. The imprint includes commentaries, doctrinal studies, examination of current issues and church history.

Christian Heritage contains classic writings from the past.

Christian Focus Publications, Ltd
Geanies House, Fearn,
Ross-shire, IV20 1TW, Scotland, United Kingdom
info@christianfocus.com

For details of our titles visit us on our website
www.christianfocus.com

'There can be no more important issue than that of worship. There can be no more important question than that of how God is to be worshipped.

'In the 21st century, as has been the case throughout history, different interpretations of worship continue to divide churches and denominations. Worship expresses our theology and if we are to worship in truth we must submit to scriptural revelation.

'The Worship of God' offers an invaluable companion to those seeking to enhance their understanding of the purpose, history and different forms of worship. Dealing with subject areas from the regulative principle of worship to the distinctives of reformed liturgy, from Heart worship to the place of Psalms and contemporary worship music, this book gives us unique insights on an issue that demands our attention.

'Convinced of the importance of worship for the health of the Church, we offer this book to the public. The purpose of this book is to address a number of the major issues that create tensions in our practice of worship. Our intent, however, is not simply to critique those who differ from us, but also to offer a blueprint for a more biblical, God-honoring worship. Thus we deal with the purpose of worship, the rule for worship, and the practice of worship.'   **Dr. Joseph A. Pipa, Jr.**

This collection of Essays was presented at the annual Greenville Spring Theology Conference. The contributors are:

Rev. Cliff Blair	Pastor of Redeemer Orthodox Presbyterian Church in Charlotte, North Carolina.
Dr. Robert S. Godfrey	Professor of Church History and President of Westminster Theological Seminary in California.
Rev. Terry L. Johnson	Senior pastor of the Independent Presbyterian Church in Savannah, Georgia.
Dr. Joseph A. Pipa, Jr.	President and Professor of Systematic and Historical Theology of Greenville Presbyterian Theological Seminary.
Dr. Morton H. Smith	Dean and Professor of Systematic and Biblical Theology at Greenville Presbyterian Theological Seminary.
Rev. Brian Schwertley	Pastor of Covenanted Reformed Presbyterian Church in Bear Creek, Wisconsin.
Rev. Benjamin Shaw	Dean and Assistant Professor of Hebrew and Old Testament at Greenville Presbyterian Theological Seminary.

ISBN 1-8455-0055-5

G10 WORSHIP
& HYMNOLOGY
CHM/CHU/WOR

9 781845 500559